Chopin's Funeral

Chopin's Funeral

Benita Eisler

ALFRED A. KNOPF   NEW YORK   2003

THIS IS A BORZOI BOOK
PUBLISHED BY ALFRED A. KNOPF

Copyright © 2003 by Benita Eisler
All rights reserved under International and Pan-American
Copyright Conventions. Published in the United States
by Alfred A. Knopf, a division of Random House, Inc.,
New York, and simultaneously in Canada by Random
House of Canada Limited, Toronto. Distributed
by Random House, Inc., New York.
www.aaknopf.com

Knopf, Borzoi Books, and the colophon are registered
trademarks of Random House, Inc.

Grateful acknowledgment is made to the following for
permission to translate from French to English
previously published material:
Editions Garnier: Excerpt from *Correspondance de George
Sand.* Reprinted by permission of Editions Garnier.
Hermann Editeurs des Sciences et des Arts: Excerpt
from *Correspondance de Frédéric Chopin,* v. 1–3.
Copyright © 1981 by La Revue musicale, Paris. Reprinted
by permission of Hermann Editeurs des Sciences et des Arts.

Library of Congress Cataloging-in-Publication Data
Eisler, Benita.
Chopin's funeral / by Benita Eisler.
p.   cm.
Includes bibliographical references and index.
ISBN 0-375-40945-9
1. Chopin, Frédéric, 1810–1849—Death and burial.
2. Chopin, Frédéric, 1810–1849—Last years.
3. Sand, George, 1804–1876. I. Title.
ML410.C54 E38 2003
786.2'092—dc21
[B]   2002073097

Manufactured in the United States of America
First Edition

Frontispiece: *Eugène Delacroix's portrait of Chopin, 1838*

Contents

PART I: *Departures*

ONE: *Lacrymosa dies illa:* "What weeping on that day" 3
TWO: First Meetings 11
THREE: A Genius in the Family 19
FOUR: The Education of an Exile 26

PART II: *Arrivals*

FIVE: The Capital of Desire 43
SIX: Preludes to Paradise 56
SEVEN: Homecoming 68
EIGHT: Labors of Love 78
NINE: Earthquakes and Harvests 89
TEN: Children of Paradise 99
ELEVEN: Deaths Foretold 110
TWELVE: Forty Pounds of Jam 121
THIRTEEN: A Victim of Time 133
FOURTEEN: *Lucrezia Floriani* 147
FIFTEEN: Winter Journeys 157
SIXTEEN: The Expulsion from Paradise 171
SEVENTEEN: "The Abyss Called London" 180
EIGHTEEN: *Recordare* 190

Appendix: Chopin's Photograph 205
Notes and Sources 207
Selected Bibliography 217
Acknowledgments 219
Index 221

PART I

Departures

ONE

Lacrymosa dies illa:
"What weeping on that day"

On a sparkling Paris morning, Tuesday, October 30, 1849, crowds poured into the square in front of the Church of the Madeleine. The occasion was the funeral of Frédéric Chopin, and for it, the entire facade of the great neoclassical temple had been draped in swags of black velvet centered with a cartouche bearing the silver-embroidered initials FC.

Admission was by invitation only: Between three thousand and four thousand had received the black-bordered cards. Observing the square with its crush of carriages, the liveried grooms and sleek horses, the throngs converging on the porch, Hector Berlioz reported that "the whole of artistic and aristocratic Paris was there." But another who surveyed the crowd, the music critic for the *Times* of London, suspected that of the four thousand who filled the pews, a large number had been admitted just before noon, strangers to the dead man, mere bystanders even, "many of whom, perhaps, had never heard of him."

If death is a mirror of life, Chopin's funeral reflected all the disjunctions of his brief existence. The most private of artists, his genius was mourned in a public event worthy of a head of state. Canonized as "angelic," a Shelleyan "poet of the keyboard," Chopin seemed to personify romanticism, and before he was buried, its myths had already embalmed him: a short and tragic life; an heroic role as Polish patriot and exile; doomed lover of the century's most notorious woman; and finally, his death from consumption, that killer of youth, beauty, genius, and of courtesans foolish enough to fall in love.

In reality, he was the least romantic of artists. While the generation that had come of age just before his own in France, including the Olympian Victor Hugo, had defined romanticism as a holy war of the "moderns" (themselves) against the "ancients" (their literary elders), setting off riots in theaters to make their point, Chopin clung to the past. His musical touchstones were Haydn, Mozart—but especially Bach. He harbored doubts about Beethoven's lapses of taste, was incurious about the music of Schubert, and generally contemptuous of his other contemporaries: Schumann, Berlioz, and Liszt, towards whom his feelings were further tangled by rivalrous friendship. In art, he preferred the marmoreal neoclassicism of Ingres and his followers to the radical inventions in color and form of his friend Delacroix. Socially and politically, he was still more conservative.

The same aristocratic circles that had embraced Chopin the child prodigy in Warsaw were waiting to welcome the twenty-one-year-old sensation of Paris. Chopin arrived in France in 1831. One year before, revolution had replaced the Bourbon Restoration with the Orleanists swept in by Louis Philippe and his July monarchy. It was still a world of fixed hierarchies: of titles, birth, and breeding, buoyed by a flood tide of fresh money coined by the financiers and industrialists whose entertainments outshone the Sun King in splendor, if not in style. Chopin made some friends among the professional middle class—a less grand banker or diplomat, a few fellow musicians. He had a horror of "the People" as a force of upheaval or even change (which he dreaded in any form), and he was suspicious of those who championed their cause. He was appalled by that quintessentially romantic belief, whose most ardent proponent was George Sand, that art must serve the cause of social justice—or, indeed, any other cause except itself.

Like many who have thrived as "exceptions," propelled by talent from modest origins to a place among the privileged, Chopin was repelled by marginality: by poor Poles, by Jews, by the ill-dressed and ill-mannered, by coarseness or slovenliness, in art or life.

Most likenesses of the composer suggest that he was far from handsome. He had pale, colorless hair, a thin, hooked nose, a pursey mouth, and rabbity, lashless eyes. In these images, Chopin bears only a glancing resemblance to his famous portrait by Delacroix—the portrait of romantic genius itself, with his tousled chestnut mane and burning inward gaze. Chopin's famous dandyism, then, must be understood as another labor of creation, like his music an imperious quest for perfection. The dandy enlists distinction—in dress, speech, manners—along with distance, to create a masterpiece: himself.

What appeared to many—then and now—as the snobbery of a provincial, self-invented aristocrat and aesthete, had deeper sources. Chopin needed the reassurance that a fixed social order provides. Dependent and childlike in many ways, he clung to the security of protective institutions—the monarchy, the Church, and the family—which defined themselves proudly as patriarchal, stern but loving fathers keeping watch over children, dedicated to exalting an ideal past and to keeping present chaos at bay.

Two years and only two public concerts after his arrival in Paris, Chopin ranked among those few artists who moved in every circle that counted. Ignoring protocol, older, established musicians called upon him. He was a fixture at the grandest houses, where, arriving in his own carriage, he was welcomed as a lionized guest who never failed to charm and amuse; if he could be prevailed upon to perform, he hypnotized every listener. The musically knowledgeable drew close to the piano to study the wizardry of his technique and his famous inventions in fingering, third finger crossing the fourth, that made his impossibly difficult compositions appear effortless. Fellow exiles heard laments for a homeland in the languorous rubato of the mazurkas, with their heart-catching drop from major to minor keys, but the mood of elegy was as often shattered by discordant salvos of unleashed rage. Even those guests whose attendance was simply an occasion to wear the new diamonds, to remark casually at the bourse that the reception last evening at Baron James's had been more than usually delightful, stayed well past midnight, straining to hear the final note, when the pianist, pale and exhausted, rose wearily to take his bow. It was uncanny how Chopin's music spoke so intimately to their most private, long-buried thoughts and memories, evoking childhood happiness and lost love; innocent, nobler selves trampled by the harsh rules of life.

Seventeen years later, he died, destitute, in an apartment paid for by friends at the most fashionable address in the most expensive quarter of Paris.

Now, at the funeral, emissaries from the world of music were outnumbered by mourners from the ranks of the rich and titled. The Polish émigré aristocracy and its French counterpart among the old *noblesse* were in turn outshone by new money: bankers and speculators whose wives and daughters had also been among Chopin's pupils. Certain of the fashionable, one reporter noted, appeared indecorously attired in brilliant colors, glittering with jewels.

While the crowd filed through the portal, the closed casket was carried from the sanctuary and placed under an elaborate catafalque ("utterly pretentious," in the view of Paris's leading music critic) at the transept. Chopin's embalmed body had lain in the crypt for almost two weeks since his death on October 17, aged thirty-nine. His dying had been long and terrible, the disease that killed him still not diagnosed with certainty: tuberculosis of the larynx, cystic fibrosis, mitral stenosis, or a rare viral infection?

With a dandy's discipline, in his final agony of slow suffocation, Chopin had planned the musical program whose principal offering was to be a performance of Mozart's Requiem. Unknown to the dying man, women were not permitted to sing in the city's parish churches; it had taken days of pleading on the part of Chopin's most powerful friends before a special dispensation was issued by the Archbishop of Paris. The decree allowed female participation provided it remained invisible; thus the women singers, including Chopin's friend Pauline Viardot among the featured soloists, were hidden from view behind a black velvet curtain.

As the mourners took their places, the organist played the funeral march from Chopin's own Sonata in B-flat Minor. Then, the choir of the Paris Conservatory sounded the opening notes of the Requiem's Introitus, followed by the first solo—"Te decet hymnus, Deus," Viardot sang, her glorious mezzo-soprano soaring above the chorus and orchestra. Then, voices and instruments were stilled while the priest chanted the High Mass for the Dead.

The pallbearers emerged from their pews. Two princes, Adam and Alexandre Czartoryski, represented the community of Polish exiles. The painter Eugène Delacroix mourned the friend he had both loved and revered, calling him "the truest artist among us." From the world of music, the composer Giacomo Meyerbeer, decorations glinting against his dark mourning attire, appeared the personification of success. He had been the merest acquaintance, but Chopin, passionate for opera, had been a fan, like millions of others who had made Meyerbeer a rich man. In contrast, cellist and composer Auguste Franchomme was known to few. But the modest, scholarly professor at the Conservatory had been the inspiration for the only music Chopin would ever write for an instrument other than the piano. Franchomme was followed by a collaborator of another kind, Camille Pleyel, manufacturer of the pianos that Chopin, more than any other composer who ever lived, had made the instrument of genius.

Shouldering the massive coffin, the six men moved up the nave to the sounds of the organ playing Chopin's Preludes in E Minor and B Minor. Many of those now leaving had heard the composer play these pieces—his favorites—in their own houses, in the salons of friends, or in Pleyel's concert rooms. The familiar notes on the somber instrument spoke of the voice they would never hear again, and they wept.

Outside the church, the mourners gathered around the *corbillard*, the wagon hearse particular to Paris. Drawn by black plumed horses, it aroused shivers of dread, but also of excitement: Parisians loved a funeral. By this time, most of the mourners had dispersed; Chopin had forbidden any graveside ceremony. With the exception of the pallbearers, freed now of their burden, those who remained were women. They surrounded the small figure of the composer's older sister, Ludwika, summoned from Warsaw by the dying man at the end of June. "Please come, if you can," he had begged, even if she had to borrow the money, of which, he, alas, had none to advance. "Apply for a passport immediately," he urged, and lest he should sound like his familiar hypochrondriacal self, he invoked the advice of others close to him and concerned for his health who had agreed that no medicine would help him as much as the sight of his sister. At the same time, he tried to deny the urgency of his condition. "I don't know myself why I yearn to see Ludwika," he wrote, with a wan coyness, to the rest of the family. "It's like those whims of pregnant women."

Chopin might have spent the last twenty years in the most emancipated company of Paris, but it was still natural to him to ask permission of his brother-in-law for Ludwika to make the journey: "A wife must obey her husband," he wrote. "Thus, I am asking you as the husband to accompany your spouse." With the intervention of the czar's ambassador to France, whose wife was Polish, the endless passport process was hastened and Ludwika, accompanied by her husband, Józef Kalasanty Jedrzejewicz, and fifteen-year-old daughter, arrived in Paris in August. But the grumpy Kalasanty returned to Poland in September; it was only Chopin's sister and his little niece Louisette who remained with him to the end.

Another young mourner, Adolf Gutmann, thirty years old, was one of Chopin's few pupils training to be a professional musician. Others, including pianists said to be more talented, could not have performed by virtue of birth; they were women and aristocrats of title or wealth; indeed, the most gifted of all Chopin's students was a princess, Marcelina Czartoryska, who had walked to the cemetery accompanied by Countess Delfina Potocka. Sumptuously beautiful of face and body, her golden hair as bewitching as her soprano voice, Delfina, long separated from her husband, was so prodigal with her sexual favors that she had been crowned "the Great Sinner"—no small distinction in the Paris of the July Monarchy. Chopin was rumored to have been one of her many lovers. She had rushed to Paris from her villa in Nice at the news that he was dying. With only hours to live, he had begged Delfina to play and sing for him. A piano was moved to the open door of his bedroom. But the sounds of the voice so dear to him or the music she played or sang caused spasms of choking and he motioned for her to stop.

Sending their carriages ahead, the Polish noblewomen walked the three-mile distance, east along the grand boulevards skirting the slums of Paris to Père Lachaise Cemetery. Others, arriving earlier in hired cabs, stood waiting by the open grave: a brawny red-haired sculptor, Auguste Clésinger, and his young wife, Solange, daughter of George Sand. Clésinger had been summoned to the dying man's bedside to mold the death mask, but the resulting likeness—bald head, drooping eyes, mouth contorted by agonized efforts to breathe—was rejected by the horrified Ludwika. Working swiftly, the sculptor had applied another layer of wet plaster, which, after removal, he reworked, smoothing away all evidence of struggle and pain until the dead man's features were composed into an expression of Christian peace. Clésinger's reward was the commission for a funerary monument, and he now surveyed the site where his marble tribute, featuring a Muse holding a lyre, would rise above a small oval profile of the composer.

Towering over the Clésingers, Ludwika, the priest, the Polish nobles, and the pallbearers was the angular figure of Miss Jane Stirling, a Scottish heiress, Chopin's pupil and patroness, who had supported the composer in the last year of his life. It was Stirling who had paid the bill for the funeral—five thousand pounds—of which two thousand were spent on the orchestra and chorus alone.

In the silence ordained by the dead man, his coffin was lowered. The mourners pressed closer together for a last look. But they also seemed to close ranks, filling an empty place among them.

Absent from the small circle of those who had been closest to the dead man was George Sand.

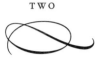

TWO

First Meetings

Countess Charlotte Marliani, battling grippe through the last icy weeks, had gone to bed early. But at 9:30 on the night of October 17, wakened by pounding at her door, she was astounded to find a weeping Solange Clésinger—so physically transformed, Charlotte reported to George Sand, she would not have recognized the rosy, buxom girl she had known from infancy. Solange had come to tell her mother's friend that Chopin had died in her arms in the early hours of that same morning. She had wanted to spare Countess Marliani the shock of reading of his death in the newspapers. Despite her estrangement from her mother, Solange added, she wished to tell Sand, too. Did Madame Marliani know where her mother was staying?

Stunned by Solange's news, Marliani explained that Sand was at her country house in Nohant. No, that could not be, the girl insisted; only a few days ago, she had seen her mother wandering alone in Paris, along the quays. Marliani stood firm in her disbelief, but Solange stuck to her story: "I can still recognize my own mother," she said, and claimed that others had seen her too.

"She must be crazy," Marliani wrote to Sand in Nohant the following day. But how could she be so sure that Solange was not speaking the truth? It would not be unlike George Sand, hearing that Chopin was dying, to impulsively make the two-day journey, only to lose courage at the last, cowed by the prospect of confronting Chopin's sister and the friends who blamed her—unjustly, she would always believe—for their separation, for having abandoned him, for his rapid decline, even for his death.

Gossipy, generous, and incurably romantic, Countess Charlotte Marliani was a friend to all artists, but she was especially devoted to George Sand. Married to a retired Italian diplomat long settled in France, the childless Marliani assumed a maternal role in the lives of her circle. The Marlianis lived at the Square d'Orléans, eight buildings constructed around a central courtyard—an oasis off the bustling rue Saint-Lazare, with a fountain set in the middle of trees and grass. Its expensive apartments, some with separate studios, were home to a number of more successful artists and musicians. Sand and Chopin had taken two apartments there in 1842, one on either side of the Marlianis' larger establishment. Their buffered living arrangements were chosen partly in the interest of respectability, but the separate quarters linked by their friend's household was also evidence of the older woman's nurturing role. "The kind and energetic Marliani," Sand later said, "made us a family." With Sand paying the cost of food for her little household, they all gathered together for dinner each evening at the Marlianis'. Afterwards, joined by other friends, the group would often drift back to Sand's salon, dominated by the green baize of the billiard table, whose size had caused Chopin to move his small upright piano into his bedroom. His own apartment, with its elegant salon, had been intended as a sanctuary, a place to be alone, to compose or dream. But more and more, Chopin had come to hate solitude; he was out every night, and it was often past midnight when his hosts asked him to improvise at the piano. Mornings were spent in bed resting before the hours of teaching to come, followed by another engagement—or several—in the evening. Since he and Sand had been together, he no longer tried composing in town, secure in the promise that early spring in the southerly Berry region, surrounding Nohant, would bring the renewal of his energy and his art. Now, the salon stood empty until, late in the afternoon, his pupils arrived for their lessons.

After two years of spending the winter months at the Square d'Orléans followed by long summers at Nohant, Marliani's cherished neighbors went their separate ways. Both apartments, however, remained intact, rents paid, contents hardly touched. Sand's furnishings, including clothing, were all left as though she planned to return shortly. But she never did. From Nohant, friends were besieged with urgent requests to rummage for this skirt, that fur piece. Precisely why the pair, who had settled into their own oddly domestic existence, had parted was a mystery to Marliani still.

Since that time, two years before, Marliani herself had separated from her husband and left the Square; that bright and music-filled utopia of artists now seemed a century ago. Meanwhile, she had heard that Chopin's health had deteriorated, that he had returned from a tour of Britain so weak and ill that he had been moved by friends from Paris to the sunny heights of suburban Chaillot. But in the turbulence of recent months, with cholera sweeping through whole neighborhoods, revolution in the streets, teenage students and workers massacred by the militia, and the king fleeing to England, it was hard to keep track of any of one's friends. So many, besides Chopin, had left the city or even the country. Sand herself, after reporting upon the bloody events as a journalist, had retreated to Nohant in May, five months before.

Still, as she comforted the distraught Solange, Marliani felt waves of disbelief. It was all so strange. Poor little Chopin, Sand's frail "Fryk-Fryk" and "Chip-Chip"—her friend's pet names for him always suggested the sounds of a bird—had been ill since she had known him. His vulnerability to the miserable Paris winters had led Marliani's estranged husband, the well-meaning Emmanuel, former consul to the province of Majorca, to propose their ill-advised escape to that island eleven years ago. Could he have forgotten what these months—the rainy season—were like in as primitive a place as you could find without setting off for the wild Americas?

As soon as Sand received word of Chopin's death, she wrote to Marliani. Justifying her failure to come to Paris at the news of this last illness, she pointed to Majorca as the first of many proofs that Chopin had always recovered, even from the worst of these "pulmonary attacks." The island had defeated them, the barbaric natives and relentless freezing rains. On the boat trip back to Barcelona, it had hardly seemed possible that Chopin, delirious with fever, choking on his own blood, would disembark alive. Somehow, they had gotten him to Marseilles and installed in a suite in the most luxurious hotel in the port city. There, with her unremitting care and daily visits from a saintly physician (a friend of the Marlianis') he was restored to better health than he had enjoyed in a decade. For the next eight years, his attacks had been seasonal; the cold and damp brought on coughing and, occasionally, hemorrhaging. But always, by the dry sunny days of the ripening Paris spring, Chopin had shaken the symptoms that drained his strength and depressed his spirits; then, he was all impatience to leave on the arduous overnight journey from Paris to Nohant.

Now, defending herself with reminders of her role in these remissions, Sand only managed to sound defensive. Since their rupture two years earlier, she reminded Marliani, a wall of silence had risen to further separate them. On Chopin's side were arrayed his few intimates, including those Sand had believed to be her friends. They had failed to inform her that the miraculous seasonal recovery would not happen this time—or ever again. He had not left his bed for months.

When it came to depicting herself in letters and memoirs, Sand produced one of her most memorable heroines. Revising, even rewriting the evidence (including copies of her own earlier letters), her self-portraits are particularly memorable for their omissions. In this instance, she knew that the dying man had sent for his sister in Poland to be with him. It was too humiliating to have to admit that shortly after Ludwika's arrival in Paris, Sand had written to her—a woman she had loved and treated as her own sister—for news of Chopin's condition, and Ludwika had not replied.

Marliani remembered seeing Chopin and Sand together for the first time; what an ill-assorted pair they had seemed then! She recalled the occasion perfectly: the first of an endless flow of parties, raucous affairs that lasted all night, whose hosts were another couple wrapped in an aura of glamour and sin.

Countess Marie Catherine Sophie de Flavigny d'Agoult, daughter of an aristocratic French mother and, on her father's side, heiress to a German banking fortune, had left her husband and two children to live openly with the twenty-six-year-old Franz Liszt. After eloping to Switzerland and Italy, a stay that expanded to include the birth of two children, the pair had returned to Paris. There, in the spring of 1833, they set up in the Hôtel de France, at 23, rue Lafitte, an establishment of opulently furnished rented apartments, whose *ton* was assured by neighboring mansions of the Restoration's richest bankers, soon to include Baron James de Rothschild. A pariah to her former world, that of the blueblooded salons of the Faubourg Saint-Germain, Marie d'Agoult was determined to replace the aristocracy of name and pedigree with that of talent, if not genius. Her timing was perfect: She harbored intellectual ambitions of her own, while Liszt, subordinating his brilliance as a composer, had yielded to the more profitable career of concert virtuoso. Now was the moment to cultivate those who might be of help to both of them.

Literary and musical Paris flocked to the Countess d'Agoult's free-flowing soirées. Among the distinguished men of letters who came to pay their compliments were Balzac; Sainte-Beuve; Heinrich Heine, poet and resident alien from Hamburg; and Victor Hugo. Of the music establishment, Their Eminences Rossini and Meyerbeer made appearances, along with newcomers in the ascendant: Hector Berlioz, the young Turk of vast orchestral ambition, and Frédéric Chopin, a Polish exile whose two Paris concerts had announced a rival to Liszt. Orbiting these stars, there swirled a large cast of extras, including journalists of unkempt appearance, loud voices, and radical politics.

When Marie d'Agoult left her forbearing husband and two little daughters to make her life with Liszt, the lovers became inseparable friends of another rebel. Aurore Dupin Dudevant, newly arrived in Paris, was trying to extricate herself by degrees from a miserable marriage to Baron Casimir Dudevant and a life of rural isolation in the Berry. Dudevant gave his wife a small allowance, along with tacit permission to establish herself, their two young children, and Aurore's younger lover in the capital—a vacation of sorts from marriage. Shortly, Madame Dudevant—not yet thirty—was managing to support her new household by writing. She started with journalism, then wrote her novel *Indiana,* followed by *Lélia,* a strange hybrid of manifesto and autobiography serialized in the *Journal des Débats,* which launched her as a celebrity with thousands of eager readers awaiting the next installment. Working frenziedly to meet the newspaper's deadlines, she was losing patience with her lazy, if good-natured, lover. Before he was dismissed from her life, Jules Sandeau left Aurore an invaluable legacy: the syllable of his surname that changed the restless provincial wife and mother into George Sand.

In Geneva, where Liszt and d'Agoult were awaiting the birth of their first child, they greeted with delight the arrival of Sand, accompanied by her two children and their nurse, but not M. Sandeau, on a brief holiday to celebrate the legal end of her marriage. For several weeks, the group, joined by new Genevan friends, had a riotous time, and the expatriates were saddened when Sand and her entourage were obliged to return to France. Her presence was required in the Berry to make certain that the court's judgment in her favor was implemented; she had wrested from Dudevant her childhood home in Nohant, a small eighteenth-century manor—more farmhouse than chateau—with a ravishing park, woods, and three farms whose boundaries extended to the river Indre. Nohant, along with Sand's other assets, had become, with marriage, the legal property of her husband.

By the fall of 1836, Liszt and d'Agoult had tired of provincial Geneva and were happily re-established in Paris. Their first thought was that Sand must join them; the Hôtel de France was just her style. Leaving her children with Dudevant this time, she moved into rooms on the floor just below her friends. Together, they entertained a constant stream of mutual friends in a common sitting room: "Those of mine you don't like," joked Sand, "will be received on the landing." The two women, at least, thrived on the constant tumult of egos clashing in loud political argument, critical judgments on the latest offerings in art, music, and theater, leavened by rowdy jokes, laughter, and freely flowing wine.

There was another attraction of the endless party at the Hôtel de France. "We heard wonderful music there," Sand recalled. The cacophony of voices fell silent when the host or one of his guests settled at the piano. It was here that Liszt introduced George Sand to Chopin and where she heard him play for the first time.

For months, she had begged her friends to introduce them. But from all that he had heard of Baroness Dudevant, Chopin had been in no hurry to make her acquaintance.

Daughter of a bird seller turned camp follower, granddaughter of an illegitimate daughter of the Marechal de Saxe, the most brilliant military commander in French history until Napoleon, George Sand was already notorious when Chopin arrived in Paris five years before. He may not have read a line of her writing, but he would have heard about their shameless revelations of women's sexuality—and, implicitly, their entitlement to pleasure equal to their obligation to please. Chopin anticipated with distaste her strident expression of radical social views, including impious denunciations of marriage and religion. She would be mannishly large, coarse in manner, her somber, trouser-clad form wreathed in her own cigar smoke like Laocoön half-obscured by the serpent.

He found her even more repugnant than he had imagined—and more frightening. She was not, however, the looming giantess that he envisioned; for a large-breasted and wide-hipped woman, Sand was startlingly small. But everything about her was dark: the wings of jet hair and swarthy skin; the huge, slightly bulging black eyes—"devouring," some said—whose fathomless gaze under a swoop of inky brows cast a spell over men. Her silence was more unnerving still; she hardly spoke. For Chopin, used to the musical sibilants of Polish women and the Parisiennes' twittering soprano,

Sand's mutism was unfeminine—unmanning, even. Her intense listening pierced the veneer of playful ironies and empty gallantry.

"Is that really a woman?" he asked a friend as they strolled home from the party. "I seriously doubt it."

Writing to his family in Warsaw, he shed the armor of the Parisian dandy to reveal his dread—of what precisely, he could not say, only that "something about her repels me."

Marie d'Agoult did not give up; she needed another couple as foil. On the verge of social rehabilitation herself, she hoped that diverting some of the limelight to another pair of the moment, one who also represented talent, celebrity, and sin, would ensure her own forgiveness. When Liszt and d'Agoult next called on Chopin, they brought with them, unannounced and uninvited, Mme Dudevant. Chopin's disapproval softened, yielding to Sand's ardent love of music. A musician of talent herself, she played the harpsichord and guitar, and collected folk songs of the Berry region; she attended nearly every concert and opera. Indeed, her passion for music and theater had dictated her masculine dress. Unable to afford expensive seats in the orchestra or loges and, as a woman, forbidden to sit in the balcony, Sand had adopted this disguise in order to see and hear all that Paris offered.

"I'm having a few people over today, among others, Madame Sand," Chopin wrote to a Polish friend passing through Paris on December 13, 1836. Almost as a postscript to his invitation, he added that Liszt would play and the celebrated tenor Adolphe Nourrit would sing. For the occasion, Sand compromised. Instead of her black trousers and frock coat, she wore billowing white pantaloons and a red sash—the sexually ambiguous costume of a houri *or* pasha and, more important, the colors of the Polish flag.

THREE

A Genius in the Family

C hopin's apartment was small, but the light-filled rooms, papered in his favorite colors of white and oyster gray, gave an illusion of infinite space. White silk and muslin hangings set off decorative objects that had come to crown his musical triumph: a silver gilt tea set, a pair of Sèvres vases and a Sèvres dinner service had been presented to him following each of three concerts he had given before the royal family at the Tuileries and the castle of Saint-Cloud, just outside Paris. (In keeping with the bourgeois style of "the Citizen King" and his family, the queen and the princesses knitted while he played.)

His ascent in the five years since he had arrived in France was reflected in his new address: the rue de la Chaussée d'Antin* was in the heart of fashionable Paris, now established on the right bank, and it was Chopin's third move, a progress drawing him ever closer to the center of money and style. He had ordered expensive new furniture, daringly upholstered in pale brocade; its cost, according to Liszt, was already giving Chopin attacks of "worry and nerves."

Success imposed other ongoing expenses: a manservant, along with the cabriolet and coachman that waited on the street below. It

---

*Today, the street flanks the Galeries Lafayette in what is now the commercial center of Paris, behind the Opéra.

would not do, he explained to his father, to arrive at the front door of the great houses where his pupils lived in a rented cab. Entertainments like the one at which he now played host on this winter afternoon required vases of hothouse flowers and ices from the best caterer in Paris, which Marie d'Agoult helped to pass around after the musicmaking had finished.

The "few people" Chopin had casually mentioned in the invitation to his friend recently arrived from Warsaw turned out to be a crowd in which, his awed guest noted, the obscure were outnumbered by the distinguished. Besides Liszt and Sand, there was the German émigré poet Heinrich Heine, whose waspish cultural reporting spared no one, excepting Chopin; the successful novelist Eugène Sue; the Marquis de Custine, exiled by reason of his open homosexuality from the salons of Saint-Germain which were his birthright. In opulent surroundings in Paris and his chateau in Saint-Gratien, near Chantilly on the lac d'Enghien, he had created an alternate world where Chopin was welcomed as a cherished friend for whose genius and sufferings he had particular sympathy. If Chopin's compatriot now felt out of place, two other Polish émigrés were there, who together had become the composer's family in exile: Count Albert Grzymala, the dashing and mysterious ex-soldier, revolutionary, womanizer, diplomat, and, most recently, financier and art collector, who, at forty, acted as Chopin's worldly father figure; and Jan Matuszynski, childhood friend, now a medical student, who shared the expensive sublet. Jan's maternal solicitude, urging his friend not to stay out so late every night and to wear heavier shoes in the cold weather, was more important than his help with the rent.

Now, as host, Chopin declined to take the spotlight in performing. He would only agree to a play a duet with his most celebrated musical guest. Together, he and Liszt dazzled with a sonata for four hands by an admired contemporary, the nearly forgotten Ignaz Moscheles.

To their rapt guests, they played as one. For the performers, it was a collaboration of architect and painter. Liszt assumed the *primo* melody part, permitting full display of his glittering virtuoso style, while Chopin provided the structure, with his preferred *sec-ondo* bass. As they sat side by side at the piano, their musical roles were dramatically—even comically—at odds with their physical appearance. Liszt's bony frame made him appear even taller than his six feet. His angular form, together with his shoulder-length ash-blond hair, long pale green eyes, and white face, seemed to miniaturize his partner's slight body still more: just over five feet tall, weighing less than one hundred pounds, Chopin appeared no larger than a child. Their startling contrast in size was exaggerated by the reversal of musical roles; the giant Hungarian tossing delicate sprays of fioritura and the frail Chopin bearing the weight of the sonata's architecture.

Enthralled, Sand yielded to her worship of genius, doubled now by their duet: the familiar brilliance of her friend Liszt and the revelation that was Chopin's playing, "angelic" sounds detached from the forgettable music itself. Envy was foreign to her; she took only pleasure in friends' talent and success. In anticipation of Liszt's earlier visit to Nohant, she had sent to Paris for a piano; and she used her connections to further the literary efforts of Marie d'Agoult. Chopin would complete their magic circle. She saw the four of them, a Parnassus unto themselves, at Nohant, writing, reading, walking, making love and music.

Liszt, in turn, had taken Chopin in hand when the dazed twenty-one-year-old arrived in Paris from his trampled homeland. At twenty-two, the Hungarian was the matinee idol of the concert stage, but his devotion to music left no place for jealousy; he seemed instead to revel in Chopin's genius. Introducing him to everyone who counted, he then wrote glowingly of his protégé's first Paris performances, never failing to include his friend's compositions in his own mobbed recitals. And he played Chopin's work as no one else did or could. To a mutual friend, the gifted pianist Ferdinand Hiller, Chopin confessed: "I am writing without knowing what my pen is scribbling, because Liszt is playing my Etudes and banishing all other thoughts from my head"; and he went on to "wish I could rob him of the way he plays those same pieces."

With its majestic striding arpeggios, the first of the opus 10 etudes seems uncannily made for Liszt's giant keyboard reach. This set and the following opus 25 are the first unmistakable works of Chopin's genius, and he dedicated them, respectively, to Liszt and to Marie d'Agoult. But the tribute marked not the beginning, as Sand joyfully hoped, of friendship and love exalted by art, but the end.

They were such extreme opposites as to seem representatives of different species. Massaging his celebrity, the young Liszt was a public artist whose turbulent life has a quality of having been conducted on a world stage. Prodigal in his talents and energies, he placed all he had on the altar of music, women, fellow musicians, and, ultimately, God. Reserved, proud, mysterious, Chopin inspired love by withholding its expression: He gave, Liszt observed, "everything but himself."

Each had survived the prodigy's star turns, child marvels anointed by royalty of blood or celebrity. (Chopin was ahead in trophies; he had started with a gold watch as tribute from the diva Angelica Catalani when he was nine, followed by the more politically compromising diamond ring from the czarina, Maria Feodorovna herself.)

His parents were exceptional in nurturing the talent without exploiting the child. Both Mozart's and Beethoven's precocious genius had been promptly converted into cash; Liszt's father had given up a secure position as manager of one of the Esterhazys' far-flung Hungarian estates. Moving to Vienna to further the boy's musical education, he was reduced to beggary until he, too, put the prodigy to work.

Chopin was never allowed to perform for money. Instead, his parents' aspirations dropped soundlessly, a gossamer net around their only son. He would be a great artist, not a professional musician. His talent would be the more valued because it was not for sale.

Exile was Chopin's legacy. His father, Nicolas, a peasant from the Vosges region of northern France, had left his home and country in 1787, probably to avoid conscription into the army during the violent years of the revolution. He seems never to have communicated with his French family again. On his arrival in Poland, Nicolas found work as a clerk in a tobacco factory. Just before floods of refugees fleeing the Terror would provide more qualified competition, he saw that his native tongue was his greatest asset. In his adopted country, as in neighboring Russia, French was the language of culture and of the ruling class. He was hired in turn by two families of minor nobility as tutor to their children; it was in the service of the second, Count Skarbek, that he met and married, in 1806, Tekla Justyna Kryzanowska, a poor relation of obscure parentage employed by the family as a housekeeper.

The newlyweds moved to a small farmhouse on the Skarbek estate in Zelazowa Wola; with its thatched roof, whitewashed walls, and dirt floors, it was far from the comforts of the main residence. Here their first child, a daughter, Ludwika, was born, followed, three years later, by Franciszek Fryderyk, on March 1, 1810, named for his father's employer, who was also his godfather. Count Skarbek was a university official, and when his own children outgrew their need of a tutor, he helped Nicolas to find other work. The young family moved to nearby Warsaw, where the private tutor began a new career, first as assistant, then as master of French language and literature at the Warsaw Lyceum, recently established as a boarding school for sons of country gentry. The modest salary required him to moonlight at another institution, the Cadet School of Artillery and Military Engineering.

The Lyceum, soon to be relocated to the shabby grandeur of the Saxon Palace close to the city's fashionable Cracow suburb, provided living quarters for the faculty in order that each teacher could board five or six boys. As Nicolas and Justyna assumed the functions, respectively, of director of studies and house mother to their boarders, they seem to have been allotted the most spacious apartments—a welcome perk, as the family was increased by the birth of two more daughters.

An only son and second child, Fryderyk had two older women to mother him and two younger ones as worshipers. Justyna was his first teacher, followed by his sister Ludwika. By the age of six, when he required a more sophisticated level of musicianship than the family could provide, he was turned over to Professor Adalbert Zwyny, at sixty, a sweetly eccentric Czech pianist and violinist who claimed to have studied with a pupil of Johann Sebastian Bach. Whether this musical pedigree had any truth to it, the master inculcated his own classical taste in his young pupil: a passion for Bach, Mozart, and Haydn, a measured skepticism about Beethoven's genius, and warm encouragement of the small boy's delight in improvisation. Two years after he began lessons with Zwyny, Chopin, aged eight, published his first composition: "Polonaise for Piano-Forte," dedicated to "Mademoiselle the Countess Victoire Skarbek," sister of his father's former employer, Fryderyk's godfather. Along with the development of his musical gifts, he was learning the courtier's skills, essential to the survival of French masters, poor relations, and artists.

Disheveled and tobacco-stained, speaking every language badly, Professor Zwyny had been court pianist to Prince Sapieha, a connection able to ensure that the precocious gifts of "the new Mozart," as he heralded his pupil, were talked of in the loftiest circles. Invitations were showered upon the child of such marvelous abilities. The first issued from the most feared man in Warsaw: The czar's brother, Grand Duke Konstantin Pavlovich was the *Gauleiter* of the Russian conquerors. Probably insane, he tortured his own officers when he wasn't galloping through the streets shooting randomly at the terrified citizenry. Like other power-mad despots, he was prey to fits of depression, when, he claimed, music alone could soothe him. Then, he summoned the prodigy of whom he had heard such amazing accounts to the vast Belvedere Palace, where, like David playing for the mad King Saul, the boy's effortless keyboard technique and delicacy of touch tamed the grand duke's demons. He was asked back repeatedly, followed by invitations from Prince Sapieha, Count Potocki, Prince and Princess Adam Czartoryski; most exalted of all, he was invited to perform at Princess Radziwill's famed salon in the "Blue Palace." Then, in February 1818, before he had yet turned eight, Countess Zofia Zamoyska arranged for his first public performance.

Justyna did not attend her son's public debut, and we must always wonder how her absence is to be explained. It may be that some occasions are burdened with such hope that they require more strength to face than adversity, and Justyna was not a strong woman. Or perhaps the reason was more banal—an untimely illness, either Justyna's or frail three-year-old Emilia's, that kept her at home. Although his mother was not there to see and hear him, he had a talisman from her hands: the wide lace collar that she had made for his debut costume, setting her son apart from the uniform of all musical prodigies—black velvet suit with short trousers and white stockings.

His pride in this lavish evidence of maternal devotion became the stuff of Chopin myth: how he reported compliments about his collar, forgetting praise for his playing. Even if apocryphal, the story of Justyna's lace enjoyed a long life, woven into the dandy's distance from the mass of lesser creatures, a distance maintained through an obsessive insistence upon the very best: the Parisian tailor whose cut, together with the special gray of his suiting, was of such legendary perfection that his clients were instantly recognizable by their trousers alone; Chopin's famous collection of kid gloves, which launched the fashion for his favorite shade—palest lavender; his friendly rivalry with Delacroix for the most subtle variety of somber yet richly figured silk waistcoats; the caressing fit of boots made by the most fashionable bootmaker in Paris.

The concert was held in the Théâtre Français, located in the Radziwill palace. Despite the countess's raptures over "my little Chopin," he was not the only gifted child to take his bows; other fledgling musicians, including another pianist, had been invited to play, even if none was so young as Chopin. Professor Zwyny had learned not to put his trust in princes; before there would be any public performance of Fryderyk's first polonaise, he made certain that the press treated the publication of the piece, in 1817, as a newsworthy event: "The composer of this Polish dance, a young lad barely eight years old, is the son of Nicolas Chopin . . . and a true musical genius."

FOUR

The Education of an Exile

For all its splendor of palaces rising from the banks of the Vistula, Warsaw was always a provincial outpost in someone else's empire—a part of Russia or Prussia; a province under Napoleon or Metternich or the czars. As in any village, the schoolmaster enjoyed a certain prestige. The Chopin household received not only Nicolas's fellow teachers, but also the small circle of local intelligentsia: poets, folklore collectors, philologists from the university, along with musicians attached to the conservatory.

From earliest childhood, then, along with an introduction to the harpsichord and pianoforte, Fryderyk heard discussions by those Warsovians who remained connected to the intellectual and artistic flowering of the European Enlightenment and pursued a romantic passion to explore and preserve what was uniquely Polish: in language, folklore, and, particularly, music. Inevitably, for a subject people, the historical shaded into the nationalist and the patriotic. To the younger ones, especially, the first measures of the polonaise did not announce a courtly dance, but a coded call to arms. Beyond Nicholas Chopin's high-minded household, however, other worlds vied to welcome his son. The boy slipped into the easy manners of the gentry whose children were his schoolmates and intimates, but from an early age, he was also at home with the formal rituals of table and ballroom, of the grand families whose palaces he regularly visited in town. To their courtly polish and refinement he added a grace entirely his own. "He was as supple as a snake and full of charm in his movements," observed his fellow émigré, the German pianist Ferdinand Hiller, when they met in Paris.

Language was another matter, rooted in anxiety passed from father to son. A foreigner concerned with proving his Polishness and shrouding his peasant origins, Nicolas was as cautious as a spy dropped behind enemy lines; he never seems to have mentioned the existence of his French family to his Polish children. French was the lingua franca of the nobility and the subject Nicolas taught to others' sons—but not to his own. (Did he fear that the accents of a former vineyard laborer would betray him at home?) Consequently, Fryderyk's grasp of French grammar and spelling would always remain shaky. Surprising for one blessed with an extraordinary "ear" and famed from earliest childhood as an uncanny mimic, his pronunciation, too, was poor. More telling was his own unease in his adopted tongue: Half-French, living in Paris, the paradise of expatriates, Chopin would always feel twice exiled—from his country and from his language. Imprisoned by foreign words, the expressive power of music unbound him.

Father and son wrote to each other in Polish. Intended to be read by the entire family, Fryderyk's letters are tender, reassuring, lighthearted, and evasive. From Paris, he details glitterng invitations, well-received performances, his triumphs over grasping publishers, and news of other Polish émigrés. Nicolas's letters are direct, straight from the heart, scattered with proverbs. He clings to the peasant's anxiety about money, to saving as an article of faith, fearing debt and the dangers of yielding to costly pleasures of the moment. His son's rejection of these same warnings, his need for extravagance and luxury as bright armor against emptiness and despair, staked a defiant claim to the carelessness of the aristocrat.

Although he was an autocratic father, Nicolas never felt the need for harshness towards his son, not even in adolescence. Dependent, deferential, anxious to spare his elders worry or disappointment, Fryderyk's role of "the good child" was fixed by tragedy. His sister Emilia, two years his junior, a promising poet and the most gifted of the three Chopin daughters, died of a massive tubercular hemorrhage at age fourteen, her family at her bedside. Fryderyk's "weak lungs," noted from his sixteenth year, were linked to his sister's terrible death; in 1826, the year before she died, he had accompanied Emilia and their mother to the Silesian spa Bad Reinerz, in the hope that both children's health would improve. His was the burden of the survivor; along with his sister's talent, dread of her disease shadowed him. As a measure of his parents' grief and, possibly, their fear of contamination, the thrifty Nicolas gave up the free apartment in the lycée where Emilia had died, moving to one across the way.

For the only son, it became harder to leave home. Staying put, however, allowed him to absorb all that musical Warsaw had to offer. He moved from the beloved Professor Zwyny to his next and last teacher, Jozef Elsner, the director of the newly established conservatory. Secure in what he had already learned, he started to work seriously and independently, applying his own musical ideas to familiar harmonies and rhythms—notably, the folk melodies and dances of the Mazur, the region near Warsaw, the mazurka and the sweeping march of the polonaise. Both had been exported and recast by masters from Rameau to Mozart into an international style of court dances with a rustic flavor. Chopin heard them at the source—simple harmonies on crude instruments accompanying peasant weddings and harvest celebrations on his friends' estates. His first published work had been a polonaise. For the rest of his life as an artist, he applied his endless inventiveness and ingenuity to extending the possibilities of these forms, the mazurka in particular; its plangent harmonies and heart-catching rubato became Chopin's most intimate musical voice.

By degrees, he inched out of his chrysalis, from child prodigy to teenaged marvel and . . . then? He himself was waiting to see what happened next. He had long since outgrown the black velvet suit and Justyna's lace collar; he had graduated from the smart cadet's uniform of the lycée student—navy blue with gold buttons and buff stockings—that he wore when playing the organ for Sunday mass at the Visitandine Church. He had done the salons and benefit concerts. Like all of Europe, he was mesmerized by the Paganini phenomenon, the new experience of hearing a musician who seemed to reinvent his instrument. Then there was the violinist's inhuman physical endurance: He had given ten concerts in Warsaw in as many days. No wonder that gossip held him to have made a pact with the devil! After Paganini, Chopin cheered the new local attempt at grand opera, more enthusiastically when he became infatuated with a pretty soprano, Konstancja Gladkowska. At nineteen, Chopin was ready to fall in love, but not to risk declaring himself. He raged while other gallants swarmed about the flirtatious young diva.

He was impatient for his own career to begin. He had tasted the excitement of two centers of musical life in Europe: a brief trip to Berlin when he was eighteen had disappointed him. Anticipating opera memorable for splendid voices and opulent productions, he found both mediocre. On passing the final exams at the lycée, richer boys did a version of the grand tour. But for the son of a schoolmaster, there was no money for extended travel abroad, not even the Italian pilgrimage that had come to be the required experience of every serious young composer.

He had to be satisfied with a visit to Vienna. In the company of a few friends, he arrived on July 29, 1829. Here, everything he heard and saw delighted him: Meyerbeer opera, church concerts, cafés and promenades. On this trip—his first without an adult presence as companion or host—he was pushed into looking after himself. He presented letters of introduction; he called on piano makers and music publishers. He had earlier sent to Haslinger, the foremost Viennese publisher, the score of his variations on a duet from Mozart's *Don Giovanni*, "Là ci darem la mano." But he had heard nothing. Now, when he played the same piece in Haslinger's shop, the publisher was ecstatic and, putting on his impresario hat, he arranged for Chopin to participate in a concert at the Kärntnertor Theatre—"the Imperial and Royal Stage," as Chopin described it to his family—where he played the variations and his "Kra-

kowiak" Rondo. It was an adolescent's triumphal fantasy come true: the wild applause, shouts of "Encore," followed by the emperor's director of music, Count Dietrichstein himself, mounting the stage and paying homage to the young visitor's talent, begging him to stay longer in Vienna and to give another concert. Even the orchestra, which had threatened to walk out during rehearsal over Chopin's illegible scoring, now applauded him.

"I don't know what it is, but all these Germans are amazed by me, and I am amazed at their being so amazed," he wrote to his parents. Following the second concert a week later, the ranks of the astonished included jaded Viennese critics who hailed him as "a true artist," a "master of the first rank"; his youthful compositions, they wrote, burned with "the stamp of great genius." Even the more judicious recognized qualities in both the music and Chopin's performance never heard before, a form of "genius" that one writer attributed to his "unconventional forms and pronounced individuality." The more astute had heard in Chopin's variations on the famous Mozart duet, and in the traditional rondo using scraps of Polish folk melodies, early instances of the way his most radical innovations would be embedded in traditional structures. This was his particular magic: assaulting with the shock of the familiar, as in a dream.

He returned to Warsaw in early September 1829 to face the malaise of the recent graduate: a student no longer, friends and classmates scattered, career plans uncertain. He had arrived home expecting a hero's welcome after his Vienna triumph; instead, he felt relegated to a group of talented young people biding their time, while they talked art and politics at cafés and coffeehouses whose very names—the Hole, Cinderella—described a state of mind. There, he heard talk far removed from the latest musical gossip from Europe, the currency of his daily visit to Brzezina's music store.

For fifteen years, Poland—what was left of it after a series of successive partitions by the Great Powers at the Congress of Vienna—had been lulled into illusions of autonomy by the benev-

olent despotism of Czar Alexander I. Under Russia, the Polish state had no sovereignty; the czar was also king of Poland. A tradition of intermarriage between Russian and Polish nobility, along with the privileged role of Prince Adam Czartoryski, author of the Polish constitution but also one of the czar's resident inner circle, had assured the "Congress Kingdom," the territory including Warsaw, of a position of favor relative to Russia's iron rule elsewhere. With Alexander's death in 1825 and the accession of the autocratic Nicholas I, all this changed. Within five years, Poland had become a police state. Universities were closed, books and plays censored, the hated Russian troops were in insolent evidence everywhere, while, less visibly, agents of the czar's secret police spied on every aspect of citizen activity, with particular scrutiny of student radicals and other subversives. And indeed, they soon had a considerable amount to report. By 1829, talk in the cafés, much of it involving Chopin's old school friends, was of plots and meetings, conspiracy and revolution.

Chopin saw himself as a patriot. But for him, this vague term did not embrace any activist role. His sympathies lay with the cause of Polish sovereignty. Together with his aristocratic patrons and the most hotheaded of his fellow students, he was outraged by the suppression of individual rights, the gutting of institutions, the flouting of constitutionally guaranteed laws. Yet, at heart he was indifferent to politics. The conservative loyalties of his family, pious Catholics and servants of the ruling class, and his own rejection of any forms of adolescent rebellion suggest that his apolitical stance was a way of remaining loyal to radical friends while accepting authority whatever its source—his parents, Saint Petersburg, Rome, or the local Russian garrison.

Now, avoiding politics isolated him. As an escape from loneliness, he plunged into work, and discovered the collaborative pleasures of chamber music. Playing Beethoven trios brought him to acknowledge the genius whose "lack of taste" he had dismissed only a short time before. Otherwise, he worked hard at his own compositions, taking up his F Minor Concerto, laid aside before his Viennese trip, and struggling with the first set of etudes.

His public debut in Warsaw as an adult performer took place on December 19, 1829, in a gala concert at the Merchants' Resource Hall. Chopin was one of several soloists, but for the first time, he displayed the full range of his inspired ingenuity and the flawless technique required to pass romanticism's ultimate test of the virtuoso: free improvisation.

Lying somewhere between a skill and a stunt, invention and pastiche, circus and concert hall, improvisation offered its own frisson of suspense: the theme or form could be proposed by anyone in the audience. Improvisation was the perfect showcase for Chopin as both composer and performer. He loved improvising. Later, he would confine this marriage of free association and constraint to the salons of his circle; there, he could always be persuaded, at the end of a long evening—especially, a friend teased, "if there should be a pair of beautiful eyes among his fellow guests"—to come to the piano for "just a few improvisations." But soon he would be lost in the sheer joy of invention, adding his own arabesques to the bel canto line of an aria that was all the rage, yielding to the infinite possibility of the keyboard and the harmonies in his head. He would stop only when he was so exhausted, he had to be helped from the piano.

Now, after the first public concert in Warsaw following his Viennese triumph, audience and critics alike went wild. But their excitement crackled with new nationalist fervor: Chopin stood as proof that a provincial Russian satrapy could produce a great artist, his music the voice and spirit of the old heroic Poland and a clarion call to a new nation in the making. More was expected of him than small charming pieces or audience-pleasing improvisations: "Mr. Chopin's works unquestionably bear the stamp of genius," exulted one reviewer; "among them is said to be a concerto in F minor, and it is hoped that he will not delay any longer in confirming our conviction that Poland too can produce great talent."

His first performance of the new work took place in the protective setting of home, his piano and a chamber orchestra crowded into the Chopin salon. Soon, the guests would be grander, but this would always be his preferred setting: familial surroundings with a chosen audience. On this occasion, critics were among the invited guests. Those from the more radical papers echoed more stridently the possessive rhetoric of earlier reviewers.

Poland needed him. Her territories whittled away, her leaders either suborned by Russia or persecuted or setting out upon the great diaspora of exile, the promise of a great Polish composer—more than any other artist—inspired collective exaltation. Heralded as the nation's poet of the pianoforte—itself a new instrument—Chopin, at twenty, held out the promise of youth and renewal, of operas and symphonies to come.

It was not the moment to acknowledge the inevitable: Talent worthy of such hopes would not long remain at home.

He gave three more public concerts in Warsaw, the first to his largest audience ever—a sold-out crowd of eight hundred people. The reception was ecstatic, but Chopin was unhappy. The source of his dissatisfaction was one that would plague his performing career: His music could barely be heard.

Clarity was his grail. But the chromatic runs in which each note was transparent and distinct—the marvel of Chopin's acrobatic fingering with scarcely a touch of pedal—became, in a large hall and played on the light-action piano that Chopin preferred, inaudible. For his next concert, he accepted the loan of a heavier-action Viennese piano from a Russian general; but the improved sound did nothing to lift his spirits.

Away from the piano, he remained inaudible to himself. Writing to the friend of his heart and only confidant, Tytus Woyciechowski, he described a sense of mounting frustration, loneliness, and abandonment, of feeling blocked wherever he turned; but his unburdenings, too, sound muffled—he is tracking a stranger who keeps eluding him. He was no closer to declaring himself to the seductive singer. He struggled despairingly with the second concerto, in

E minor (published as no. 1), whose adagio, along with "a little waltz," was inspired by Konstancja, he told Tytus—the only time he acknowledged love as a wellspring of his art. The adagio, he added, "should give the sensation of gazing at a place which brings back a thousand cherished memories."

Tytus, meanwhile, had left Warsaw to learn the duties of a country squire on his family estate. Chopin made plans to travel to Italy and France, but one friend after another proved unable to accompany him. Political turmoil in Paris reverberated throughout Europe and provided further reasons to delay.

His third concert was also his last public appearance in Poland. After a trial performance in the Chopin salon, he aired the E Minor Concerto and the Fantasia on Polish Airs, a work he had played in concert more times than any other. Perhaps because he had finally made travel plans, he boldly asked Konstancja to participate. Exceptionally, he was delighted with the event: the singers, orchestra, even his own playing. "For once, the final mazurka called forth terrific applause," he reported. But there were many empty seats and the concert received only one offhand review. It was more than time to leave.

His departure took place to a musical farewell. The sounds of a surprise cantata, composed and performed by Professor Zwyny and Chopin's friends, followed his coach as it lumbered through the Warsaw suburbs, headed towards the border.

He did not have to travel alone after all. He had arranged to meet Tytus on the way, and they arrived together in Vienna on November 22, 1830. Finding elegant rooms at the most stylish address in the heart of the city put him in high spirits. His sense of being welcomed on a return engagement seemed confirmed when, the very next morning, he received a call from Johann Nepomuk Hummel, the most eminent composer and pianist left in Vienna. Primed to build on the success of his earlier visit, Chopin called on Haslinger, the music publisher and impresario who had launched him the year before, confident of selling his newest compositions and arranging further concerts.

One week to the day after his arrival, Warsaw erupted in revolution. Aggravated humiliations of the Poles by their czarist rulers had played into the hands of the most radical of the insurrectionists. An attempt on the life of the hated Grand Duke Konstantin in his Belvedere Palace chambers was followed by a failed attack on the Russian garrison. Retaliation was swift and brutal. A full-scale uprising seemed inevitable.

In Vienna, seat of the Hapsburg Empire, city of Count Metternich, architect of the partition of Europe among the great powers, any threat to the established order was a criminal act. Foreigners, especially, were suspect as fugitives or agents of revolution. Polish visitors—whatever their stated business—might be either. Chopin heard loudly voiced anti-Polish remarks in cafés; the same Austrian families with ties to the court who had received him warmly a year earlier were "not at home." Letters of introduction went unanswered. A new director of the Kärntnertor Theatre had no interest in engaging Chopin; Sigismund Thalberg, said to be Count Dietrichstein's illegitimate son and a powerful technician of the keyboard known as "Iron Wrists," was the new toast of Europe. Without concerts to publicize his newly issued music, Haslinger could not see his way to publishing any of Chopin's new work. But these disappointments were nothing compared to the loss of Tytus, returned to Poland to join the insurrectionary forces. Chopin had agonized about going with him and their other friends, all of whom were enlisting, but Tytus had persuaded him that his art—a Polish art, after all—had greater claims. There was no need to add the fact of Chopin's frailty, his undersized body and frequent bouts of illness. Compared to his contemporaries, he saw himself as a child. Following a dismal Christmas, more homesick than he had ever been, Chopin wrote to his only other close friend, Jan Matuszynski, who had interrupted his medical studies for military maneuvers: "Oh, why can't I be with you, why can't I at least be your drummer boy?" He wrote to his family and Warsaw acquaintances, pleading for advice on where to go next: Berlin? Paris? Italy? Isolated and preoccupied by preparations for war at home, neither his parents nor his friends could advise him.

Limbo, it turned out, had its virtues. With no fixed travel plans, no major concerts to prepare, no energy to be expended on ambassadorial receptions, Chopin immersed himself in music. He attended the opera as often as the programs changed, and tried to hear every concert, sacred and secular, that promised to enlarge his musical education. He spent time with other talented musicians; together they lamented the taste for the trivial that had come to characterize Viennese music, personified by the ascension of Johann Strauss the Elder: "Here, they call waltzes *works*," he raged. But he could not help trying a teasing jewel of his own. The Waltz in E-flat, op. 18, is the promise of a polonaise seduced into a waltz. He began to question his musical ideas—his own and others'.

In Vienna, he composed his final work for piano and orchestra, the Grande Polonaise Brillante, op. 22. Already, he deployed instruments more as punctuation than text, sounding short bursts to mark a polonaise beat, privileging the pianist to plait his melodic arabesques.

While he still struggled with a third piano concerto, he played versions of his E Minor arranged for solo piano in the only two performances he gave in Vienna; in the first, his role was relegated to "Herr Chopin—pianist" at the bottom of a program whose star was an undistinguished singer, Mme Garcia-Vestris. Chopin received no reviews at all. Before the second, he reported feeling "so indifferent . . . that I wouldn't care if it never took place."

This was no pose. He had gone from taking an adolescent delight in attention and applause to dreading the entire process. Concerts devoured him: the planning, the strain of performing, the fickleness of audiences with their adulation of prodigies and other freaks, and, afterwards, the preening ignorance of critics.

Chopin was free of the need to perform, socially or artistically, and musical ideas crowded his mind. He had brought with him to Vienna the two piano concerti that counted, in Emanuel Ax's words, as "his passport to the great world." But his trunks were also filled with rough sketches, pieces in which he had begun to reinvent and expand forms that time and lesser talents had exhausted.

The etude, or study, had enjoyed a dull if honorable life as an exercise to develop young pianists' technical dexterity while sustaining their interest through a variety of harmonic and rhythmic settings. For the composer and performer, these short pieces were occasions for the display of invention and mastery of the keyboard. Chopin chose this form to proclaim that he was a student no longer. With the magnificent cascading arpeggios that introduce the first set of etudes, opus 10, his authority was established. Eleven more studies flow by, in a constant play of contrasts: The tender inwardness of Etude no. 3 in E Major, the vivace's witty provocation in the "Black Key" Etude, no. 5, until the final note that stops rather than ends the "Revolutionary" Etude, the last of opus 10. At twenty-one, the apprentice was reborn as sorcerer. Chopin became Chopin. He recognized this himself: "I've written a "grand *Exercice en forme*," he told Tytus, "but in my own style."

By the middle of May, he had roused himself to make new travel plans, only to discover that he was stranded in Vienna. The Austrian authorities, as loyal allies of the czar, were pledged to prevent his enemies from carrying the republican plague elsewhere; still roiled by revolutionary turmoil following the deposition of Charles X in July 1830, Paris had no need of foreign agitators. Italy was on the brink of civil war. Chopin could no longer return home. Polish borders were closed to those now branded as fugitives, along with their fellow travelers. The Austrian police had marked Chopin as one of those guilty by association; they managed to lose his Russian passport, now required of all Poles. Only when an astute compatriot advised him to apply for permission to travel to London—by way of Paris—did the document turn up again. By then, a cholera epidemic in Vienna threatened to detain anyone trying to leave the city.

Finally, on July 20, armed once more with a traveling companion, a naturalist, Norbert Kumelski, Chopin left Vienna for Paris. In Munich, he discovered that needed funds from his father had not arrived. For the first time, he found himself obliged to perform for money. He participated in a program where he played his now-standard E Minor Concerto and Fantasia on Polish Airs. Afterwards, he was greeted by another admirer and visitor, Felix

Mendelssohn. Funds finally arrived from Warsaw. But now Kumelski decided to head for Berlin. Chopin pressed on alone for Stuttgart.

Arriving to find no news of his family or of the fighting in Warsaw, he was gripped by alternating bouts of depression and what would now be called panic attacks. In a journal, he imagined those who must have died in his very bed, comparing himself, in his abandonment, to an unclaimed corpse. Like a drowning man, he surveyed his life, whose every act and impulse now seemed a cause for remorse, for *żal*, that rich, untranslatable Polish word freighted with every shade of sorrow, from regret to mourning— and guilt. His discovery that he had contracted a venereal infec-tion, proof of the shame attached to sexual encounters, confirmed his unworthiness.

On September 8, one week after he arrived, he learned of the fall of Warsaw. The Polish forces had been crushed by the hated General Paskevich, infamous for training the most brutal Cossack troops, now charged as military governor of the Congress King-dom, to teach Varsovians the folly of rebellion. At this news, Chopin fell apart. His outpourings, scrawled into the same jour-nal, spool a horror movie of images run and rerun obsessively on his private screen: fantasies of violation, voyeurism, and his own impotence; the rape of his sisters and of Konstancja, ravished and strangled at the hands of "enraged Muscovite troops let loose."

Recently engaged to a rich landowner, Count Grabowski, Kon-stancja appears in Chopin's fantasy as a helpless victim of Cossack bestiality. Too frightened to resist, the beloved's paralysis mirrors Chopin's passivity. If the terrified girl will come to *him*, he promises, he will take her into his arms, wipe away her tears, and distract her from her wounds of violation with memories of their innocent past. At this point, the Cossacks descend to tear her away, "but now you can mock them because I'm there—me, not Grab[owski]," he crows.

As powerless a son as he is a lover, Chopin projected images of his parents' despair: his father's collapse as he sees his family starve; his mother forced to watch while Russian troops trample the bones of her dead daughter. Meanwhile, far away, "empty handed and incapable of action," their son "can only sigh, stifling his grief at the piano."

But there is another, guiltier than he, of abandoning Poland.

"God, my God . . . may you inflict the cruelest tortures upon the French who failed to come to our aid," he wrote. A week later, Chopin was in Paris.

PART II

Arrivals

FIVE

The Capital of Desire

A mirage in a bend of the Seine, Paris was a blur of light that never admitted darkness. Chopin reeled at the dizzying contrasts of opulence and squalor. Fashion and vice were inseparable; purveyors of obscene images and real-life whores accosted passersby, all lit as on a stage by shop windows and cafés whose temptations he could never have imagined, certainly not in Warsaw, not even in Berlin or Vienna. (Only his venereal infection, he told Tytus, kept him from answering the siren call of the local "sisters of mercy.") In no time at all, he found an apartment in one of the brand-new neighborhoods that seemed to spring up all at once, fruits of a new partnership of builders and speculators spawned by the July Monarchy.

Number 27, avenue de la Poissonière was a six-story building where, gasping from his climb to the fifth floor, he could catch his breath to panoramic views of Paris, from the windmills of Montmartre to the Panthéon dome. Not only that, he exulted to his family, his rented room was furnished in real mahogany! In balmy mid-September, he did not concern himself with the absence of a fireplace.

Socially and musically, he was soon launched. Between Liszt and Ferdinando Paër, director of the royal concerts, he met everyone in the musical establishment. To his relief, many compatriots had preceded him in the "great migration" from Poland, including his aristocratic patrons, old school friends, and artist contemporaries. The exile community offered both refuge and entrée, eager to introduce a newcomer whose talent and charm reflected brilliantly upon all of them.

In Vienna, the refugees had been as welcome as carriers of the cholera epidemic. In Paris, where the hated Bourbons had been overthrown only months earlier, with most Parisians cheering on the insurgents, exiles from Warsaw—at least, the noble, gifted, and patriotic among them—were embraced as heroes. Polish aristocrats, many with blood ties to the ancien régime, were in the vanguard of the more than four thousand Poles who had streamed across the border in the wake of the failed November uprising. Many nobles, including Prince Adam Czartoryski, leader of the Polish government in exile, had been sentenced to execution or Siberia in absentia. Unlike their Russian counterparts a century later, rich Polish landowners—Radziwills, Sapiehas, Potockis, Platers, and the Czartoryskis themselves—managed to leave with much of their wealth intact in the form of liquid capital. Prince Adam bought and refurbished the palatial seventeenth-century Hôtel Lambert on the Ile Saint-Louis, whose Salle Lebrun became the setting of glittering benefits, balls, and bazaars held by his wife, Princess Anna. Other grandees took houses in the fashionable Faubourg du Roule, now the Faubourg Saint-Honoré.

Chopin became part of this world. Homesick, he could grieve for Poland in the midst of fellow Poles, speaking the language he longed to hear. He joined family celebrations of traditional feast days, performing at benefits to aid the many more impoverished Poles crowded in their own slum. Riddled with crime and disease, "Little Poland" festered behind Notre-Dame on the Ile de la Cité.

Soon, his well-connected hosts presented him to their counterparts among the French elite.

"I have been introduced all around the highest circles," he wrote to his family. "I hobnob with ambassadors, princes and ministers. I can't imagine what miracle is responsible for all this since I really haven't done anything to bring it about."

He felt uneasy that his father was still supporting him, the more so now that the Russians had closed the lycée and Nicolas Chopin's income, much reduced, depended upon a few private pupils. Discreetly, his son let it be known that he, too, was available for lessons. His fee was 20 francs*—highway robbery from a mere piano teacher, but when the instructor was a genius (hadn't a German named Robert Schumann said so in an important review?) as well as a sought-after guest and, since he was to be entrusted with wives and daughters, utterly reliable as to morals, it was a bargain.

Chopin's own musical progress faltered. His debut concert took place on February 26, 1832—five months after his arrival in Paris. The planned event, always a responsibility of the principal performer, had to be put off four times. On the appointed Sunday evening, the Salle Pleyel attracted barely more than the loyal Polish colony, with two eminent exceptions: Liszt and Mendelssohn. As was the custom, Chopin shared the program—on this occasion with two singers and ten other musicians. His role was limited to a performance of his Concerto in F Minor (probably arranged for two pianos), his Mozart variations, and participation as one of six pianists performing a Grande Polonaise by Kalkbrenner, part of the Viennese exodus of talent and now Paris's reigning virtuoso. Despite the large cast, sparse attendance, and even mixed reviews (Chopin's inaudible touch was noted once again), the twenty-two-year-old pianist had begun his ascent.

By the end of the evening, the musically astute in the small audience recognized that Chopin's genius as a composer lay precisely in his subversive use of innovation. His "abundance of original ideas," the editor, critic, and pianist François-Joseph Fétis declared a few days later, found expression in a "renewal of forms": Enlisting counterpoint, including internal voices, weaving ornamentation with washes of color, Chopin gently led his enchanted listeners from the familiar into uncharted territory. Torn between pride and envy, his fellow émigré and musician Antoni Orlowski helped beat the drum: "All Paris was stupefied,"

*Estimates of the French franc of 1830–1848 and its equivalent in today's U.S. dollar, British pound sterling, or Euro vary dramatically, ranging (to take the dollar) from $2.50 to $4.80. For a more useful idea of the franc's value during this period, note that the average daily wage of an unskilled Parisian worker was one franc. Thus, Chopin's fee for one lesson would have represented three weeks' wages for a laborer—many with families to feed.

he reported of the hundred or so stalwarts who had huddled together in Pleyel's elegant new rooms, adding that Chopin had "wiped all the others off the stage."

Then, in March, the dreaded cholera reached Paris; by April 10, the death toll was two thousand a day. Before the epidemic ended in late spring, twenty thousand had died. Musical opportunities withered as audiences and musicians alike fled the stricken city. The only follow-up to Chopin's debut was a minor role in a concert to benefit the victims' families arranged by a rich amateur, Prince de la Moskova, who took over the auditorium of the Conservatory for the occasion. Chopin's application to perform in an event sponsored by the Société des Concerts, the Conservatory's official series of concerts and the certificate of musical talent, was rejected. Kalkbrenner now proposed that Chopin consider a course of expensive master lessons—with him.

Ignored or patronized by the concert establishment, his success was ensured by another, invisible audience. Following the sale of the first two sets of Chopin's etudes and the E Minor Concerto, op. 11, thousands of amateur pianists—almost all of them women—rushed to buy the sheet music that enabled them to play these pieces, and soon the tender, swaying rhythms of the mazurka became, along with all things Polish, the rage in Paris.

But the unexpected reach of his music—beyond the world of his own exclusive performances or the envied status of his pupils, themselves an elite of wealth or talent—was made possible by another phenomenon. A new instrument, the pianoforte, was fast becoming an indispensable furnishing of middle-class households; little more than a decade later, a contemporary survey would find that sixty thousand of these instruments had been purchased in Paris alone.* Replacing the aristocratic harpsichord and the deeper-toned clavichord, the rich sonorities of the piano were suddenly, it seemed, heard everywhere. Thanks to technical advances in hammer action, pedal, and materials (from the beginning, the new instrument was almost as regularly improved and "updated"

---

*The same 1845 survey calculated that 100,000 persons were capable of playing the piano, or one-tenth of the Paris population of one million.

as present-day computers), the piano's range of tone could suggest an entire orchestra. Moderate competence could pass for artistry. Arriving at this extraordinary moment, then, Chopin was the first artist to devote himself to exploring every possibility of the piano and to inventing more.

Demand had also transformed the role of piano manufacturers. Sons of skilled artisans, they were now members of the newly moneyed class of entrepreneurs and impresarios that mushroomed under the July Monarchy. Erard (maker of Liszt's preferred instrument) and Pleyel (Chopin's favorite) were also competitors, flogging a growing consumer need for the latest and newest with advertisements of their exciting refinements of existing models, while their new showrooms added small, elegant concert halls for the display of fresh talent.

This explosion of pianos, in all sizes, shapes, and degree of luxury, required a constant supply of music, pieces within the reach of thousands of "accomplished" or "musical" wives and daughters: thus, the metamorphosis of the son of a small Berlin music publisher, Moritz Schlesinger, into Maurice Schlesinger, the foremost French publisher and retailer of music, editor of an influential musical review, and a cultural power in his own right. With the sale in 1833 of Chopin's opus 10 etudes and E Minor Concerto and the best-selling success of both, the composer and publisher were bound, for the next thirteen years, in a stormy partnership of friendship and commerce.

By the middle of the 1830s, Chopin's conquest of Paris was complete. Success and celebrity followed each other in a seamless spiral. Sales of his new work fed his cachet as a teacher; appreciation of the composer was reinforced by the magic of the performer and the charm of the man.

"He is turning the heads of all the ladies," his friend Orlowski reported. "He sets the fashion. Soon we shall all be wearing gloves à la Chopin. Only sometimes he suffers from homesickness." He kept worse pain to himself. Returning to his rooms late at night, Chopin removed his courtly amiability along with his evening clothes. Then, he yielded to "tormenting memories, sour, bitter feelings"; at other times, he felt only indifference or the desire for death. Outwardly, he no longer needed Orlowski's help; envy divided them. But his friend's ironic tone points to Chopin's troubled relations with other Polish émigrés who were also artists. Chopin had vaulted into the walled precincts of the rich and aristocratic—a world where he was already at home. Now, his handsome income stood in stark contrast to his fellow exiles', who were scratching desperately—often with growing families—merely to survive. Chopin's explanations of why high life was impoverishing him were ill chosen: "You probably think I'm making a fortune," he told an old friend, "but you're wrong. My carriage and white gloves alone cost more than I earn." His little jokes—signing letters home, "Frédéric Chopin, pauper"—were apt to mystify more than amuse those living close to the bone in Russian-occupied Warsaw, especially his mother, who had secretly sent him 1200 francs from her small savings. That both his extravagance and his humor cloaked deep anxieties about money was apparent to Liszt, well aware of the high cost of rich friends; but the Poles—poets especially—were unsympathetic.

Money and social success were not the only reasons for Chopin's estrangement from most of his fellow exiles. The younger ones, his contemporaries, tended to be liberal—when not radical—in their politics. Chopin, "more royalist than the King," proudly declared himself a Carlist. Named for the absolutist Spanish pretender Don Carlos, brother and would-be successor of Ferdinand VII, Carlism was synonymous with all the forces of reaction: antiliberal, antiparliamentary, xenophobic, intolerant of non-Catholics (to the point of pressing to revive the Inquisition), and, most crucially, against all forces of change.

His own dread of change was personal, more than political: a reflex of fear. He longed for absolute stability, and it would always elude him—or bore him, the same thing. He never shared the faith of the Polish diaspora in a triumphal return to a liberated homeland. He no longer wanted to go home. In 1833, the czar granted a general amnesty to exiles. Those who had not been revolutionary activists were allowed to return—either to stay or to visit. Chopin never availed himself of this opportunity.

While waiting for Poland's freedom, the expatriate colony had splintered along religious or political lines: millenarian fanatics, revolutionary plotters, diplomatic negotiators. The intelligentsia were at least united in their belief in an engaged art: It was up to the artists among them to keep the presence of Poland alive in exile, to celebrate her heroic past, to give voice to their suffering compatriots crushed into silence at home, to remind her allies that the present martyrdom of the "Christ of Nations" was a sign of divine favor to come.

Chopin's worst sin, then, was his continued rejection of an explicit musical nationalism. The same obstinacy he had shown in Warsaw—ignoring the call to compose a great national opera which would dramatize Poland's past; insisting upon the sufficiency of the pianoforte as an instrument of his art—became, in exile, nothing less than betrayal. (His musical settings of poems by various compatriots sound perfunctory; the art song, with its linguistic confinement, was uncongenial to him.) To his more fervent fellow Poles, it was unforgivable that Chopin, this lukewarm patriot and religious apostate who rarely set foot in any of the several churches from which Polish prayers for deliverance rose at every mass, had been anointed, by all of Paris, to personify Poland's genius.

Consciously or not, Chopin engaged these resentments from the exile community. He had always loved opera. The expressive power of the human voice stirred him as no instrument ever would. He had first fallen in love with Konstancja singing, only to be enthralled by the siren song of Delfina Potocka. Now, it was Paris that intoxicated him with its richness of operatic offerings. Days after he arrived, he was transported, along with all other Parisian music lovers, by the marvelous special effects and cast of thousands in Meyerbeer's operatic spectacle *Robert le diable*. (Capitalizing on the success of both the opera and his newest composer, Schlesinger commissioned from Chopin variations on a theme from Meyerbeer's popular work.) In letters home to Warsaw he enumerated the great vocal artists he heard night after night. In terms of his own music, Chopin's momentous discovery was the "never-ending melody" of Vincenzo Bellini's cantabile line. Soon, he had become a friend of the Sicilian composer; they spent occasional Sunday afternoons making music together with other singers and musicians.

Chopin's homage to Bellini and to opera incorporated bel canto elements and techniques into a genre that was new to him. The nocturne has come to be the form most closely identified with Chopin's musical style without Polish origins. Its inventor, however, was John Field, an Anglo-Irish composer and musician whom Chopin had admired as a student. In its earlier life, the piece functioned as a conventional salon offering. Soon after his arrival in Paris, Chopin saw the nocturne's supple possibilities as open to borrowings from the new Italian opera, notably the melodic line of the aria. At he same time he recognized the confessional capacity of the solo—that of the human voice itself. With his first nocturne, in B-flat minor, sudden shifts from minor to major, then back to minor chords, catch us off balance, unaware, like an intimate revelation overheard. It seems no coincidence that Chopin's reinvention of the genre began with his first years of exile in the city Walter Benjamin called the "capital of the nineteenth century." The nocturne breathes an urban sensibility: the voluptuous melancholy of the *flaneur,* the sudden descent of night in deserted streets, the solitary's dreaded return to empty rooms. Baudelaire's first title for his cycle of prose poems *The Spleen of Paris* had been *Poèmes nocturnes:* "I love you, O infamous capital" was the poet's ambivalent homage to his city of night.

Visual imagery, too, clings to the nocturne as urban pastoral. Chopin's lyric meditations on regret, Baudelaire's hymns of love and hate, evoke Whistler's later compositions of London's Thameside softened by moonlight. Nor can it be coincidence that these three great poets—of music, words, and paint—defined the figure of the Dandy. Chopin and Whistler, especially, armed in opera cape and white gloves, perfectionists in their art, mordant and melancholy exiles of romanticism, enemies of progress and conquerors of its capitals, expatriates of uneasy hyphen: Anglo-American, Polish-French.

In Paris, especially when it rained, Chopin said, nostalgia drove him "close to madness."

The nocturne offered Chopin an escape from this nostalgia, suffered as solitude. As he had reinvented the etude, he took another familiar form and, leaving the husk intact, he replaced the innocuous content with a coded message: "You know how I've always tried to express the feeling of our national music and how, in part, I've succeeded," Chopin wrote to Tytus on Christmas Day, 1831. To a recent interpreter, the expanded form of the Chopin nocturne stands as glorious proof of his success. Harmonies familiar only to Polish listeners pierce the isolation of the exile through communal memory: wisps of folk song, loops of mazurka. Summoning far-off church bells and drifts of chorale to recall Poland's sacred mission, Chopin affirms, with painful intimacy, their collective loss.

It's unclear how Chopin's fellow exiles heard this allusive music and whether ill feelings towards the composer were dissolved or ties strengthened by invocations of a musical language with special meaning. The nocturne's reminders of a shared past would not have compensated for the message conveyed by his present behavior. With the exception of close friends and grand patrons, Chopin was given to describing his compatriots as a "pack of imbeciles." Then, at the height of the composer's success, Stefan Witwicki, a poet and regular of George Sand's salon, arranged to call on Chopin, bringing two other Polish poets, one of them only passing through Paris. They waited for more than half an hour in the street below Chopin's apartment. Monsieur was "not at home." Nor did he trouble to explain his absence. Would he have forgotten an invitation extended to Baron de Rothschild or Prince Czartoryski, or failed to alert these gentlemen that he was unavoidably detained?

Among those left waiting in the cold that day was Poland's greatest poet. Adam Mickiewicz was recognized and honored in exile, even as his masterpieces, *Forefathers* and *Pan Tadeusz*, suffered the fate of most poetry uprooted from its native language and readers—its power and originality fated to be lost (and unread) in translation.

Mickiewicz's life in exile was marked by griefs and burdens beyond those suffered by his fellow refugees. Shortly after arriving in France, his young wife began to suffer periodic mental breakdowns, and in addition to caring for their young children, he had to regularly escort their mother back and forth to the women's insane asylum in the Salpêtrière. In 1838, the poet was honored by his adopted country with a chair in Slavic studies at the Collège de France. Before darkening religious fanaticism ended his appointment six years later, attendance at Mickiewicz's lectures was deemed essential by everyone who counted in Paris. Among the faithful was his devoted friend and admirer George Sand, who hailed the poet as "cousin to Byron and Goethe." Mickiewicz reciprocated Sand's esteem and affection. Now, he held it one of the duties of friendship to warn her against Chopin. The man was a "moral vampire," he said.

His warning came too late.

In the six weeks that followed Chopin's first reluctant invitation to Sand, late in 1836, they saw each other six times. Spanning the old year and the new one of 1837, the season of festivities and bright beginnings ought to have smiled on the new couple, a union deemed inevitable, this time, by all their friends. Now, however, new obstacles loomed, at least one of them entirely foreign to George's experience of men. All that attracted her in Chopin, and set him apart from the others—his genius, his intellectual subtlety, his delicacy of perception, his refinement and reserve, his fastidiousness of manner and dress—were inseparable, so it appeared, from the shame, disgust, and guilt he felt about sex. Sand was horrified. In a forty-page letter she wrote to Albert Grzymala, she revealed the outrage she felt on discovering that her beloved had been so revolted by earlier sexual experiences as to recoil from the sensual as a defilement of love. What unspeakable woman had done this to him?

Two years before—in August 1835—Chopin had joined his parents in Karlsbad. Their reunion at the fashionable spa was the last time he would see them again. Stopping in Dresden on his way back to Paris, he had fallen in love with sixteen-year-old Maria Wodzinska, sister of his friend and classmate Antoni Wodzinski. Seeing his family return to Poland had revived Chopin's home-sickness, and the Wodzinskis gathered him in "like a fourth son," Madame Wodzinska said, tacitly encouraging his interest in her daughter. He extended his stay with them for two weeks.

A pretty, dark young woman, Maria was musical, but remark-able only in that she seems to have been more innocent, sheltered, and passive than other girls of her age and class. On his return to Paris, Chopin corresponded with both mother and daughter, car-rying out commissions that ranged from sending them the latest French novels to the expedition of a Pleyel piano. Matters looked promising, and in late July of the following year, 1836, Chopin rejoined the family in Marienbad, staying for the entire month of August. Now, in what was to be encoded in their correspondence as "the Gray Hour," Chopin and Maria declared their love, and subject to parental approval, the two young people considered themselves unofficially engaged. Madame Wodzinska appears to have supported her daughter's choice, while pointing out that the final decision would, of course, rest with her husband. Joyfully, Chopin returned to Paris. Then, for reasons that remain mysteri-ous, paternal approval was not forthcoming. Maria's letters cooled, becoming impersonal and infrequent. The romance seems not so much to have broken off as to have dwindled away; if mother or daughter offered an explanation, it has not survived.

Chopin was devastated. He accompanied Camille Pleyel on a trip to London in July of 1837, where his friend hoped the distrac-tions of a new musical scene would cheer him, but the foreignness of his surroundings, the fog and damp, deepened his isolation and gloom. Reports of his ill health had circulated in Warsaw, includ-ing an erroneous obituary. Would Maria's protective parents have sent their eighteen-year-old child to Paris to shoulder the burdens of wife to a sickly artist, dependent upon his earnings for every franc? That on some level the failure of his suit was predictable—

possibly to Chopin himself—would not have consoled him. Among the effects found at his death was a bundle of Maria's letters and a dried rose, tied with a ribbon and a scrap of paper with the words "My Sorrow."

He had told Sand of this attachment, leaving unanswered the question of whether he was still in love with the younger woman. Thus, in the same letter in which George elaborated her concerns about Chopin's sexuality to his older and more worldly friend Count Grzymala, she also set forth her doubts about her role in the composer's life *if* his affections were still engaged elsewhere. Sand saw clearly the symbolic roles that she and Maria played at this turning point in Chopin's life: the pure child sweetheart, an icon of old Poland whom he could romanticize from afar, and the Frenchwoman, independent, infamous, powerful, and demanding—his past and future. She had reason to fear her rival. Unformed and unattainable, Maria Wodzinska embodied Chopin's flight from adult passions. Although his reply has not survived, Grzymala seems to have reassured and encouraged Sand to proceed with her task of re-education.

Only Chopin was not reassured. He could not bring himself to accept that silence from the Wodzinskis spelled the end of hope. Sand's imperious certainty that swept aside any obstacle to desire filled him with dread as much as longing. The reserve and distance he maintained between himself and the world was no romantic posture; with his limited energy, he saw preserving and protecting himself as crucial for his art, above all. And what Sand demanded was nothing less than that he abandon this wary stewardship, and yield his fears of loss, of waste (connected certainly to sexual terror), to embrace her own faith that extravagance—in money, politics, friendship, work, and love—promised not death but rebirth.

In turmoil, Chopin sent an urgent message to Grzymala: He must see him—immediately—no matter the hour. The two met in the fashionable Maison Dorée café. This time, a trusted friend dismissed his case for caution and delay. In the spring of 1838, nearly two years after their first meeting, Chopin and Sand became lovers.

The incumbent in Sand's life, Félicien Mallefille, took it badly. A playwright who had been hired as tutor to her son, Maurice, he began behaving like a character from a boulevard melodrama. He took to stalking the lovers, staking out a place near Sand's lodgings. When he waylaid her one evening, waving a gun, it was clear that Sand's vows of a love that ended only with death had been taken literally. Mallefille's threats, Maurice's rheumatic pains, and Chopin's dread of the impending cold decided Sand in favor of flight and a winter in Majorca.

Before they left, she accompanied Chopin—established now as her lover—to a concert he had agreed to give at the Marquis de Custine's chateau at Saint-Gratien. Enamored of Chopin himself, Custine's turbulent feelings surged at the sound of his guest's playing: love, pity, jealousy, spite. Custine saw in the frail composer and heard in his music the marks of certain death: "You have no idea what Mme Sand has managed to do with him in one summer! Consumption has seized that figure and turned it into a soul without a body," he crowed.

Whether Chopin looked this ill or whether this was wishful thinking on the marquis's part, the end of his musical program suggested that the composer's thoughts, too, had turned to death. As Custine wrote to a confidant, Chopin played "funeral marches that, despite myself, made me dissolve in tears." One of these, the most famous of all funeral marches, Chopin later incorporated as the third movement of the Sonata in B-flat Minor, op. 35: Played by the frail artist in the worldly company and precious decor of Custine's salon, its effect was the more shattering. The composer now appeared as the ghost at the banquet, evoking "the cortege that led him to his final abode," his host said. That Chopin had earlier discarded the word "funeral" from the title of his march* only intensified the music's painful impact, confirming Custine in the belief that his friend, by joining his life with Sand's, had embraced death: "The poor creature does not see that this woman has the love of a vampire."

Much to their friends' relief and enemies' disappointment, the two "vampires" did not drain each other to the death in Majorca, after all.

---

*Chopin's march was indeed played at his own funeral.

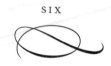

SIX

Preludes to Paradise

In the summer of 1838, a few months before Sand and Chopin left Paris, Delacroix had a piano brought from Pleyel to his studio, where he painted a double portrait of the lovers, both friends of his. All we can see of Chopin are his head and shoulders, just enough to reveal the dandy; he wears a black velvet jacket, and a spread of dark blue silk cravat all but covers his white shirt front. Even though his arms and hands are invisible, we know from the intent unseeing gaze and slight frown of concentration that Chopin is seated at the piano, playing. Sand stands next to him; her full body, shown from just below the waist, faces front, but her profiled head is almost completely turned towards the pianist. She stares down, looking at what we cannot see: Chopin's hands on the keys. Delacroix's double portrait is a duet in paint: the composer playing his own music and his rapt mistress who makes of listening an act of love.

At the same time, Delacroix evoked Sand's androgyny. In one hand, she grasps a white handkerchief, iconic accessory of female singers in concert, while in the other, she holds between thumb and forefinger, masculine style, a small cigar or cigarette, smoked down to the end.

. . .

Eugène Delacroix's unfinished double portrait of Sand and Chopin was cut as shown. Hers is now in the Ordrupgaard Collection, Copenhagen, his in the Louvre, Paris. The area that appears in gray is lost.

Reflecting its subjects, the portrait has had a troubled history. The loosely painted background and sketchy rendering of Sand's gown, along with her arms and hands, are evidence that the picture remained unfinished: Someone—artist or sitter—was dissatisfied with the work in progress. The portrait stayed in Delacroix's studio until after his death, when it was purchased by another painter, whose heirs apparently were responsible for cutting the canvas into two unequal parts. Bought by a Danish collector, the portrait of Sand has remained in Denmark; Chopin found his way into the Louvre. The amputation has always been considered an act of unspeakable vandalism, but when the two halves of the canvas were reunited for a recent exhibition, we can understand why an earlier owner saw his painting as individual portraits that did not belong together. The scale of the heads, the position of Chopin's bust and of Sand's torso, their relation to each other and to the background and foreground of the composition, are all puzzling—a problem that could not be solved. Even as great an artist as Delacroix could not order his subjects to inhabit the same space.

Chopin and Sand's four-month interlude in Majorca has taken on a mythic life of its own. Beckoning with the shimmer of a mirage, the island lured them with promises of a semitropical paradise where it is never winter. They set out to worship the miracle of sun that cures the incurable, conferring strength, health, and immortality. Instead, the largest of the Balearic Islands has come to stand for the perfidies of climate, as the setting for the longest-playing trope on consumption consuming the artist, of fatality hastened by carnal passion, of the flesh laid waste.

In reality, Majorca was the place where Sand was transformed from sexual outlaw to nurturing parent, beginning the slow drip of dependence. Here Chopin, orphaned by exile, was reborn into the Oedipal dream: the favored older son who shared his mother's bed.

Theirs was no wild flight of lovers. For the first time, George's bohemian disdain for appearances yielded to Chopin's implacable correctness. Like diplomatic missions, they traveled separately, Sand accompanied by the two children and a maid, Chopin escorted by the brother of the Spanish ambassador, meeting in Perpignan.

Chopin's first impressions of Palma de Mallorca were, indeed, of an island paradise: "I'm surrounded by palm trees, cedar, cactus; lemon, orange, fig and pomegranate trees everywhere. . . . The sky is turquoise, the sea lapis-lazuli, the mountains emerald and the air smells of heaven. The sun shines all day long."

Serpents, in the form of the local population, were not long in appearing. No sooner had Sand found the only house to be rented on the island than Chopin succumbed to a respiratory infection. Visits by three local doctors only succeeded in spreading the word that his illness was indeed tuberculosis. ("One said I'm going to die, the second that I'm dying, the third that I'm already dead," he reported.) A recently passed Spanish law decreed that those so infected be promptly evicted, the cost of burning and replacing all household effects added to their bill. Hostility to the foreigners as a public health menace was further justified by their suspect morals. Their failure to attend mass was duly noted. Word spread that even the little girl in this un-Christian family wore pants. The carriers were banished to the remote beauty of an abandoned Carthusian monastery in Valldemosa, perched among mountain crags where the nearest neighbors were the eagles circling overhead.

Provisions and medicine were sold to the pariahs at extortionist prices. Food cooked in rancid olive oil by a local peasant woman added chronic diarrhea to Chopin's respiratory problems. Now, Sand's competence and grit became crucial to their survival. She dealt fiercely with every obstacle, human and material. She took over the cooking; in between tutoring her children, she set in motion the superhuman feat of getting Chopin's Pleyel piano shipped from Paris. She was desperately behind in finishing her novel *Spiridion*, but the demands of householding, tutoring, and nursing left her no time to write.

Sick, demoralized, without a decent piano, still Chopin worked. He had not come to this primitive paradise for a long holiday, but to regain the strength to compose. Before leaving Paris, he had borrowed money from publishers, friends—even a moneylender—to finance an indefinite stay abroad. Lessons were his only regular source of income, and without them he was entirely dependent upon the sale of his music. If he did not complete works he had already sold and make solid headway on new compositions, he would return more heavily in debt. He had taken with him the uncompleted twenty-four preludes of what would become opus 28, for which he had received an advance of five hundred francs from Pleyel, who had led Chopin—wrongly—to believe that as a friend he would do better by the composer than Schlesinger. He had also borrowed fifteen hundred francs on a short-term loan from his friend the banker Auguste Léo, ceding him the German rights to the preludes as credit.

Dealings with his publishers—Schlesinger, Pleyel, and others—reveal an unknown side of Chopin. Next to the familiar images of the composer—the frail, hypersensitive artist, unworldly, even naive; the dandy, proud, reserved, and mysterious—emerges another Chopin: the tough and shrewd negotiator, aware of the market value of his music and determined to wrest the highest possible prices from its sales. (In fact, the works that had gone to Schlesinger five years before had been sold earlier to a less important French publisher—a contract that Chopin simply decided to ignore.) From now on, in all of his bargainings, he sought to flog competition, playing one offer against another for the best price in France, while trying to keep foreign rights and profits for himself by dealing directly with his German and English publishers.

From our perspective, these negotiating strategies are accepted professional practice employed by all artists' representatives. Chopin, however, was the last artist who should have represented himself. With his low tolerance for frustration, uncontrollable outbursts of anger and aggression, and a peasant's suspiciousness, negotiating on his own behalf exposed him at his worst. When

Schlesinger would not give him what he wanted, or demanded work for which he had already paid a substantial advance, the composer flew into hysterical rages, reviling the publisher to others as a "Jew dog" and summoning vengeful fantasies of what would happen to him and his kind if there were any justice.

Money considerations apart, he wanted and needed to work for himself, too. His new surroundings reminded him that in work lay salvation: "Here I am, hair uncurled, no white gloves, just white face, as usual," he told his friend and factotum Julian Fontana. The former cell that now served as his bedroom and study made him think of an upended coffin; the small space had a high vaulted ceiling and one tiny window that looked onto the garden, with its cypress, orange, and palm trees. There was a folding camp bed, and beside it, a schoolboy's square desk, uncomfortable for writing, with just enough surface to hold a lead candlestick with a candle—a great luxury in these parts, Chopin noted sourly. On top of a moldering pile of papers left by the last inhabitant of the cell, he placed his own scrawled manuscript pages and his well-worn copy of Bach's *Well-Tempered Clavier*.

Pillars of Chopin's musical life, the baroque master's great preludes and fugues, complex and inevitable, were always with him. Since his student days in Warsaw, he had begun his daily practice with these works; he played them to warm up before concerts. As a teacher, he insisted that his pupils study their architecture, the teasing voices of Bach's counterpoint, now hidden, now revealed. But he also used the two books as their author intended: to extend the pianist's capacities—technical and physical—to master the full range of the keyboard.

His own preludes, collected as opus 28, would become Chopin's dazzling chromatic homage and challenge to Bach. He had continued work on these and had begun other compositions on the primitive little piano that Sand had managed to rent in town. But this local treasure hunt was nothing compared with her superhuman efforts to procure a first-rate instrument, which included the Pleyel's long-awaited arrival in the harbor of Palma on

December 21; three weeks later, the piano appeared at the monastery door. Days of pleading, threatening, and haggling were required just to release the instrument from the clutches of extortionist customs officials, who were holding them up to the tune of four hundred francs—nearly the cost of the piano. Reducing that by half, Sand then had to arrange to transport this delicate mechanism—with its hundreds of movable parts—over the five inaccessible miles of mountain roads which, as Chopin decided, had been dug by streams and repaired by avalanches. Its delivery—intact and even in tune—from an unsprung cart could only be explained as a miracle performed by his guardian angel.

At last he was able to hear the new preludes. But precisely which of the twenty-four were new—that is, composed since his arrival in Majorca—is uncertain; estimates range from half of them to only four. It would seem, then, more than poetic license to propose that such a collection of pieces, written at different times, unified by formal considerations—their chromatic design, and deliberate contrasts of alternating major and minor keys—also reflects a sense of place. Yet two of Chopin's contemporaries reached for the same image to convey the music's feel of impending tragedy: a great creature in flight, free, fierce and powerful, brought to ground. Baudelaire saw "a brilliantly feathered bird circling the horrors of an abyss," and Schumann shuddered at "ruins—, single eagle feathers in wild confusion." These hearings return us to Chopin's own first impressions of Valldemosa—"the poetry breathed by everything here"—but also the sense of dread.

"Even when he felt well, he found the cloister full of terrors and phantoms," Sand said. And she later recalled a night when she and the children, coming back from town, were delayed by a storm; on their return, they found Chopin at the piano "in a kind of frozen despair, playing his wonderful prelude and weeping." At the sight of them, he leapt up, as from a waking nightmare in which he had seen their violent deaths. "I knew you were dead," he told them. He was greeting ghosts.

Twenty-three bars long, the Prelude in A Minor, second of the twenty-four that make up opus 28, has received more critical scrutiny than any of the others. The piece has been called "disturbing and disturbed" and one of late romanticism's "impossible objects." Forged of disjunctions, the prelude's harmonic clashes in the bass accompaniment, the melody's ominous descents followed by silences, have seemed to expose an artist riven by oppositions: of body and spirit, classicism and romanticism, naked introspection bound by constraints of mathematical precision.

A serious amateur pianist, André Gide experienced the prelude as trauma—visceral and psychic. The music's intensity of feeling assaulted him with "something close to physical terror," he said. The repetitive rocking in the first two measures of unaccompanied bass mimes the compulsive back-and-forth motion characteristic of certain mental disorders. In contrast to the left-hand ostinato in the later Barcarolle, op. 60, with its lulling wash of waves, the beat of the prelude's opening marks time with foreboding.

Disjunctions wrenched the prelude into life. Following the upheavals of travel, Chopin suffered a leper's banishment to Valldemosa. There, even as he was cradled by the intimacies of family life, he felt the tenderness of his care accuse the cruelty of sickness and pain. Surrounded by youth, health, and love, he suffered every absence as an intimation of death.

Composed in these months, a draft sketch for a prelude in E-flat minor has been deciphered and reconstructed by the Chopin scholar Jeffrey Kallberg. Its thirty-three measures reveal a vocabulary of terror not heard again in music until our own century. From beginning to end, continuous trills twitter in the upper register while the lower part of the keyboard keeps its own time to a rocking triplet motion. These are the warring vibrations of madness, of two metronomes ticking in the head. Stripped of melody, Chopin's "experiment in pure ornamentation" draws us into the obsessiveness of pattern, abstract and static. It may be that his abandonment of the piece, composed in sickness, reflects Chopin's sense that the prelude was possessed of a *mal'occhio*. Once the "terrors and phantoms" had disappeared, and with his own health briefly restored, it would be tempting the devil to summon its demonic sources once again.

He had brought with him other works begun in Paris, the first each of what would ultimately number four ballades and four scherzos.

The ballade began as a medieval poem, the favorite verse form of the troubadour-poets. Lyrics to be recited or sung, the ballade's stanzas end with a refrain of regret or bitterness: "Where are the snows of yesteryear?" They are songs of experience, tales from a heedless youth recalled by a battered survivor: of lovers unfaithful or dead, of family and companions never to be seen again. Chopin was the first to call works for the piano "ballade," and he retained the narrative associations that clung to the name.

With its seductive scrap of recitative that breathes "Once upon a time . . ." Chopin's first ballade draws us into his story. The second needs no such introduction. In both ballades the wistful opening melodies evoke a fleeting innocence, before we are swept into a drama of musical episodes and personae: racing chromatic pursuits, lyrical encounters, cold silence and wrenching separation; tension and sudden release. Then, the turbulent codas remind us: There are no happy endings.

Chopin's scherzos, on the other hand, lay bare the ironies buried in the title, whose literal meaning is "joke": The joke is on us, played by the fates against whose senseless malice we rage unheard. Chopin hears us. He gives voice, achingly, to the pain inflicted by memory, that cruelest of torments inflicted upon the sinners of Dante's *Inferno;* the remembrance of past happiness recalled in present sorrow. He invented music that whipsaws between poles of feeling. From strident discord, in the First Scherzo, he retreats to the tender harmonies of a Polish children's carol. Stranded in childhood himself, its raw emotions—savage, shifting, direct—remained available to his art.

Ultimately, the climate's treachery defeated them. (Is there any crueler lie of nature than the dark skies and freezing rain of Goethe's "lands where the lemon trees bloom"?) The northerner's dream of a life-restoring South more often ends in death—in Venice; or in Rome, like Keats; or, like Lawrence, in Ravallo. It was Sand who, ill advised by the unreliable ex-consul, Emmanuel Marliani, had brought Chopin on this "catastrophic voyage"; now it was Sand who saved and, briefly, strengthened him.

Fear only made George stronger and more decisive. Each attack left Chopin weaker than the one before. Soon after the new year of 1839, she knew he would not recover in these primitive, hostile conditions. Not even her energy and resourcefulness could render a place intended for prayer and penance a family dwelling. (She and the maid had constructed an outdoor kitchen so that the choking fumes would not poison the air in their rooms.) By the middle of February, Chopin was coughing blood; he was feverish, refusing to eat and too weak to leave his bed. Swiftly, she booked passage for them on the next boat, the famous cargo vessel where their only fellow passengers were pigs headed for market. She packed up her little household, and they made the agonizing descent to Palma. A carriage with springs had been promised them, but the owner then reneged, fearing he would have to destroy his infected vehicle. In the cart and again on board the boat, Chopin coughed "basins of blood." Following a week in Barcelona, he was well enough for the trip to Marseilles. There, installed in suites in the best hotel, Sand supervised Chopin's convalescence as minutely as she had nursed him during the despairing days of sickness. She found a competent and solicitous doctor, hovered over his diet and rest. Like a Mozartian duet where the hero and heroine sing of their love at opposite ends of the stage, Sand and Chopin wrote to friends, extolling, in identical phrases, the perfection of the other:

"My God, if you knew him as I do now, you would love him even more," Sand told Charlotte Marliani; and to his friend Grzymala, Chopin confided: "You know, you would love her still more if you knew her as well as I do at this moment." Each was anointed an "angel" by the other, George of devotion and self-sacrifice, and "Chip-Chip," as she called him, for his "kindness, tenderness, and patience." George confessed to Marliani, "I imagine that his sensibility is too finely wrought, too exquisite, too perfect to survive for long in this rough life." While Sand fretted over Chopin's angelic innocence of the real world, the angel himself was hysterically reviling his publishers, past and present. Word reached him in Marseilles that Pleyel, far from topping Schlesinger's terms, was offering less; he had not yet received payment for his piano, and until the five hundred francs arrived from Palma, Pleyel refused to release funds for other works under consideration, even should Chopin agree to his offer—lower than the price named by the composer. This still left him the publisher of the preludes, "with the right to wipe his ass with them," Chopin raged to Fontana. Chastened, Chopin now sent Fontana back to Schlesinger, but although the composer had lowered his price since his first offer, the publisher now wanted to renegotiate the terms. Chopin's first impulse was to agree—"better to deal with one Jew than with three"—but ultimately, he decided to wait until he returned to Paris, when he would try his luck with yet another publisher.

His confident plans for the future were evidence of restored health. He celebrated his own return to life by playing Schubert at a memorial mass in Marseilles for his friend the tenor Adolphe Nourrit, who had fled Paris and a failing career to leap to his death from the window of a Naples hotel room. Chopin's efforts at the church's untuned organ honored a fellow artist martyred by the fickleness of audiences. The suicide's warning was not lost on him. Sand was more horrified by the little group who had accompanied the body home to France: the singer's six children and his young widow, visibly pregnant with a seventh.

She felt blessed that their own ordeal had drawn them closer: "We became a family, our bonds tighter because it was us against the world. Now, we cling to one another with deeper, more intimate feelings of happiness. How can we complain when our hearts are so full?"

SEVEN

Homecoming

C ome and create a new motherland at Nohant."

It had been Marie d'Agoult who had teasingly issued that summons to Chopin two years earlier, when she and Liszt were Sand's guests in the Berry. At that time, Chopin—still stubbornly "chaste," Liszt reported—had, more than once, refused. Now, on June 1, 1839, he gratefully allowed his "angel" to take him home, embracing her faith that the place that had always healed her would confer its blessings upon him as well.

Built by her grandmother Marie-Aurore Dupin, beginning in the late 1760s, Nohant is, first and always, a house, elegant, graceful, and welcoming—*souriant*, smiling, the French say of such houses, a reminder that certain arrangements of stone can present a human face. Other local gentry, Sand's friends and relatives among them, were barricaded in forbidding chateaux that loom throughout the region, legacies of the dukes of Berry, their dungeons and moats still intact: Montgivray, where her half brother, Hippolyte Chatiron, was drinking himself to death; the Château d'Ars, home of George's childhood friend Gustave Papet, now her doctor. Surrounded by feudal remnants, Nohant seems to greet the visitor with open arms; the soul of an earlier farmhouse still alive in the modest front courtyard and great-hearted kitchen, smokehouse and stables only a parterre away.

Sand loved Nohant because it was her first refuge, far from

Paris and the chaos of life with a crazy mother, who was actually paid to stay away from the little girl by her grandmother, Madame Dupin. The elder Aurore herself was a starchy relic of the ancien régime, but she set her namesake free to play with the tenant farmers' children. Sharing their games and chores, the young Aurore absorbed an intimate knowledge of everything grown, raised, slaughtered, and cooked on the property. More important still, she was exposed to the harshness of human lives lived on the land. She observed closely the maimed, misshapen bodies, the vulnerability to natural catastrophe, and the farmers' hatred of the speculators whose profits were based upon the creation of scarcity and starvation. These struggling peasant families remained her friends, just as the Berry would always be her country.

Now, Chopin and Sand, accompanied by the children and a maid, traveled by ferryboat down the Rhône from Marseilles to Arles, and then, by leisurely relay of carriages, they approached the gates of Nohant on June 2, 1839.

Chopin's first impressions were musical. Instead of Valldemosa's circling eagles, they were greeted by the songs of "nightingales and larks," he wrote to Grzymala. Berry in midsummer recalled Mazovia, the region around Warsaw that Chopin had visited countless times as a boy. The same pollarded willow and chestnut trees line low roads spooling invisibly through pastureland mirrored in still ponds and streams whose presence is hidden by flowering hedgerows. The manor houses of his friends were more rustic versions of Nohant, walls and facade of local stone softened by climbing roses and clematis. After Majorca, he was grateful for a nature that seemed to embrace them. Still, Chopin was not a country person. He was more delighted by the provisions indoors that Sand had made for his arrival. Next to her bedroom, she had created a little apartment for him, a library and bedchamber freshly hung with festive red and blue Chinese paper. Downstairs, in place of the upright piano Sand had installed for Liszt's visit, a small Pleyel grand awaited Chopin's return to work. These were his ideal accommodations: a private retreat surrounded by the reassuring sounds of a busy household; children, servants, dogs; carriages with friends and neighbors arriving and leaving. Secure in a solitude without loneliness, he rarely made the effort to join Sand on the excursions that she and the children planned and discussed with such gusto. No corner of the "Black Valley" would be left unexplored: There were trips to prehistoric sites and Merovingian ruins; nature expeditions where Maurice, fifteen, pursued his avid collecting of minerals and meteorites, butterflies, reptiles, and insects. On these explorations, his sister Solange could display her progress in riding: a fearless jumper with easy mastery of her mount, the ten-year-old's advanced equestrian skills were the only talents that found favor in her mother's eyes. Very occasionally, Chopin set off with the rest, riding on the back of a gentle donkey. But when the others dismounted to explore the area on foot, he remained behind, to pick wildflowers or doze in the sun.

The charming young Dr. Papet had examined Chopin thoroughly and reported himself satisfied. Despite recent weight loss and episodes of coughing blood, the lungs were sound. True, the patient was prone to chronic infections of the larynx, but the doctor was optimistic. With an orderly, healthy life—regular meals, plenty of rest, and, above all, the vigilant care of his dear friend—even these symptoms would diminish, if not disappear entirely. He rejected completely the Majorcan doctors' gloomy diagnosis of mortal illness.

Jubilant, Sand felt confirmed in her own positive view of Chopin's condition, the more so as, within weeks, he returned to composing and playing with a concentration and energy she had never observed before. "He enchants all of us from morning till night," Sand reported, and it says much for Chopin's own feelings of strength and possibility that his earlier march, whether conceived as "funeral" or simply heard as such, was now given an expansive sonata setting. Its dark and terrible opening bars sound a prophecy of lament; then, as it spirals into a *doppio movimento*, anguish ebbs into pastoral calm. Possibly the first pages Chopin composed in Nohant, the opening "double movement" of the Sonata no. 2 in B-flat Minor, op. 35, enfolds death as part of life.

Buffeted between restlessness and languor, Chopin typically

found pushing troublesome works to completion more difficult than beginning new ones. A measure of his sense of well-being, then, in this first summer at Nohant, was his will to finish what he had started earlier and put aside.

He had begun the first of the two nocturnes of opus 37, no. 11 in G minor, in Palma. Islands are famous for disorienting the traveler, and in Majorca, Chopin had dangled between past and present. He was sicker than he had ever been; yet, nursed by Sand, he relived a cosseted childhood while confronting the reality of dying. The choralelike interlude introduced into the first nocturne has been heard as both hymn and funeral march. Composed in Nohant, the second nocturne of opus 37, no. 12 in G major, weaves bold experiment into the gentle rocking of a barcarolle; from the first bars, the lapping rhythm of waves emerges from the overlapping, out-of-phase measures played by right and left hand.

Defying certainties of rhythm or key, the opening gestures of the Third Scherzo, in C-sharp minor, begun in Majorca and completed in Nohant, present Chopin as lion trainer. With confidence bordering on arrogance, he opens the cage and faces down the beast. Violence is courted only to be elegantly controlled. Brutal double-octaves subside, rising as airborne arabesques in a contest whose plays are displays of mastery. When Sand listened to Chopin at work on the scherzo, she heard an agony of creation new to her. This was her first exposure to Chopin's obsessive perfectionism, and it recalled the intimacy of the sickroom: the endless repetition of a troublesome phrase, worked and reworked; the angry, despairing sounds of frustrated effort—cunning, desperate, exhausting—to retrieve a composition that had earlier come to him, complete and unbidden, only to evaporate. This was art as blood sport, or human sacrifice. She was humbled, but also mystified and frightened. "Why couldn't Chopin manage to save intact the work he had earlier conceived all of a piece?" she asked.

A journeywoman scrivener, covering reams of paper nightly while the rest of the household slept, she wrote the way others breathed. She wrote to pay bills and pay off debts, "to feed twelve mouths," to satisfy her ever more impatient publisher for work owed him and to extract needed advances against future novels:

"I'm working like an old rat, gnawing my brains," she wrote to her half-brother, Hippolyte, thanking him for seeing to their small income from property, freeing her to write. And she later told her great friend, that other slave to perfection, Gustave Flaubert, that even had she been blessed with his brilliance, she never had his luxury of time, to chew each word, prod and pare every sentence. But she harbored no illusions about herself; she was not an artist. Her success simply enabled her to provide for all those dependent upon her and, where Chopin was concerned, to pay the tribute owed by one of modest gifts to genius. Flaubert had had first his mother and old nurse, then his niece, to care for him; Chopin had only her.

They had been at Nohant for a little less than three weeks when Sand, using a penknife or hard sharp pencil, scratched a date on the paneled embrasure of her bedroom window: June 19, 1839. Originally, the mysterious graffito—the only known notation of the kind ever attributed to the writer—was followed by a line of verse in English. The line doesn't survive and no one has ever identified the poetry, which seems to have been obliterated first; the date itself has since been plastered, painted, and papered over many times. Theories about the meaning of the lost words abound: What do they commemorate? The editor of Sand's twenty-five-volume correspondence and most of her other autobiographical writing believed that the tracing paid homage to the new life of peace and happiness that opened before them, affirming the optimism she had first expressed in Marseilles: Majorca and its trials had forged deeper bonds of love and intimacy between them. Others have argued that so precise a date must signal an anniversary. Its location in Sand's bedroom has encouraged two divergent views of supposed sexual significance: The day marks either the passage of a year since the consummation of their love or the reverse, the end of Sand's physical relations with Chopin.

There are few clues from either that shed light on the meaning of the graffito. Medicine in the nineteenth century held sexual activity to be dangerous for consumptives. Sand, however, was persuaded that Chopin was free of the disease; and she believed, almost alone among her contemporaries, in sexual fulfillment as natural—indeed, as the *most* natural, both physically and spiritually, expression of human love. She had come to take's Chopin frail constitution for granted; he would always feel "not quite ill or yet entirely well," continuing to suffer periods of lassitude, she said. As soon as he felt the least bit energetic, he was in high spirits, and even in the grip of melancholy "he threw himself upon the piano to compose some of his most beautiful pages."

Whether conceived in sadness or gaiety, the last three mazurkas of the four that would become opus 41 are among those "most beautiful pages" Chopin composed at Nohant. Even their creator, who so rarely expressed any satisfaction with his work, admitted to a certain pride in these pieces: "They seem as lovely to me as only youngest children can be to an aging parent."

The form most intimately expressive of a self hidden from intimates and the fullest expression of his genius, the mazurka offered Chopin a freedom to take stylistic risks. With his second set, opus 7, the first that he composed in Paris in 1831, the mazurkas became the alchemist's laboratory, a place to experiment with expanding the traditional structure of the dance form, but also to play with fire. Here, the composer conjured musical forays into the grotesque—the off-balance and asymmetrical, the ugly and misshapen flowers of evil cultivated by the romantics. In Chopin, what Charles Rosen has called "sinister sonorities" imprint the final mazurkas of both opus 24 and opus 30. Harsh dissonances accelerate before collapsing or just trickling away.

Certainly, the last three mazurkas of opus 41, Chopin's "lovely . . . youngest children," fulfill the ultimate romantic requirement: beauty touched with strangeness. Marked by hammering percussive repetitions that promise no relief in resolution, they expose, like flayed flesh, the anatomy of obsession that so disturbed Sand.

Chopin's generally improved health and steady productivity allayed George's principal worries, but she continued to fret over his spirits. She feared the slide into an enveloping ennui, that toxic mix of melancholy and boredom whose only antidote was diversion in its true sense, the turning away from care. He needed spectacles, opera and theater, concerts and cafés, balls and soirées; but most important, he missed other people, friends, acquaintances, and strangers, the swirling, shifting human panorama of Paris. Life at Nohant, with its country rhythms, was monotonous, "austere," Sand acknowledged. Estate manager, housekeeper, children's tutor, breadwinner writing into the night to make up missed deadlines, she could not help failing him as an available companion; her other obligations often left him without company when he least wanted to be alone. Separately and sometimes together, in the same letter, they wrote beseechingly to Grzymala to come for a visit. Since turning to him for counsel in her successful siege of Chopin, Sand had adopted "Gryz" as godfather to their union; a standing joke was to address the dashing former military officer turned financier as "dear husband," with "Fryk-Fryk" discussed as their "little one." Since Chopin was certainly in on this playful scenario, there is no reason to read this epistolary role-playing, as some have done, for evidence that their relations as lovers had ended. More to the point, Sand's salutation may be a reminder that she, too, had enjoyed a fling with Grzymala, whose official mistress was never included in these invitations. By way of substitute, he was promised the canopied bed formerly occupied by the temptress Marie d'Agoult.

Sand might be deemed the most fascinating woman in Europe by many, but she humbly confessed to Grzymala the fear that, even when she was free, her company was insufficient to her lover's happiness. "I'm the last one to whom he'll complain of being bored," she told their friend, imploring him to come and "take the pulse of Chopin's morale." Finally, at the end of August, Grzymala appeared, and for two weeks the two friends chattered and joked in Polish. Their high spirits buoyed the whole household; the children now had two accents to imitate, rolling their r's and making up long Polish words. Sand invited the favorites among her Berrichon stalwarts to meet the ebullient houseguest; brilliant talkers all, the men had in common those double and even triple careers that flourished in French provincial life. The convivial bustle eased the tensions that accompanied the visit of Sand's publisher, François Buloz, and his wife. From Majorca, letters between George and Buloz had become increasingly acrimonious, with accusations and counteraccusations about money owed and withheld, manuscripts long overdue, pleas for patience and another advance. Unlike Chopin, whose rage towards his publishers was vented to third parties only, Sand, true to form, insulted Buloz directly: "You've become so ambitious, you now claim to understand what you publish!" she sneered, going on to accuse him of a host of other sins, from bad faith to outright theft. Along with his influential role as publisher and editor of the *Revue des Deux Mondes,* which serialized his authors' novels before these were issued as books, Buloz had recently been promoted from commissioner to director of the Théâtre Français. In this capacity, he now urged Sand to write a play, pointing out the huge earnings that success on the stage had won for playwrights like Dumas *père.* She could easily claim a piece of this pie. Excited by the challenge, Sand plunged into writing her first drama, *Cosima, or Hatred at the Heart of Love.* At the least, she brought wide experience to her subject.

Finally, the guests were gone. Their first summer at Nohant, with its "temperate heat in daytime and evenings of delicious cool," was almost over. After weeks of constant company to satisfy his need for distraction, Chopin was grateful now for the strolls alone in the gardens with his Aurore—"Dawn," a name he loved both in French and in Polish. But it was the soft twilight hour that they both preferred. Then he would play for her alone.

By the middle of September, the chill drove them indoors ever earlier, infecting Chopin with his seasonal sense of dread; it was more than time to think of returning to Paris. Sand had revisions and rehearsals. Chopin must see to dealing with his publishers; he had deputized these negotiations to his friend, fellow musician, and copyist Julian Fontana for too long. Now, however, he would exploit the latter's fraying good will yet again, assigning him the task of finding apartments for both of them.

Neither Sand nor Chopin had a place to live. Chopin had given up the expensive Chaussée d'Antin rooms while he was in Majorca, his furniture parceled out among friends for storage. And in her recent Parisian visits, Sand had alighted with the Marlianis. Chopin bombarded Fontana, enlisting Grzymala as well, with lists of their respective housing requirements, detailed as to location (his had to be both fashionable and central), number of rooms (including their disposition), views, neighbors (quiet and few), and, not least, rent. As a bachelor, Chopin's needs were met with less difficulty: Fontana found a suitable apartment at 5, rue Tronchet, the wide street behind the Madeleine. Next to a splendid new town house, it was a perfect location for his lessons. Next, he put Fontana to the test of readying his quarters for their new tenant. He wanted the two rooms hung with dove-colored wallpaper with a glossy finish and dark green border, not too wide. But if Fontana should see something prettier, or in the latest style, he should get that instead. "The important thing is a simple, modest and clean look . . . nothing commonplace, loud or vulgar that suggests a grocer's taste," he warned. He should also see to having the bed and desk refinished and the upholstered furniture freshly slip-covered to match the wallpaper. Oh, yes—and could Fontana please find him a Polish manservant? Grzymala would advance all the costs.

Decorating his new apartment reminded Chopin that in the year he had been away from Paris, styles in men's fashion had changed, particularly hats. Fontana was to go to Chopin's hatter and order this season's model, and while he was about it, he should stop by his tailor to replenish his wardrobe with trousers (dark gray, no stripes), with a visit to his haberdasher for a new waistcoat (he preferred velvet with a small pattern).

Sand's needs were complicated by the two children and the several servants required for her household, but also by the reality, discreetly unmentioned, that Chopin would be spending the private hours of his life with her. In dramatic contrast to his assigned part of unworldly angelic child, he assumed the role of man of the family, taking Sand's house hunting entirely upon himself— hardly a promotion that suggests banishment from her bed. He fired off to Fontana and to Grzymala lists of Aurore's preferred addresses, and diagrams (drawn in his own hand) of her desired floor plan. Other requirements: peace and quiet (no whores or blacksmiths); no smells, especially not smoke; and preferably, a location on one of the higher streets leading to Montmartre. The rooms themselves must be light, ideally with a southern exposure. And if at all possible, he and Sand preferred an entrance of their own, one not shared with the children and servants.

In case his two friends took the fact of separate apartments literally, Chopin reminded them delicately that it was a matter of appearances: They must be diligent in finding the perfect apartment for Sand, "just as if it were for me."

By spending every waking hour on Chopin's needs, Fontana acquitted himself brilliantly. In the rue Pigalle, he found Sand a double pavilion in eighteenth-century style, its two wings separated by a garden. When he was in residence, Chopin would share one part with Maurice; the other was for Sand, Solange, and the servants.

Having achieved the impossible in real estate, Fontana was now urged to more challenging feats: "Since you're so clever, can't you make sure that I have no somber thoughts or coughing fits in my new apartment? And how about erasing a number of episodes from the past. It wouldn't be bad either to arrive and find a few more years of hard work finished. Finally, while you're at it, I'd be grateful to discover that I'm younger on returning than when I left or better still, that I've yet to be born."

EIGHT

Labors of Love

They did not go to Nohant the following summer of 1840. Sand's persistent financial troubles made opening the house—which for George meant keeping open house—a luxury she could not afford.

Deep in debt, Chopin, too, needed to think principally of earning money. He took over negotiations of his sales from the overburdened Fontana, selling six pieces to a new French publisher, Troupenas, probably for an offer of cash on signing. Haggling with the Paris representative of his German publishers, Chopin justified the high prices he wanted for recent work by claiming that he was too ill to teach and thus completely dependent upon sales of his music. But Sand had earlier reported at the end of 1839 that he was giving five or six lessons a day, and that his nightly social calendar was more crowded than ever. Indeed, Delacroix worried that exhaustion was dissipating the gains his friend's health had made over the past summer in Nohant.

His increased earnings allowed Chopin to make generous gestures. He gave an allowance of fourteen francs a month to an impoverished Polish youth; with this, the boy was able to redeem his belongings from the pawnbroker. Thinking to do a good turn at the same time for an old friend, Chopin arranged for his protégé to be tutored in French by Stefan Witwicki, at ten sous a lesson. Naively, Chopin had not anticipated the rancor caused by the contrast between his own fees and the poet's pittance. Witwicki's bitter letter to the composer did not even trouble to offer the most perfunctory word of thanks for Chopin's help.

Sand's efforts to resolve her financial troubles proved more frustrating. The promise of success in the theater, dangled alluringly by Buloz, turned out to be a humiliating failure. On opening night in April 1840, *Cosima,* starring Sand's adored friend Marie Dorval, was greeted with boos, catcalls, and a hailstorm of rotten tomatoes. Explanations for the resounding flop ranged from the underrehearsed cast, to Sand's refusal to pay for the cheers of a claque, to the audience's rejection of Dorval—worshiped in her prime—as too old and overweight to play a romantic heroine. The play closed in a week.

Ever the professional, Sand put defeat behind her, starting work immediately on two new novels. *The Journeyman Carpenter,* with its apprentice hero, reflected her growing faith in the working class as the future of France. *Horace,* a social critique of another kind, took as its target the excesses of romanticism, as reflected in the self-induced madness of a Byronic poet, whose languor and ennui (symptoms the author might have observed at first hand) were encouraged by his aristocratic sycophants. Buloz detested both works; he refused to serialize the first and rejected *Horace* outright.

The labors of both Sand and Chopin made George less indulgent towards Maurice. The sixteen-year-old's summer visit to his father in Gascony had lengthened into months during which the son had clearly been converted to Baron Dudevant's philosophy of avoiding work in the company of like-minded country gentlemen and local servant girls. From Paris, his mother now wrote to Maurice, recovering from his dissipations in Nohant, to remind him of how hard others were working: Chopin was giving five lessons a day while "I write from eight to ten pages a night." Now that Delacroix had returned to town, she announced her plans to apprentice Maurice to the artist as a studio assistant. The long holiday was over, she warned.

The week before Christmas, Napoleon's ashes were brought back from Saint Helena and deposited in the crypt of the Invalides.

A steady procession of mourners, beginning with the entire house of Orléans and including the highest ranks of the church, military, and civil orders, streamed into the vast chapel. There they heard the Archbishop of Paris eulogize the deposed emperor who had defied them all. Chopin came especially to hear his friends Pauline Viardot, Luigi Lablache, and Alexis Dupont, accompanied by a choir and a three hundred-piece orchestra, sing the solo parts of Mozart's Requiem. Their performance honoring Napoleon would be a dress rehearsal for Chopin's funeral, eight years later.

So far, Chopin had resisted playing in public, but his evenings out continued to end at the piano. His admirer the Marquis de Custine, just back from Russia, heard Chopin play, either as a guest of mutual friends or, once again, at Saint-Gratien. "Time, along with the influence of genius," had led Chopin to become "all that you can be," Custine told the composer, adding that "maturity in a time of youth is sublime; nothing less than art in all its perfection." And Custine concluded by thanking Chopin for an emotion which the composer alone had inspired in the amateur: "gratitude for the pleasure which art aroused in me."

Jouissance—Custine's word for his reaction to Chopin's playing—most often denotes sexual pleasure. And indeed, their archness and precious language notwithstanding, Custine's letters to Chopin are love letters. Chopin's replies have not survived, but the presumption behind Custine's outpourings has assumed a certain encouragement on the part of the composer. A stronger case for Chopin's homosexuality has been made on the evidence of his own erotically charged imagery in the early correspondence with his friend Tytus Woyciechowski. This reading of the letters makes no allowance for the nineteenth-century rhetorical conventions of same-sex "romantic friendship" between young people whose passionate expressions (such as Chopin's favorite sign-off, "I kiss you on the mouth") are typically formulas of special affection—unless they signify something more. Certainly, among his contemporaries, the perception of both his temperament and his music has emphasized the delicate, feminine, otherworldly qualities of both.

His frail physical presence, the "short form" of his most popular compositions and the lightness of touch at the keyboard evoking "small faery voices," fused into a single impression: Chopin was not a man. Sand herself called him an angel in the early, most passionate days of her love. In the 1840s, Parisian slang gave only one meaning to the word "angel" (*ange*): homosexual. As unlikely as it seems that Sand consciously exploited the double entendre, her racy, idiomatic letters, freely spiced with both Parisian street speech and regional patois, make it equally unlikely that she was unaware of the word's underground connotations.

At the end of the year, an elderly friend of the Dudevant family died, leaving Solange a gold watch and chain. In reporting the bequest, her father, Casimir, explained that, given his daughter's age, he would take the valuable timepiece for safekeeping, along with fifty gold ecus that the same lady had bequeathed to Maurice. When he reached his majority, Maurice could decide whether he wanted to spend the money on a watch like his sister's or an Arabian horse. Baron Dudevant's New Year's gift to his children— the traditional *étrenne,* or good-luck offering, given instead of Christmas presents—consisted of six pots of jam from his estate. Their mother found this latest example of paternal miserliness a cause for hilarity. Identifying with the children, however, Chopin felt only pain. Particularly in his father's treatment of Maurice, Chopin, another only son, was sensitive to the infantilizing lack of trust along with the stinginess. No wonder the seventeen-year-old was showing few signs of progress towards manhood. Chopin now bid to exchange his role of older brother for one of paternal authority. At the New Year, he presented Maurice with an elegant gold pocket watch.

To his own family in Warsaw, Chopin had written in vague terms of the great woman who had been "taking care of him." Underlining Sand's maternal role did not allay the moral concerns of his devout parents: Nicolas Chopin wanted to "know something about this intimate relationship."

In the freezing Polish winter, in occupied Warsaw, the gloom of the Chopin household seeps through Ludwika's letters to her beloved Frycek. The closeness of brother and sister echoes in their every exchange; they speak the same language of melancholy and delicate irony. It fell to Ludwika to deliver the painful news of Maria Wodzinska's engagement to Joseph Skarbek, son of Chopin's godfather. The bridegroom-to-be struck her as a poor specimen, looking for a wife to take care of him, rather than the other way around. Despite his fortune of 400,000 florins and substantial property near the Wodzinskis, it was agreed that young Count Skarbek, not Maria, was the one making an advantageous marriage.*

The new year of 1841 began with a challenge from Chopin's rival. In March, after a triumphal concert tour, Liszt returned to Paris. At every performance, his legions of fans, their fervor, the sold-out halls, had convinced him that the traditional organization of concerts as a kind of musical variety show was a waste. Franz Liszt was the virtuoso that audiences wanted to hear—and see. Beginning in Rome, he inaugurated what he called "musical soliloquies" (the allusion to *Hamlet* by no means inadvertent). His first solo flights ecstatically received, Liszt continued to appear alone in London, where he muted the romantic melancholy of his Roman billing to the more restrained "recital," thus inaugurating the modern performance by a single artist.

His Paris one-man recitals launched another Liszt innovation. At a gala evening at the Salle Erard, he played only his own compositions. The most rapturously received were the composer's "reminiscences," or free piano transcriptions, from Meyerbeer's operatic blockbuster *Robert le diable*. Hearing about Liszt's concert and the acclaimed centerpiece of his program, Chopin could not have failed to recall his own variations on the same opera, published eight years earlier to no fanfare whatsoever.

---

*Ludwika's remarks about Skarbek were not made simply to assuage her brother's feelings; the marriage was a disaster and the couple soon separated.

For months, friends had been working to convince him to brave a return engagement. He had not played in public since the spring of 1838, before their stay in Majorca. His horror of performing before strangers—akin to feelings of violation—had worsened since he had confided to Liszt: "I am not fit to give concerts; the crowd intimidates me and I feel suffocated by its eager breath, paralyzed by its inquisitive stare, silenced by its alien faces."

Against these fears, intensified by the debilitating bouts of illness he had suffered since his first Paris concerts, Chopin's practical side reminded him of the profit—both direct and indirect—sure to flow from a return engagement, from the sale of tickets to the increased value of new works through audience word of mouth and glowing reviews.

Whether Liszt's series of recitals in March 1841, Chopin's constant need of money, or the reassuring certainty that Sand would manage the entire event was the deciding factor, he let himself be persuaded.

George was jubilant: "A great, no, the greatest piece of news is that little Chip-Chip is going to give a grrrrand concert," Sand informed her friend and protégée Pauline Viardot, then in the whirl of her own triumphal tour of England. Chopin had agreed only because he assumed the event could never be arranged on such short notice, at the end of the musical season, Sand reported. But he had not reckoned on her efficiency. Scarcely had he uttered "the fatal 'yes,' " George added, when, as if by magic, everything was done, with three-quarters of the tickets sold before the actual date of the concert had been announced. Could anything be funnier, Sand demanded, than the sight of their friend, so famously finicky and indecisive, trapped in the impossibility of changing his mind?

Chopin panicked. "He doesn't want posters, he doesn't want programs, he doesn't want a big audience, he doesn't want anyone to talk about it. He's so terrified by the whole thing that I suggested he play in the dark, with no one present, on a dumb keyboard!"

Sand conquered fear by appearing fearless. She refused to

accept the reality that anyone—let alone a man who was also a great artist—could succumb to terror. Her mocking surrealist scenario of Chopin's ideal concert—the hall dark and empty, the keys mute—was a measure of her well-honed skill in facing down her own terrors.

She had thought of everything, even a pacifier. Only now did George reveal that the forthcoming concert was public in name only. Tickets had been carefully "placed"—offered only to those already part of Chopin's world.

The occasion was more brilliant than any manager could have hoped. Tubs of hothouse flowers massed at the foot of the red-carpeted double grand staircase of the Salle Pleyel to welcome the glittering throngs, before their ascent to the auditorium on the floor above: "the most elegant women, the most fashionable young men, the most celebrated artists, the richest financiers, the most illustrious peers, indeed all the elite of society, all the aristocracy of birth, fortune, talent and beauty," Liszt reported.

Fighting a throat infection, Delacroix had remained in bed for days before to make sure he would be well in time to escort Chopin from rue Tronchet to the back entrance of Salle Pleyel.

Rivalry notwithstanding, Chopin was unprepared to engage Liszt on the grounds of that virtuoso's latest innovation: the solo recital. Following convention and conserving his strength, he shared the evening with the noted singer Laure Cinti-Damoreau and an undistinguished violinist, Heinrich Ernst.

For his own performance, Chopin spared himself nothing; he would never play a more arduous program. There were the four mazurkas of opus 41: the expansive, even athletic no. 1; the second, with its relentless hammering attacks; the acrobatic leaps of no. 4. There was the second Ballade, in F major, op. 38. The one work on the program that read most directly as a challenge—not only to Liszt, but to a new generation of emerging composer-musicians— was the Third Scherzo. From its first measures, the demonic savagery unleashed upon the delicate Pleyel had to remind his audience of Liszt's shattered pianos. Although Chopin's instrument did not require replacement in the course of the evening, the scherzo's vicious double octaves declared a defiant stamina and strength.

The first of the two polonaises of opus 40 that Chopin performed that evening, the "Military" Polonaise, has become one of his most famous and popular compositions. Like words repeated over and over by young children, the music has lost its meaning. For the audience in the Salle Pleyel that evening, many of them fellow exiles, the clarion notes were heard for the first time, their significance urgent and unmistakable: The stirring triple rhythm, homage to Poland's glorious past and martyred present, was also a summoning of hope. As composer and performer, the messenger and message were one: Chopin himself, fragile and steely, toughened by physical attack, was a living embodiment of defeat turned to triumphal heroism.

"The 'bravos,' the 'encores,' the ladies fainting away"—by every measure, Sand reported, Chopin's "Great Concert" had been his greatest success. And it was not lost on all those who knew them both that the works performed by Chopin on this historic evening had all been composed since his liaison with Sand. Along with her organization of the event and her role in his restored health, the occasion was also acknowledged by their circle as a homage to George.

Marie d'Agoult was among those who recognized Chopin's triumph as a tribute to Sand, but her despair at losing Liszt took the form of a poisonous malice towards the other couple, happy and successful together. She tried holding on to her lover by isolating him, injecting him with her own paranoia: Chopin's concert was a plot by Sand and her cabal to destroy Liszt. "A malicious little clique is trying to resurrect Chopin," she wrote to Franz shortly before the Pleyel performance. "Madame Sand hates me. We no longer see each other." And she tried to goad Liszt into being the first to strike.

In the process of getting rid of his mistress, importunate and increasingly unstable, Liszt attempted to placate her with promises that he would deal with their "enemies" later, urging good behavior in the meantime. Now, however, he indulged in some extreme theatrics of his own. At the end of Chopin's concert, while the final note still hung in the air, Liszt rushed to the stage, where, cradling the exhausted performer in his arms, he tried to carry him from the piano. This scene-stealing gesture was much mocked by the satirical press.

Then came the still more perplexing issue of Liszt's review. Writing in the *Revue et Gazette Musicale,* where he had asked to take over from its regular reviewer to cover this event, Liszt's analysis of the concert touched on every aspect of Chopin's program and performance. He painted the brilliance of the occasion as a showcase of fashion and celebrity before evoking, as only a fellow musician could have done, Chopin's magic as a pianist, concluding with the heart of his genius as a composer:

"Even before the concert began, people were settled and ready to listen, telling themselves they could not afford to miss one chord, one note, one nuance or thought, by the person who would seat himself there. And they were right to be so avid, so attentive, so devoutly moved, for he whom they awaited, whom they longed to see and hear, to admire and applaud, was not only a consummate virtuoso, an artist in full command of the technique of his art, a musician of great renown, he was all that and more; he was Chopin."

As a virtuoso who included Chopin's music in his own recitals, Liszt understood how the listener's experience of Chopin the pianist was intensified in hearing him perform his own works: "Music was his language, the divine tongue through which he expressed a whole realm of sentiments. . . . As with that other great poet Mickiewicz . . . the muse of his homeland dictates his songs, and the anguished cries of Poland lend to his art a mysterious, indefinable poetry which, for all those who have truly experienced it, cannot be compared to anything else."

His own most daring works still before him, Liszt grasped the complex interplay of tradition and innovation wielded by Chopin. "Without any specious striving for originality the composer has remained himself in both the style and conception of his works. To new ideas he has given new forms." And Liszt pointed to the tension between Chopin's "bold dissonances and strange harmonies, while the delicacy and grace which characterize his personality are apparent in the endless shadings and ornamentation of his inimitable imagination."

Singling out the preludes as "unique compositions," Liszt disposed of the connotation of their titles; these were not "introductions to something further" but marvelously structured short forms, complete unto themselves: "Admirable in their diversity, they require scrupulous examination of the workmanship and thought which have gone into them before they can be properly appreciated. Even then, they still retain the appearance of spontaneous improvisations produced without the slightest effort. They possess that freedom and charm which characterize works of genius."

Chopin found the review offensive. Reading the unstinting praise as either sarcastic or patronizing, he pounced upon one innocuous sentence as proof of Liszt's real point: After a polite comment about the performances of the soprano and the violinist, Liszt concluded: "Chopin, however, reigned as king of the evening."

" 'King,' yes, but within *his* Empire," Chopin wrote.

If the review was, even in part, dictated by jealousy, we would say today that Liszt deflected envy with adulation. Chopin's reaction appears the more troubling, a misreading that seems perversely determined to turn praise into censure. Whatever feelings the concert stirred on both sides, their friendship was effectively ended. Other causes besides the review have been advanced for the rupture. Chopin had apparently been incensed to discover that while he was away, Liszt, to whom he had given the key to his apartment, had used the rooms for assignations with his new lover, Marie Pleyel, the beautiful pianist wife of the much-cuckolded Camille. Some believed that Chopin was more offended by Liszt's lack of musical taste, and the vulgar cadenzas he inserted when performing Chopin in place of the composer's chaste ornamentation. Then there was the matter of d'Agoult's mischief-making; the woman scorned had poisoned the friendship between the four of them.

As it happened, from this period on, Liszt would spend little time in Paris; but for Chopin, the loss of a friend who, in his own extravagant way, had been his most generous and powerful supporter among musical figures of rank, was a loss he could ill afford. His world narrowed, and his dependence upon Sand deepened.

NINE

Earthquakes and Harvests

C hopin was now so rich, Sand joked, that he could afford to
laze away the summer. He may not have been rich, but he
was certainly richer. The sold-out success of the concert—with
tickets going for an unheard-of twenty to thirty francs—netted the
composer six thousand francs.

With his spending habits, there was no question of saving;
money just disappeared. First, he had old loans to repay. But from
Nohant, where they repaired in June 1841 after a nearly two-year
absence, Chopin's letters to Fontana could serve as a shopping
guide for rich visitors to Paris. He consoled his footsore errand
boy with the reminder that most of these fashionable purveyors
were clustered in the same Right Bank area around the Palais
Royal.

Even in rustic Nohant, Chopin needed to replenish his supply of
suede gloves, his two favorite colognes from Houbigant-Chardin,
and his special soap. There was a bill to settle at the florist and a
new commission: He wanted a back scratcher "for my head," one
of those carved ivory hands on an ebony wand sold by the most
fashionable "notions" shop in the Galeries Royales. "Shouldn't
cost more than 10, 20 or 30 francs," he told Fontana airily.

More crucial, he needed a new piano. The Pleyel that had
delighted Chopin on his arrival that first summer at Nohant he
now found unsatisfactory. He instructed Fontana to compare the

best instrument that Pleyel would make available with what he could get from Erard and, once he had made his choice, to oversee shipping the piano express to Châteauroux via the most reliable— and expensive—expediter in Paris.

Out of tune after two years of silence, the flatted notes of the old Pleyel seemed to presage the heavy weather that followed their arrival. Then, on the first clear night, July 5, an earthquake erupted whose rumblings were felt as far away as Paris. In Nohant, live-stock bellowed, walls trembled, pictures shook. Chopin's "poor nerves were shattered," Sand reported. The "idiotic little quake" unleashed an entire month of rainstorms, spoiling all of July, she complained. Indifferent to outdoor pursuits, Chopin worked upstairs in his little study, or downstairs, making do with the tinny sounds he could coax from the keyboard.

In June, with a sense of urgency, he sent to Fontana a tar-antella. As Chopin knew, this rapid-fire, rollicking dance was the height of fashion; Rossini had launched the style for the Neapolitan-inspired showpiece and Chopin, following the market closely, was determined that his contribution to the popular genre should be sold for a top price—he was asking 600 francs. The tarantella was followed in the next months by the Polonaise in F-sharp Minor, op. 44; the Prelude in C-sharp Minor, op. 45; the intimate Third Ballade, in A-flat; the last two nocturnes of opus 48; and the Fantaisie in F Minor, op. 49. This summer alone con-firmed Marquis de Custine's observation that Chopin had arrived at the fullest expression of maturity while still young; he was thirty-one. If the composer was more obsessively perfectionist than ever, confessing, as he did to Fontana, to acute disappoint-ment with work in progress, he was also more fully aware of his capacities, chafing at the frustration of falling short of his own expectations of his art.

In August, clear skies greeted both the new piano—another Pleyel—and two eagerly awaited guests. Pauline Viardot, accom-panied by her husband and manager, Louis, returned from her tour directly to Nohant in time to unwrap and try the beautiful new instrument. Pauline, at twenty, was as complete a musician as

Chopin had ever known. Her thrilling voice was matched by a rare dramatic gift and musical intelligence; she was a talented pianist and inventive composer with a special interest in vocal arrangements of folk songs, both Spanish and the local bourrées, as well as Chopin's mazurkas, which she included in her concerts. Chopin loved hearing Pauline sing and making music with her. The Viardots stayed for the first two weeks in August, and during that time he accompanied Pauline as she sang her way through all the Mozart operas (her Paris debut had been as Zerlina in *Don Giovanni*), along with their favorite Handel, Gluck, and Haydn arias. But it's in the pure song of Chopin's Prelude in C-sharp, op. 45, that we seem to hear the long melodic line of Viardot's sinuous mezzo with its three-octave range.

Beyond her musical gifts, Pauline had a depth and generosity of spirit that was at the polar opposite of the diva. Sand adored her "Fifille," the nickname expressing the singer's place in her heart as a beloved older daughter; and when the Viardots' first child was born the following December, George would act as grandmother and baby-sitter for little Louise while her parents were on tour. Most important, Pauline was probably the only friend that Sand and Chopin held in equal affection and esteem. For Chopin, though, she was irreplaceable. There was little other than music that interested him. Through their common language, she unburdened him of solitude.

Like the unexpected earthquake, the summer revealed fissures beneath the calm surface of country life.

One of Fontana's errands for Chopin required him to collect at the Susse foundry outside Paris two plaster busts of the composer by the brilliant caricaturist in sculpture, Jean-Pierre Dantan, for shipment to Poland. But Fontana, thinking to save money, instead entrusted the pieces to Antoni Wodzinski, Chopin's boyhood friend and brother of the girl he had hoped to marry. Antoni was about to visit his family, who had resettled in Warsaw from Dresden, but he was returning as something of a black sheep. Notorious among the Polish colony in Paris as a wastrel and libertine, infamous for unpaid debts, including two loans from Chopin, Antoni had, meanwhile, acquired a most unlikely lover.

Marie de Rozières, one of Chopin's more talented students, came from a family of impoverished provincial nobility, and her need to earn money had led Chopin to recommend her as a piano teacher for Solange. She was a great success with her pupil and charmed Sand, who swept her into the magic circle she called "the Family." Chopin now came to rely on Marie, writing her effusive letters of thanks for taking on such errands as Fontana would or could not manage. Then he learned that the respectable music teacher, hovering on the brink of spinsterhood, was a passionate woman who had fallen wildly in love with his young friend. The affair was no secret; the besotted Marie flaunted their intimacy all over Paris. But when Chopin heard that Sand had invited the lovers to Nohant he became hysterical. An embarrassed Sand had to rescind the invitation, while confessing to Marie that she was mystified, not least by Chopin's refusal to explain his sudden and irrational hostility—anger that erupted into "impatience and irritability" towards Sand herself. Holding Antoni blameless, he turned on Marie with a fury that defies explanation—still. She had "manipulated" and seduced a naive boy, he raged to Fontana, reviling her as a "mischief-making old maid" who had "insinuated" herself into Sand's household to exploit her intimacy, an "old sow" rooting for dirt to spread about their menage. Sexual puritanism and misogyny inflamed Chopin's attacks upon Rozières, and her behavior seems to have activated his distrust of another sexually emancipated woman.

Antoni's forthcoming visit to his family in Poland triggered the real crisis. Chopin still brooded over the Wodzinkis' rejection of him as a son-in-law. Now, he was convinced that Antoni's gossip about Nohant as a scene of sexual license, passed on to him by Rozières, would confirm the family's doubts about him. At the same time, he feared that the gift of his plaster likeness could suggest that he was trying to revive his suit of their daughter. It was all Marie's fault; but she would get her come-uppance, he predicted. Antoni would jilt her, just as she deserved—and, of course, he did.

Sand, too, now cast Marie in the role of corrupter of innocence. From defending the music teacher's right to behave as an "independent woman," she proceeded, in the same letter, to forbid Marie to invite Solange, now an unhappy boarder in a Paris pension, for holiday outings. Sexually awakened, Rozières had become too openly seductive towards men, Sand claimed—a startling accusation coming from the most notorious woman of her time—and threatened to exercise a dangerous influence on her already rebellious daughter.

The banishment of Marie de Rozières is a drama, strange yet strangely familiar, in which a family's unresolved troubles find a scapegoat. Marie fit the part perfectly. Her dismissal, however, is significant for another reason: It marks the first time that Sand would describe Chopin's behavior as anything less than angelic. However unjust or irrational this uncharacteristic cruelty, *his* feelings are all that count for her, she informed Marie. And by way of declaring her loyalty absolute, she assumed Chopin's rejection of the music teacher as her own.

George Sand's letter to Marie de Rozières declares a love stripped of illusions. Instead of lyrical raptures elevating Chopin to the seraphic spheres, she now acknowledged loving him for his faults. He can be childish, nasty, even crazy—"impossible," she would say, more and more. She was pledged to him as inseparable from another impossible project: creating a paradise at Nohant.

For the first time, in her letter to Marie, Sand points to Chopin's illness as the cause of behavior foreign to his nature, the sulks and silences that he refused to explain. But this other, "sick" Chopin was proving infectious. Her beloved Nohant, refuge from life's griefs and burdens, was suddenly a "hornet's nest."

Sand did extract one human sacrifice from Chopin in exchange for exiling Marie: His Polish manservant, Charles (rechristened Louis), had made himself the scourge of the entire household, irritating everyone with his coarseness and stupidity. (Louis's idea of a good joke was to keep ringing the dinner bell throughout the meal.) Bowing to the inevitable, Chopin agreed to let Louis go—but he couldn't bear to fire him directly. He was shipped to Paris on the pretext of an errand in Chopin's apartment, where Fontana, temporarily in residence, was delegated to break the news and to be sure he was gone immediately.

George was convinced that Fontana was behind Chopin's venom towards Marie: Every letter that arrived from him drove Chopin into fits of gloom or agitation. Now, with a tactlessness that hardly seems inadvertent, Fontana reported that their mutual friend Jan Matuszynski had dreamt that Chopin was dead. Chopin replied by urging Fontana to dream that he, Chopin, had just been born. In fact, he felt as unsteady on his feet as a toddler; if only he could be held upright by a baby's lead strings, instead of the much likelier crutches or wooden leg! Some time ago, he had dreamt he would die in a hospital, he told Fontana, and the dream had shaken him so badly that he recalled it as vividly as though it happened last night.* "Only a few years ago, I had very different dreams, but they did not come true."

Several weeks later, at the end of August, he reported to Fontana other feelings of disablement: "As for my music, its bad."

In early September, he sent off to Vienna the work that had so disheartened him. Produced after weeks of frustrated effort, writing, revising, crossing out, scrubbing, starting over, the Polonaise in F-sharp Minor, op. 44, is the longest composition with this title he would ever write. Capacious, expansive, it is a boa constrictor of a work, seeming to have swallowed pieces of waltz and mazurka and getting longer in the process.

At the end of the month, Chopin went to Paris—alone. He called on Sand's publisher Buloz on her behalf, but the principal reason for his flying visit was to begin the process of moving from his old apartment in the rue Tronchet to join Sand and the children

---

*In nineteenth-century Europe, such a death, in nightmarish surroundings, was reserved for the indigent.

on the upper floor of the two connected pavilions off the rue Pigalle. With the move, he abandoned even the appearance—personal or professional—of a separate life; as most of his pupils were too grand to venture to the bohemian outpost of the rue Pigalle, Sand had persuaded Chopin to raise his fee for lessons from twenty to thirty francs for going to their houses. (And they would have to send their carriages to fetch him and bring him home.) "I had a hard time convincing him to do it," she said, "but with his poor health, he really has to earn much more to work less."

He basked in his lover's concern for his well-being, a solicitude that embraced all aspects of his life: her management of what George playfully called his *frélicatesse* along with prudent financial planning. Freed of worries, Chopin yielded to the unthinking bliss of the cosseted infant, with this difference: He was aware of his privileged state. "I feel as peaceful as a baby in its cradle," he told Fontana.

Returning to Nohant within days, he went back to work "with the speed of a thirty-second note." Responding to Schlesinger's pleas for the short pieces that sold so well, he sent off to the publisher a new prelude, the first since the great gathering of opus 28; he described this last only as "well-modulated," but it breathes a pastoral calm, the pause between late summer and early autumn's bright perfection. Less than three weeks later, he had eighteen pages covered with his usual "flyspecks," ready for Fontana to transcribe into the chromatic scampering of the Allegro de Concert, finally finished after seven years of sporadic efforts; its alternations of martial playfulness, far from the somber clashes of a "revolutionary" polonaise, conjure the maneuvers of toy soldiers, while the rocking motion of the opening measures of the Third Ballade, in A-flat major, included in this packet, evokes Chopin's cradled image of the summer's peace and plenitude.

Just before their return to Paris in the first week of November, he sent two new nocturnes of opus 48 to Fontana. When teaching the first of these, the majestic C Minor Nocturne, Chopin was said to devote a full hour to instructing pupils how to play the stately opening measures alone, among the simplest he would ever write. The pure melodic line and lyrical expansiveness pay homage to the operatic duets played with Viardot, but also to their surroundings: to the grace of Nohant and its long, unhurried hours guarded by Sand for cherished friends to fill with music.

At the farthest remove from the intimacy of music-making for their own pleasure was the royal concert—his third—in which Chopin participated three weeks after his return to Paris, given by the Duke d'Orléans, son of Louis Philippe. The splendid room at the Pavillon de Marsan of the Tuileries welcomed, on December 1, 1841, about five hundred guests, including the king and queen, the other royal children, and ministers of every nation. Among the composer's few guests were Delacroix and the painter Ary Scheffer, Chopin's latest portraitist; Sand, too, of course, but also her old lover Alfred de Musset. Following two arias by the acclaimed diva Giuditta Grisi, Chopin played his recent Third Ballade. As always, it was his improvisations that left audiences—kings or commoners—ecstatic. Instead of merely nodding approval (applauding was not done at royal performances), Queen Marie Amelie came over to Chopin, still seated at the piano, to "pay him the most flattering compliments." For reasons he refused to elaborate, the occasion left him dispirited. It was to be his final court appearance in France.

Early in the new year of 1842, Chopin gave another concert at the Salle Pleyel. Despite the demanding program and large, fashionable audience—a bobbing sea of jewels, satin, feathers—the collaboration of brilliant fellow musicians who were also beloved friends, including Pauline Viardot and the cellist Auguste Franchomme, lent the performance a familial feeling that seemed to flow from one of Chopin's own musical evenings. Among his new works, he played, once again, the Third Ballade, along with the second of the two nocturnes of opus 48.

He also introduced a new impromptu, the third in a genre that, like the nocturne, he had never tried before arriving in Paris in 1831. The essence of romanticism, the impromptu is linked to the piano, to improvisation or to sudden and spontaneous inspiration. Schubert composed eight of these pieces in 1827, mostly theme and variations. It seems unlikely that Chopin knew Schubert's works for piano when he composed his first impromptu around 1834, but he was too unhappy with his own piece even to tinker; putting it aside, he refused to consider publication while he lived.*

He waited three years before trying another. Composed in the early months of his liaison with Sand, the Impromptu No. 1 in A-flat Major, op. 29, was followed by a second, completed in Majorca, under conditions of privileged crisis. With this third and last impromptu, written in Nohant, Chopin had made the genre so completely his own, he may as well have invented it. More than musical improvisation, opus 51 follows the patterns of conversation; its spooling repetitions and variations breathe the switchbacks of spoken language. The briefest of encounters, seductive or merely flirtatious, they echo verbal games of hide-and-seek, a fitting tribute to his lover, that indefatigable spinner of words.

Along with the welcome five thousand francs, the concert confirmed Chopin's place at the pinnacle of musical Paris. He might still be cursed with critics stirred into bad poetry who sighed over his "infinite number of fingers" summoning "the faint voices of fairies sighing under silver bells"; more sophisticated reviewers confined themselves to observing the "pristine elegance" of pianism that was declared "more profound" and "more substantial" than Liszt's.

Amidst the swans and peacocks in the audience, only one entrance created a stir: "The real star of the evening was George Sand," noted the reviewer for *La France Musicale*. "As soon as she appeared with her two charming daughters, all eyes fixed upon her."

---

*It was left to Fontana's posthumous editing of Chopin's unpublished works. Rechristened Fantaisie-Impromptu, op. 66, the disowned work eventually became one of Chopin's most painfully famous, through its Tin Pan Alley lyrics: "I'm Always Chasing Rainbows."

But the reporter was mistaken. Only one of the girls, Solange Dudevant, now fourteen, was Sand's daughter; the other, eighteen-year-old Augustine Marie Brault, called Titine, was a young stepcousin whom Sand was helping to study music in Paris. The observer's confusion is part of Solange's story.

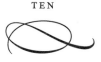

TEN

Children of Paradise

S he was born in 1828 and named for Solange, the patron saint of
Bourges, capital of Berry. But Solange Dudevant was not
blessed by divine or, for that matter, much human favor. The birth
of her brother, Maurice, five years earlier, had brought only joy to
the love match of the young parents, Casimir and Aurore Dudevant. Conceived in discord and estrangement, Solange was an un-
wanted child, probably not fathered by Casimir, but by Stéphane
Ajasson de Gransagne, Aurore's neighbor and childhood friend.
Son of a distinguished Berrichon family, Gransagne was an amateur naturalist who had given the teenaged girl anatomy lessons.
Nine months before Solange's birth, according to Casimir's testi-
mony at the separation hearings, Stéphane had arranged to be in
Paris "for his health" in order to tryst with Casimir's wife.

When the Dudevants parted and Aurore was granted Nohant
by court order, Casimir retired to his property in Guillery in Gascony. Under the terms of the separation, Maurice was to spend
vacations with his father, who also retained the right to make deci-
sions about his son's education. Solange, although given Dudevant's name, rarely saw her father. Her mother was now reborn as
George Sand. Literary success required a masculine nom de
plume. Parisian anglophilia inspired the English spelling of
George; she borrowed the new surname from her lover and early
collaborator Jules Sandeau. Launched on the life of an indepen-

dent woman, Sand retained full custody of her daughter, since, as Casimir acknowledged, he knew nothing about the upbringing of girls.

To both children, Sand was the sun around whom everything in their universe—friends (many of them famous), family, neighbors, servants, even pets—revolved. They basked in her brilliance and warmth and vied for her attentions, divided, inevitably, among so many.

Maurice alone had no need to compete for Sand's love. From birth, he was enveloped in his mother's adoration, a passion absolute and unconditional. Her maternal pride in his character and talents (distinctions not always discernible to others) was detailed often enough, but Sand also recognized that her infinite tenderness for the boy, her pain when they were apart, were more like another kind of love. When Maurice was four and George had returned to Nohant after a short absence, she described their reunion to Casimir: "I can't be away from him without grieving. I miss him so much, especially at night." Back together, Sand reported, "We are both still in the newness of our rapture, like two lovers reunited. We can't be out of each other's sight. We go to sleep together and when we awake, side by side, it's like a dream. The poor child throws his arms around me with such joy!"

In the next few years, there were many more such absences; Solange hardly knew either parent. When her daughter was two, Sand left for Paris and a new literary life with Sandeau. She encouraged Maurice to mother his little sister; he comforted her lovingly when she cried, compensating for the crossness of the overworked servants charged to look after them.

Then it was Solange's brief moment in the sun. When she was three and a half, she was taken to Paris by her mother. The little girl became part of Sand's freewheeling *vie de bohème*, sharing a series of apartments on the quays overlooking the Seine with her mother and Sandeau, and playing exotic pet to their childless circle of artists and actors. In this largely masculine company, the pretty and clever child learned early that attention and affection were more easily won from men, albeit a shifting cast of uncles and big brothers. Solange felt keenly her mother's eventual separation from Sandeau, the surrogate papa who loved to spoil her with treats, and the collapse of the carefree household of parties and laughter was another loss.

Sand's troubled feelings toward Solange emerged early. Before she was three, her mother described the little girl as "fat and lazy." She had a quick mind, a startling memory for facts, and she could already read "with considerable understanding," George admitted; but these proofs of exceptional intelligence only led her parent to expect more of her—harder work, higher achievement, larger ambition—and to be always disappointed. When Solange was four, Sand complained of her "strong will and extremes of emotion—especially her violent temper"; she feared the child showed signs of an unstable personality.

Before Sand disappeared on her Venetian "honeymoon" with the poet Alfred de Musset in December 1833, she delivered Maurice, now ten, at his father's insistence, to the Lycée Henri IV in Paris, where he was enrolled as a boarder. Seeing her leave, the boy tore away from the preceptor and, rushing back, clung to his mother, sobbing uncontrollably; Sand barely managed to contain her own weeping until she had fled the school's grim cloister. Solange was dispatched to Nohant, where she was left to the supervision of servants.

When their mother returned to France nine months later, she found the saucy, high-spirited five-year-old had become cringing and submissive: Solange, it turned out, had been regularly beaten by one of the servants. To emphasize the inherited nature of her charge's wickedness, the maid, Julie, had also filled the child's ears with gossip about her mother's sins. Sand's response to the brutalizing of Solange was to remove her to Paris, where the six-year-old was enrolled in a select boarding establishment for girls near the Etoile, then a semirural area of expensive villas.

Directed by two English sisters, the Pension Martin, Sand reassured friends, was a "jewel box" of a house, filled with sunlight and fresh air, surrounded by a large garden and run according to the healthy child-rearing precepts of Jean-Jacques Rousseau. Sand made known her firm expectations of the Martin ladies: They were to teach Solange self-discipline in terms of both behavior and application to studies, but also to discourage dependence—no complaining, whining, crying, or clinging to other adults as a mother substitute.

There was no further question of fathers, real or surrogate: Due to his "erratic" behavior in the years following her flight to Venice, Sand had forbidden Casimir the right to take Solange out on holidays. Then, without warning, in the summer of 1837, while Sand was still in Paris, Dudevant abducted the nine-year-old from Nohant. Over the feeble objections of the servants, and the hysterical screams of the resident governess at the moment, Casimir galloped off with his daughter. Had she not been terrified by the reactions of the other adults, Solange would have been glad for the unexpected and rare visitation from her papa, and the exciting, posthaste trip to Gascony.

As soon as Sand was alerted, she staged a daring kidnapping raid of her own. She enlisted the help of the local Gascon authorities, who surrounded Dudevant's property in the dead of night, demanding he turn over the child to his estranged wife, after which Sand and Solange, with their official escort, sped back to Paris.*

This dramatic rescue only confirmed Solange's sense of her mother as all-powerful; George's displays of love were as yearned for as they were infrequent. The absent mother became the emotional lodestar of her life, the focus of Solange's sense of privation and her most intense longings. From a series of boarding establishments, the little girl's letters echo with pleas for Sand to write, to visit; she had waited so long. "Please come on New Year's Day," she begged; she had made her mother a basket for the traditional gift-giving holiday. But Sand did not come, and Solange gave the basket to her godmother. Later, and most achingly, she pleaded to be allowed to come home for a visit, especially when the others were together at Nohant. Her requests, with their run-on

---

*The administrator in charge was none other than Georges-Eugène Haussmann, future leveler of medieval Paris and planner of the city's *grands boulevards*.

sentences—"I love you don't forget me"—were followed by notes sodden with grief and, always, disappointment.

Disappointment is the duet voiced by mother and daughter, addressed to each other, but also to others. Sand complained of Solange's indolence, her carelessness, her poor progress, as revealed by the badly written letters (the Martin sisters' knowledge of French was sketchy); she scolded the child for complaining about her health or conditions at school—she was exaggerating or telling lies merely to worry her mother and garner sympathy. But just as often, Sand didn't bother to specify faults; harping instead on her daughter's "bad character," she urged her to pray to God for help in overcoming her flaws. Finding that the English ladies were too tender-hearted, she demanded less leniency; they must punish Solange for every instance of poor performance—both academic and behavioral—by forbidding holiday outings. But when Sand herself needed the confirming presence of both children as proof of maternal virtue, she showered Solange with written endearments—"dearest chicken," "darling angel"—and assurances of how keenly she was missed.

Meanwhile, the miseries of Maurice at his school took more dramatic form. The fourteen-year-old developed a variety of mysterious symptoms: floating pains, loss of appetite, dizzy spells; he was listless and continued to lose weight. Diagnoses differed. Sand was terrified, but also relieved when the family doctor pronounced the first step towards a cure: Maurice must be removed from the lycée and returned to his mother's care.

"This child breathes with your breath," Sand quotes the doctor as telling her. "You are his tree of life, the only physician that he needs." Mother and son went off to Nohant, "where, for six months, we didn't leave each other's side for an hour," George recalled.

From the Pension Martin, Solange wrote adoring letters to her mother and brother. Formulas of concern about Maurice's health failed to disguise the pain of envy and exclusion; she so longed to be "seated between [them] at table" and begged for news of their doings. Then, to the girl's delight, Sand decided that her clever daughter required greater challenge and substance than the English ladies could provide. Solange, too, was dispatched to Nohant, where her mother engaged a tutor for both children.

Her choice was Félicien Mallefille, the twenty-seven-year-old Creole playwright whose prompt besotment with his employer led to the inevitable; his passion reciprocated (until he was unseated by Chopin), Mallefille soon abandoned the role of resident tutor to join Sand in Paris. In outlining to friends her requirements for a replacement, Sand revealed an objective judgment of each child's capacities, along with her own revolutionary notions of an education based upon ability and interests, not gender. In this, she may be said to have reversed contemporary notions of appropriate schooling for boys and girls. For six hours a day, Solange, ten, and Maurice, fifteen, would share lessons in arithmetic, French, and geography. Intellectually superior, Solange alone would receive instruction in English, history, and music. Maurice, she noted vaguely, would be free to follow his "artistic disposition."

More important than learning or pedagogical skills, the tutor would need natural authority to control Solange: "The girl is a demon who requires constant surveillance"—not physically (a maid attended to that) but "morally, everywhere and at all times." "He must be serious, firm and rigorous, never showing signs of weakness"—and "no intellectuals," George stipulated.

Where Solange was concerned, Sand wanted a jailer, not a tutor. When no applicants for the job appeared, she briefly took over the task herself. Then, more compelling interests beckoned her to Paris: the final disposition of her legal separation and the beginning of her affair with Chopin.

Their mother's new lover was a complete stranger sprung suddenly upon the children. When the little group convened in Perpignan to board the boat for Majorca, Chopin had never met Solange or Maurice. The remarkable fact has gone unnoticed: Under circumstances of hardship and illness, the composer became part of the family. No greater tribute survives of Chopin's delicacy and tact: deferring always to their mother as head of the family, he never tried to replace their father; nor, with Maurice, did he even presume on the rights of an older brother. Slight, frail, often sick, Chopin belonged more to the helpless world of childhood than to the universe of powerful or remote adults who controlled their lives. Although he laid claim to a large share of Sand's time and attention, Chopin's invalid state—his need for special food, for medicine, for quiet—along with the heavenly music he coaxed from the toylike piano, became part of their strange and exotic adventure. He possessed the rare ability to inspire trust in two troubled children, one still a child, the other an adolescent boy, rivals for their mother's love.

His friendship with Solange was something apart from the others. In Majorca, he began to teach her piano. If she did not show real talent, she revealed a sensitivity to music worth cultivating. By helping to focus her intelligence and energy, by gratifying a child's hunger for praise, Chopin encouraged the self-mastery that constant maternal carping and criticism had arrested. He offered an alternative to the only power Solange possessed: enraging her mother.

From the beginning, there was a nameless sympathy between them: Unloved child and homeless artist, they were both exiles; wherever they found themselves, they were there on sufferance, rewarded for performing, for charming, for summoning a sympathy that, once granted, deepened loneliness. Neither could satisfy the restless, voracious, imperial mother: her dynamism, her need, her ideals of work and love—of self, family, humanity, God, art. In her churning wake, they would be washed up, broken, on some distant shore, easily replaced.

"I love you don't forget me." Chopin would not forget.

Number 16, rue Pigalle, the paired pavilions at the back of a luxuriant garden, promised an oasis hidden from city life. Chopin and Sand's second-floor apartments, located above workshops and reached by an exterior iron staircase, had the feel of adjoining treehouses. Chopin and Maurice occupied one wing; George and

Solange were across the garden. Delacroix had agreed to take on
Maurice as one of his studio assistants; his mother hoped that the
master's genius and industry would move the indolent boy from
artistic "leanings" to a real career.

In her freshly decorated Paris quarters, Sand's entertaining
took on the permanence of a salon. From late afternoon on, the
largest room, painted a pale coffee color, filled with friends; Balzac
especially loved the tubs of flowers and plants sent from Nohant,
the walls hung heavily with paintings, and, in the middle, Chopin's
piano, as richly carved as a baroque altarpiece. The novelist nosily
eyed the hostess's bedroom and reported to his mistress, "no bed,
two mattresses on the floor, à la turque."

Once again, Solange, now thirteen, was expelled from Eden.
Enrolled in another boarding establishment, near the Parc Mon-
ceau, run by a Monsieur Héreau and his wife, she briefly appeared
to flourish. Soon, however, on Sunday afternoons when it was time
to leave rue Pigalle for school, there were terrible scenes and she
had to be taken away by force. Abject letters followed, begging
forgiveness, and pleading to be allowed to return home the following Sunday. She reported her academic progress and commenda-
tions in conduct. Chopin would be proud of how well she
performed in the school concert.

Then, Sand decided that the Héreaus, too, were spoiling
Solange: they were lax with punishments and too lavish with praise
and high marks. She was removed in the middle of the year to yet
another school. Before Solange arrived at her new pension, Sand's
letter to the director, Monsieur Bascans, alerted him to the problem
student he was about to encounter: her daughter's "flawed character," "moody, capricious, domineering, jealous and hysterical,"
tainted her qualities of intelligence, generosity, and tenderness,
along with the child's "exalted sense of justice."

The latter was tested most often by her mother. After assuring
Sand of how hard she was working to correct her faults, Solange
added, "I don't have to say that I'm no longer a liar because I never

lied; that's a fault which you accused me of having which I never had."

Solange lied if she said anything her mother did not want to believe. When she complained about school—the drafty halls, her recurrent sore throats, the skimpy food—or said that she was so homesick she would cry most of the time, if she wasn't too ashamed, Sand replied harshly, accusing her of making it all up out of egoism, to win sympathy or simply to worry her mother. Not only did Sand urge the director that laziness and poor behavior be punished by canceling weekend outings, but in the spring of 1841 she suggested that if Solange's schoolwork was less than exemplary, she should be kept after the others had left for the summer vacation. (Seeing extra tuition, the Bascans eagerly seconded this proposal.)

Cruelty—cold and gratuitous—snakes through Sand's letters to her daughter from these months. Her remarks have a vengeful, retaliatory thrust. In truth, she found Solange's presence disruptive and accusing, and dreaded it; she was the one human being who could make George feel a failure. Now, she held up to Solange the idyllic picture of life at Nohant without her, the loving tranquility that her arrival would shatter.

"Here's how we spend our time, your brother and I. Since it's been pouring rain for the last two weeks, we go to my study after breakfast at 10; there your brother paints watercolors, with a concentration and perseverance which I'd be happy to see you apply to something, even if it were just needlework. While he draws, I paint flowers and butterflies. Evenings we go back to work from 8 to 9, he copies engravings while I read to him."

Every letter from Solange ends with a rosary of those she loves and misses in Nohant, starting with her adored mother, her Didion (Maurice); Luce, a neighboring farmer's daughter and her best friend; and, always, Chopin. "Tell 'Sans-Sexe' to write to me; he hasn't sent a word since he's been at Nohant; it seems that he's become too proud, playing Lord of the Manor, just because he earns his keep."

"No-Balls"—the insolent sexual needling of a woman betrayed

came from a fourteen-year-old. Chopin, her special friend, has failed to defend her, to take her part. And why? He's been coopted by the all-powerful mother, playing Lord to her Lady of the Manor—but only because he pays his way (this last bit of nastiness surely gleaned from adult gossip).

Lest she slacken in her efforts to improve, Solange was kept in suspense about whether she would be allowed to join the family until two days before Maurice was to bring her from Paris to Nohant on August 15: "Now, I hope you're happy and that you're coming resolved to change your character," her mother warned. And she listed once again the sins she must "destroy in herself": her vanity, her need to dominate, and, worst, her "insane, foolish jealousy."

Solange had just missed Pauline Viardot's visit, and Sand made plain just what a poor substitute the real daughter was for her "Fifille." "Everyone here who saw her—even for a moment—adored her instantly, not just for her talent and intelligence, but above all, for her goodness and simplicity, her devotion to others. If you could only be like her some day, I would be the happiest of mothers."

In the first joy of her return to Nohant, Solange charmed everyone. Soon, however, the irritating adolescent re-emerged: restless, bored, sulky—she yawned, threw aside a book, fiddled with her hair, played with the dogs, and bothered anyone who was engaged in any purposeful activity, Sand said.

Chopin welcomed her interruptions. He understood the emptiness of ennui, the invisibility of the less busy in this bustling household. She came to him bringing snacks of chocolate. He tried to engage her with a little music making, but he soon gave up and succumbed to her childish jokes, her teasing and flirting, her beauty.

The plump, pretty child had become a smoldering teenager, graceful and voluptuous, with sleepy blue eyes and a provocative pout. Seeing her, Marie d'Agoult, another golden goddess, waxed rhapsodic: "When the wind blows through her long blond hair tumbling in natural curls over her Roman shoulders and the sun's rays illuminate her face, skin dazzling white with a brilliant flush of red, I see a young dryad escaped from the forest upon whom the gods smile; birds, insects, plants and flowers bow as she passes." And artists.

If she was using him as a mirror, an audience, as stand-in for a dress rehearsal of seduction, Chopin did not care.

ELEVEN

Deaths Foretold

He had dreamed of Chopin's death, but it was Jan Matuszyn-ski who died of tuberculosis on April 20, 1842, aged thirty-three. Sand and Chopin had spent Jan's last days at his bedside holding the dying man: "His agony was slow and dreadful and Chopin suffered almost as much as his friend," Sand wrote to Pauline. "He was as brave and strong as he was faithful—to a degree that I never could have imagined for such a frail creature. But afterwards, he was shattered."

Theirs had been the most passionate of Chopin's early friendships; he had as much reason to mourn the circumstances of Jan's life as to grieve his friend's untimely death. The young doctor's Paris exile had been marked by failure. He had shared Chopin's rooms until his marriage—with the composer as witness—to a Frenchwoman; their union was brief and disastrous. And Jan's medical career foundered before it began. Both defeats surely were related to the disease ravaging his lungs. Chopin and Matuszynski were patients of the same émigré, Dr. Raciborski, who bled the dying man even as he treated Chopin for assorted respiratory ailments. If Chopin was not already infected with the bacillus that was killing his friend, their common living quarters and physician provided ample opportunity for contagion. Much as he had loved his "Jeannot" and done everything he could to help him, Chopin felt the guilt of the successful exile towards his unlucky compatriot, making the loss harder to bear.

Then, Chopin's old teacher Adalbert Zwyny died in Warsaw. Chopin's last memory of this eccentric relic of the age of Mozart had been the snuff-stained musician conducting Chopin's friends—all of them weepy with wine—in a farewell cantata, as Chopin's departing coach pulled out of the last stop on the outskirts of Warsaw. His professor's death severed Chopin's final tie to his musical past. Now, both the friend and the teacher of his youth were gone.

A few weeks later he and Sand were in Nohant, deposited for the first time by the new railroad from Paris to Orléans. The rattling train had given Chopin a migraine. Then had come the ordeal of the overnight coach from Châteauroux to Nohant.

Their first guest was Delacroix, accompanied this time by his cat, Cupid, it being a mark of Sand's special favor when pets were included in her invitation. For a few days, the overworked painter rejoiced in long unscheduled hours of peace and quiet, interrupted only by billiards, walks, or his host's music. Soon, however, Delacroix, another boulevardier, joined Chopin in complaining of the monotony of rural life; friends and neighbors quite literally tended to their sheep. He would become a "fossil," he feared, if he stayed too long. Three days after his arrival, he sent to Paris for paints; then, as Sand recalled, he appropriated a length of canvas she had been saving for a corset, drafted Maurice to nail it to a stretcher, and went to work. On a walk in the meadow nearby, Delacroix had come upon Françoise Caillaud, George's much loved servant, teaching her daughter Luce to read. Their peasant faces, "pure and naive," heads inclined over the primer, touched and inspired the painter: He cast the two as Saint Anne and the future mother of Christ in a small composition, *The Education of the Virgin*.

Delacroix was an aristocrat and skeptic—most of the time. But unlike Chopin, the painter, increasingly, felt drawn back to the faith of his childhood. Now, as he listened to his host at the piano, he heard "God's presence descending through his fingers."

Of his many talented friends, Delacroix had always felt the deepest affinity for Chopin; in these weeks, the painter realized for the first time that the composer was a genius. "Of all those I've known, he is the only true artist among us," he said. Along with the music he heard with wonder each time Chopin played, Delacroix was now the beneficiary of his friend's vast musical knowledge, woven through days of one "endless conversation."

Chopin was an incomparable teacher. The twenty francs paid by those who could afford his fee was not based on the cachet of his celebrity. He had the gift of imparting what he knew to his pupils in a way that both freed and inspired them. He taught by example: During lessons, the large Pleyel was ceded to pupils while Chopin, seated beside them, played on a small upright "pianino." At the same time, he devoted rigorous and minute attention to each student's progress, particularly the proper position of the hands, on which he was implacable, helping students to master his own innovations in fingering and pedaling. On the subject of practice, he was still more radical. Taking a firm stand against the view that more was better, he warned that exhaustion was counterproductive; he advised a student who boasted of practicing for six hours to cut this time in half, and even then he urged that sessions at the piano alternate with intervals spent reading a book, looking at great paintings, or just taking a walk. The only point of technique was freedom, the liberation of interpretative faculties, not keyboard acrobatics for their own sake—the stock in trade of a Kalkbrenner or Liszt. Touch was the secret, he insisted, to "creating the most beautiful quality of sound"; Chopin's famous touch was described as a "stroking" movement which coaxed from certain final notes a magical afterlife, their tones lingering in the air.

Above the monotony of scales, or submission to the famous Czerny exercises, Chopin placed "an intense listening concentration" on the student's own playing to cultivate "refinement of the ear."

He could be ill tempered, scourging pupils with icy contempt or explosive rage (the latter when he was feeling ill or confronted by lazy or careless work from students preparing for musical careers). He possessed, though, an intuitive understanding of what to give those young pianists who, once they had reached a certain level of virtuosity, were "stuck," unable to move ahead with confidence in their own sense of the music: He urged them, "Be bolder, let your-self go more"—a reminder that along with Chopin's classical rigor, he was a romantic artist after all.

But not romantic enough to savor Delacroix's feast of color. He "detested" their friend's canvases, Sand reported. Chopin could never make the connection between the painter's freedom, earned by mastery of form and structure, with the abandon, based upon the same foundations, that he urged in musical performance.

Delacroix's passion for music made up for Chopin's color blind-ness in painting: It was the painter who found in each medium "reflections" of the other. Soon, they discovered a common lan-guage through which they could address common problems of composition: how to create contour, tones and half-tones, or fix elusive effects of shading and relief. From Delacroix's *Journals*, with their precise notations of pigments and mixes, of highlights and washes, gleam shards of his talks with Chopin; what Sand called the composer's "blue note" reverberates in the painter's records of certain effects of touch: the barest stroke of violet that quickens a coil of blond hair.

At the least, the timing of their talks suggests that his visit to Nohant played a vital role in helping Delacroix, who had strug-gled through the previous winter and spring with a large and com-plex public commission: the decoration of the cupola for the library of the Chambre des Pairs in the newly renovated Luxem-bourg Palace. By fall, the artist had settled on the subject and its plan, four groups depicting an Elysium of great men who had not received the grace of baptism. In the most important of the four, an apostolic succession of genius from antiquity through the Renaissance, Virgil is shown introducing Dante to Homer. Chopin's explicit contribution was to provide the likeness for the portrait of Dante.* Was it the genius of Delacroix's favorite poet and the composer whose music he "worshiped" or the similarity of their beaked noses that inspired him?

---

*In the second section, depicting illustrious Greeks from Alexander to Apelles, Sand is supposed to have been the model for Aspasia, brilliant and influential mistress of Peri-cles, the fifth-century Athenian statesman.

Nohant felt desolate after Delacroix left. Another visitor, Stefan Witwicki, consoled Chopin with the pure happiness of speaking Polish. The invitation, their first to the poet, seems related to Jan Matuszynski's death. As irritating as he often found his fellow Poles, Chopin did not want success to starve him of his past.

His homesickness intensified as images of home blurred. Nostalgia replaced memory. Chopin chafed at rumblings from the émigré colony that he had become too grand for compatriots who did not frequent balls at the Hôtel Lambert, home to several generations of Czartoryskis and a center for the émigré court in exile.

As a poet who remained an alien in his adopted culture, Witwicki could be counted upon to persist as Chopin's Polish conscience: He never gave up trying to recall his friend to his preordained calling, composer of the great national opera celebrating their homeland. It seems more than coincidence that among the works Chopin composed during this summer, one stands as his summa of the heroic in a genre that the composer himself had transformed from courtly processional dance to stirring call-to-arms; in the Polonaise in A-flat Major, op. 53, Chopin's final work of this title, a famous passage is often compared to the crescendo hoof beats of an approaching cavalry charge. It's said that when the composer played the work in Paris, his fellow exiles rose as one at the end to sing the anthem: "Poland has not perished yet, as long as her sons are alive."

Witwicki, at least, made no secret of his envy at his friend's triumph: Julian Fontana's rage and resentment festered silently. Inviting Chopin's exploitation, he then blamed him for his failure. Dependent as he was upon Fontana's services, Chopin found it easier to ignore his friend's feelings—along with his basic needs, such as money. Fontana never seems to have been paid for his endless errands or his exacting work as copyist. In lieu of payment, however, Julian expected—or had been led to expect—compensation from his friend in the form of help with his own stalled musical career. He allowed himself to be used by Chopin (or so he rationalized) in the belief that the latter both endorsed his talent and would further his ambitions. Then, it seems, he faced the truth.

As Chopin and Sand boarded the train for Nohant in May, Fontana wrote to his sister in Poland. He had come to the end of his resources, financial and moral. "I had always counted upon one friend who was supposed to open doors for me, who, instead, lied to me while leading me on . . . I even left Paris for a while to escape his domination—a move that damaged my career still more. I could only begin composing again on my return."

The next year, 1843, Fontana left for America.

Chopin was usually generous—to needy fellow Poles, to struggling musicians of talent. He went out of his way to promote his pupils who were preparing for careers in music, even though one of his favorites, Adolf Gutmann, was judged a complete mediocrity by those who heard him play. Thus, Chopin's apparent refusal to do anything for Fontana raises crucial issues of motivation and character: We must suppose that he found his friend so lacking in ability that supporting his aspirations as either composer or pianist would have been impossible. The questions then arise: Did Chopin try to make his views known, and did Fontana refuse to "hear" him? Chopin's horror of confrontation, as revealed in his dealings with his publishers, along with his dependency upon Fontana, argue that, far from being honest with his friend and risking losing him—and his services—Chopin was indeed guilty as Fontana had charged, of "leading [him] on," encouraging the embittered musician to live in hope. Fontana's masochism and his yearning to be part of Chopin's charmed circle, along with delusions about his own gifts, took care of the rest. He was the perfect victim. Returning from New York in 1852, Julian Fontana committed suicide in Paris, three years after Chopin's death.

At the end of July 1842, Chopin and Sand made a brief trip to Paris to find another apartment for the fall. The charming pair of pavilions off rue Pigalle had turned out to be cold and damp; climbing the steep outside staircase left Chopin short of breath. They wanted to move, but at the same time hoped to stay in the same neighborhood, which retained the character of a rural village, but one now inhabited by a yeasty mix of artists, musicians, and writers, leavened by actresses kept in great style in new villas paid for by their rich protectors. The first group had led the marginal *quartier* climbing towards Montmartre to be reborn as the "New Athens."

The Square d'Orléans, where they moved in September, was the "New Athens" in microcosm. The only apartment complex of its size, more urban than any of its neighbors, Sand saw it as a "kind of phalanstery" after the communal ideal promoted by Fourier. But unlike the socialist's vision, their own aristocratic—and expensive—utopia guaranteed the "mutual freedom" she required, offering the advantages of a commune of kindred spirits, along with separate facilities to suit the needs of individuals and families. Lured by the Marlianis, both Sand and Chopin felt at home with such notably talented neighbors as the pianists Kalkbrenner, Alkan, and Zimmerman, and the dancer Marie Taglioni.

George rented the roomiest apartment, with the famous billiard table; diagonally across the garden courtyard was Chopin's smaller retreat, to which he rarely repaired. Maurice had his separate bachelor studio on a higher floor, while Solange was given a tiny maid's room off her mother's apartment to use on school holidays when good behavior earned her a visit home.

Autumn in Paris always affected Chopin badly, but this year, thanks to a new homeopathic physician, he could at least breathe. Every other day he spent five minutes inhaling deeply from a bottle whose contents, prescribed by Dr. Molin, and probably containing morphine, suppressed his cough, even enabling him to climb stairs without collapsing. His breathing made easier, he became less anxious. Sand reported him to be generally calmer, less irritable, and with fewer attacks of nerves than he had suffered for some time (a revealing glimpse of daily life with Chopin before his new medication).

Renewed strength bolstered his confidence. With greater energy, he took on more pupils; daily lessons filled the afternoons until six. The pace of social life quickened, and although Chopin still resisted public concerts, the large audience at some of his private performances would have overflowed Pleyel's rooms. In the middle of January, together with Karl Filtsch, a Hungarian prodigy of thirteen who was his new favorite pupil, Chopin performed his Piano Concerto in E Minor for five hundred guests of Baron James de Rothschild and his wife, Betty. Filtsch played the solo, with his teacher providing the orchestral part. Even by the standards of splendid entertainments at 15, rue Lafitte, the Rothschild triple mansion, this grand musicale inspired fresh superlatives. The rooms glittered as never before: gold, crystal, paintings, and tapestries; astounding arrangements of ices and flowers. Then came the legendary array of talent: Besides Chopin and his protégé, the performers included three of the most famous singers in Europe: Giulia Grisi, Viardot, and Lablache.

Chopin had trained Filtsch for two years before their dual performance that evening. During that time, Karl and his brother, Joseph, were adopted by Sand, often staying for dinner after lessons at rue Pigalle. It was at one of George's soirées that Baroness Betty de Rothschild had first heard Filtsch perform and decided to launch the child of such marvelous gifts. Then, the summer before the joint performance, while the family was in Nohant, Liszt had poached the prodigy—already famous in Paris musical circles—for himself. As a measure of the boy's talent and Chopin's affection for him, when Liszt decided to remove to Weimar, Chopin took Karl back, forgiving both the personal insult and the likelihood that he had been "tainted" by Lisztian vulgarities.

Pride in the boy, generosity, forgiveness, along with an intuitive understanding: Chopin's feelings for Filtsch come closer than any other in his life to those of an ideal father—very different from his own wary relations with Maurice. Far from resenting the adulation that already flowed his pupil's way—or fearing that the disciple might eclipse the master—Chopin, through Filtsch, relived his own early triumphs and became, for Karl, the teacher who was both composer and performer of genius that he himself had never had. Aware of his own precarious health, he rejoiced in what he could still pass on to another in style and technique; his art would be extended by the miracle of Filtsch's talent, formed, it seemed, to complement his own.

He took infinite pains preparing Karl to play the solo part of the concerto, a piece that for Chopin had sharp emotional resonance, of early love and sorrow. According to a fellow student, the master worked with Filtsch particularly on perfecting the cantabile style. Based upon the suppleness of the human voice, cantabile requires that "the pianist must be first tenor, first soprano—always a singer and a bravura singer in the runs."

Anointing Filtsch to play the piano solo in this work approached a sacrificial gift. He had the boy study the work section by section; he was "never allowed to play the movement right through, since it would affect Chopin too powerfully." Young as he was, Karl recognized the sacred trust that informed his apprenticeship. He was devoutly Catholic, and his final preparation of the piece was accompanied by fasting and prayer. Until the last, he was not permitted to practice his part on the piano; Chopin would only allow him to read the score under his direction. On the evening of the concert, the duet of teacher and pupil emerged as an apostolic succession; the thirteen-year-old's delicacy and sureness of touch were deemed miraculous, a worthy tribute to the master. Chopin played from memory, and his power to evoke the the entire orchestra was no less inspired: "I have never heard anything comparable to that first *tutti* as he played it himself at the piano," a listener recalled. "To hear them together" remained "the experience of a lifetime."

All that Chopin had given to Filtsch—in precious time and energy, drawn from a wellspring of love and trust rarely tapped—was about to bear fruit. Karl was on the brink of a dazzling career. He had already begun touring when, two years later, at the age of fifteen, he died of tuberculosis in Vienna.

Loss makes us fearful. For Chopin, hovering over his own worrisome symptoms, skeptical of his doctors' reassurance, a believer in signs and portents, all deaths came as warnings. After Jan Matuszynski's mortal illness, so close to home, he could not have failed to observe the signs of mortality in his pupil, a small, pale boy with large dark eyes.

. . .

Eighteen forty-two marked the end of Chopin's most productive years: From now on, the number of his published works would drop dramatically. The energy and exuberance of youth—until now, always resurgent, despite periods of sickness—was running out; in their place, a psychology of self-doubt entered: critical, dissatisfied, indecisive. More often, in the summers to come, this is what Sand would hear as the dark labor of creation. Other works besides the opus 53 polonaise proved to be the last of a genre that he had stamped as his own.

Both his Fourth Ballade and his Fourth Scherzo were completed this year, the composer's final offerings in the great cycles of these extended forms. Is symmetry destiny? Chopin, himself, distrustful of words in general but particularly where these concerned his musical practice, would be the last to reveal whether this paired conclusion was an aesthetic decision or one imposed by circumstances: his health, or the beckoning of other ideas and possibilities.

Fewer would not mean lesser. Almost twice as long as the First Scherzo, the Fourth embraces amplitude to spin melodic webs that evoke pure song, while its delicate washes of color have led it to be called proto-impressionist. A light-filled buoyancy swells the work; games of chromatic tag convey a sensuous pleasure in the materials of music making that, indeed, approach the painterly; not even Chopin's painful drops from major to minor keys, those unbidden hauntings from the past, dispel an unhurried mood of celebration.

In its textural richness, complexity, and sweep, the Fourth Ballade offers a gathering of other forms—memories of a waltz, rondo, sonatas, nocturnes—and the triumphant recasting of those pylons of Chopin's musical architecture: counterpoint and canon. Every emotional state, too, makes an appearance, from the elegiac melancholy of the introduction to the tension that builds to bursting in the savage coda. But it's Chopin's deployment of variation in this last ballade that reveals with an almost eerie clarity the two faces of his genius: Listening to the dazzling display of changes wrought on one theme, some so subtle as to slip past on first hearings, we are present at both creation and performance.

At the heart of romanticism lies transformation, a magic act conferring promethean powers on the artist. By this point, Chopin stood alone, the acknowledged master of transforming genres, conjuring radical innovation from traditional materials. New ideas in the shape of forms that did not yet exist now claimed him.

TWELVE

Forty Pounds of Jam

To those waiting at the terminus of the Paris-Châteauroux coach on May 22, 1843, the six passengers who descended (having taken up all but one of the seats) could have been any solidly bourgeois household: Chopin, Sand, and eighteen-month-old Louise Viardot, accompanied by a baby nurse, a cook, and a manservant.

At thirty-three, Chopin no longer appeared younger than his companion, nearing forty; his slight form looked shrunken, the delicate features more wizened than boyish. As Sand would warn his sister Ludwika a year later, when she was about to see Frédéric after fourteen years of separation, she should try not to be shocked by her brother's appearance: He had aged so terribly.

In the absence of Solange and Maurice, Sand and Chopin slipped into the roles of being parents—together. George was always enchanted by young children. Preparing for Louisette's arrival, she had refurbished an old cradle with ribbons and lace, just as she had done twenty years earlier for her firstborn. Chopin was not normally a baby lover, but when the prodigious toddler took to calling him "P'tit Chopin" he became her slave, making faces, playing patty-cake, "spending hours kissing her little hands," Sand said. His devotion was repaid; the little princess preferred Chopin to all her other adoring courtiers. With no other visitors, their shared delight in the baby's activities—even to her "peeing on every carpet"—emerges as need: Their borrowed child joined two solitudes.

"We're alone here, Chopin and I" was a refrain that summer in Sand's letters; it was not the shorthand of intimacy, but a cry of loneliness. They worked and slept like relay runners; as one rose, the other went to bed after the night's labors. Sand missed Maurice, in no hurry to leave the good life in Gascony, where he was staying with his bon vivant father. Chopin's letters to friends in Paris—especially to Polish intimates—sound a note of abandonment.

Her fortieth birthday looming, Sand fell prey to suicidal depression, made more desolate by the sense that she had no one in whom to confide her grief at aging; all those close to her were dependents, starting with Chopin.

Deciding that a few days in the out-of-doors would raise both their spirits, Sand and Chopin set off in June for a three-day excursion in the back country beyond the Creuse River; most of the time, George walked while Chopin, using Maurice's plushly cushioned custom-made saddle, rode Margot the donkey. Sand had to dissuade him from paying Maurice for use of the seat; instead, she wrote to her son, he could expect a gift from "le Père Gatiau" ("Sugar Daddy"), who spoiled them all with his generosity. George may have misunderstood—or preferred to misread—the impulse behind Chopin's preference for paying Maurice. He did not want to feel beholden to one whose growing hostility was waiting to ignite into open warfare. They roughed it, sleeping on straw in haylofts. Chopin never felt better, Sand said. It was she who took to her bed with a bad stomach as soon as they returned. Unable to work and with a deadline looming, she sank into low spirits once again: "It's not very gay around here when the lady of the house isn't feeling well," Chopin grumbled to Grzymala.

Delacroix came for a ten-day visit in the middle of July. This was a cause for rejoicing under any circumstances, but Sand hoped, too, that the painter's imminent arrival might shame Maurice into returning from Gascony to work alongside his teacher. On the eve of his twentieth birthday, his mother said it was now or never if Maurice was to become an artist. (Imitating Delacroix's rakish beret was as close as the apprentice would come to emulating the master.)

As though on cue, Sand's old loves reappeared: the silver-tongued lawyer Michel de Bourges, tubby, bald, bespectacled, whose talk had once made him irresistible. Now, his eloquence seemed harangue, and Sand, as much as Chopin, was not sorry to see him leave after a long lunch. Another of George's former lovers, the actor Pierre Bocage, was a different matter.

Since her separation from Dudevant, Sand had rarely lied about her sexual history. With Chopin, she would not have needed even to equivocate; delicacy, discretion, and tact were his very measure—at least in the great world where he moved with such grace. He would have been the last man to interrogate the woman he loved about her past. He would have known of her famous affairs: the precocious poet Alfred de Musset; the writer and bureaucrat Prosper Mérimée. But he was unprepared now for casual revelations about the handsome actor. To Sand's astonishment, dreadful scenes erupted: suspicions, accusations, and denials, followed by icy silences.

"As for a certain younger man's jealousy about a certain old lady, it's subsided for want of nourishment," Sand wrote to Bocage. ". . . Still, I can't say that the sickness is entirely cured or that one doesn't have to be very careful about hiding the most innocent things. The old lady was wrong in believing that sincerity and trust were the best remedies. I warned him to simply stop going on about the letter of a certain older man for whom she indeed still harbors silent feelings of eternal loyal friendship."

Arch and coquettish, the tone of Sand's letter would certainly fan any suspicions Chopin harbored that old passions, far from settling into the friendship of old lovers, as she maintained, had rekindled. Sadder still is the disrespect—on both sides—revealed by her diagnosis. For Chopin, George could no longer be trusted; to Sand, her Chopinet had rejoined the gallery of other former lovers, crazed by jealousy, sniffing for evidence to confirm their fears. From now on, he must be "managed," with even the most "innocent" relationships concealed from him.

More damaging, Chopin's jealousy—retroactive or immediate—declared a fraying sense of security. In George's casual confession, he found proof, not of intimacy and trust, but of his desexualized role: he had become—what, precisely? A son? An old friend? A visitor who had outstayed his welcome? A permanent boarder, tolerated more than welcomed? If he accepted that they were no longer lovers, to swallow demotion to sexual confidant was to dishonor the past.

On August 13, Chopin left for Paris, alone. Sand was assaulted by anxiety: How would he survive without her? The troops were alerted—the Marlianis, Marie de Rozières (reinstated in the family's good graces since she had been jilted by Antoni Wodzinski). Maurice, now supposedly hard at work in his studio across the courtyard at Square d'Orléans, was charged with warning his mother should Chopin show the slightest signs of sickness. "Take care of him—just as he would do for you," she said. (Obsessed with Pauline Viardot, Maurice was laying siege to the singer in her country house near Paris while her husband was away.) All of Sand's precautions were aimed at a visit of only four days. Chopin returned to Nohant with Solange on August 17.

Less than a week later, the peaceful rural pace turned to frenzy as the household prepared for a wedding. Once again, Sand and Chopin assumed a familial role as hosts and proxy parents, this time of the bride: Françoise Caillaud, mother of Luce and Delacroix's model for Saint Anne, was remarried after seven years of widowhood to a popular local farmer.

Using makeshift straw pallets and every inch of floor space, Sand found room for sixty guests, while food, wine, and extra help for three days of feasting crammed the kitchen. With their passion for folk traditions, Sand and Chopin rejoiced in every detail of the centuries-old Berrichon peasant celebration: from the costumes, carefully handed down over generations—especially the wide-brimmed white hats worn by the men—to customs like the roast presented to the bride in a chamber pot. For Chopin the great revelation was the music; at the skirl of ancient bagpipes, the bridal couple, guests, and hosts leapt, hopped, and slid to the fast duple-meter rhythms of the bourrée, the traditional dance of courtship.

Then, Sand and Chopin were alone again.

Despite the tensions and scenes, feelings of irreparable harm on both sides, their production, in energy and concentration, would never be more richly complementary. The two nocturnes of opus 55 distill Chopin's mastery of every form of musical expression: counterpoint and polyphonic weavings, ingenuity of ornament. In both, the composer's engagement with the body informs the expressive impact of the music. The first, in F minor, leads a dreamlike dance in slow motion. Cast in limpid bel canto style, the E-flat major nocturne's pure melody, effortless trills, and arching line follow the human voice in all its glory. Once again, the magician burns away the clichés of operatic convention, and stripping the form of sentimentality, leaves only the piano's intimate reach to the heart.

Chopin called the three mazurkas of opus 56 "little stories," but "histories"—*histoires,* the same word in French—better describes their sense of vaulting cultures and centuries. In the second mazurka, in C, the strong beat of a Mazovian peasant dance is welded to recent musical memories of wedding bourrées in an imitation of bagpipes (he summoned the Berrichon instruments—the only ones he had yet heard—to evoke the sounds of Scotland, dedicating the piece to a pupil, "Miss Catherine Maberley").

With the third and longest of the mazurkas, in C minor, Chopin the pied piper dances the simple rustic form turned courtly favorite into a musical future. Attentive listeners have heard "prophetic harmonies," "premonitions" of the mature Wagner, and beyond. Literally without missing a dance beat, the composer enlists dissonance, daring harmonies, unexpected modulations, all deployed with the freest of play on the basic form. Its lack of harmonic resolution thrusts this mazurka into more complicated emotional territory, closest to the longing, regret, remorse—even anger—expressed in the word *żal.*

In these months, while Chopin directed his energy to a small number of highly complex pieces, Sand labored on a succession of novels requiring solid historical research. She continued work on

Consuelo, the life story of a singer based upon Pauline Viardot; the fictional Spanish heroine's career took her from Venice to Hungary, including revolution and romance along the way. Consuelo's talent and success collide with her high moral scruples to create the novel's dynamic. Whether Sand's heroines are singers or actresses, they are all recognizable stand-ins for the author herself, the principal reason for their popularity with contemporaries—and obscurity thereafter. Ennobled by marriage as the Countess of Rudolstadt, Consuelo reappears in a long, rambling sequel of that name, which drew heavily on the activities of Freemasonry and the conspiratorial world of secret societies. For both works, Sand depended upon friends to trawl the Bibliothèque Nationale, finding, copying, and speeding to Nohant quantities of material on a Mozartian eighteenth-century universe. The double burden of reading and writing was damaging Sand's eyesight; pained by the light, she took to wearing blue-tinted glasses, giving her the appearance of a blind woman.

While she rested her eyes, she learned of a local scandal that demanded action and redress. A retarded girl, not yet fifteen and probably pregnant, had been found wandering a deserted back road with nothing but the clothes on her back. Fanchette, it turned out, was a foundling; she had spent her entire life in the local asylum in La Châtre, whose officials had clearly given orders to get rid of her. While at the institution, she had been sexually abused—"passed from hand to hand," Sand reported—by those charged with her protection. The scandal and subsequent cover-up by the local establishment, including clergy, were immediately exposed by Sand in a pamphlet called simply "Fanchette." Now, for the first time, Sand realized the extent of government repression on the local level; no printer in the region would publish her account. Galvanized by outrage, she immediately set about gathering support for an alternative newspaper, to be called *L'Eclaireur de l'Indre* (The Watch on the Indre).

In fact, *L'Eclaireur* was Sand's second venture in what we would call countercultural journalism: Several years earlier, angered by her then-publisher Buloz's rejection of novels he feared would ruffle the conservative readership of his house organ, *Revue des Deux Mondes*, Sand had dunned friends for money to start *La Revue Indépendante*. To Chopin's dismay, their rue Pigalle salon filled with Sand's old acquaintances among radical activists and writers, along with younger journalists. But she was the first to recognize that the *Indépendante* was no disinterested strike for free speech. She needed an organ that would serialize her novels and ensure sales of the published works.

Since then, Sand's political sympathies had moved steadily to the left; she was ever more convinced of the evils of wealth and the conspiracy of the powerful to deny any rights—especially the vote—to the powerless. Swept up in the new wave of romantic socialism, she sought to discover ability and extend opportunity among the working classes, promoting young men of ambition like the artisan-poet Agricole Perdiguier. The Fanchette affair promised a larger reformist role. The provinces were worse than Paris; here, feudalism still lived. Among a less literate, scattered population, information was scarce, official authority absolute. Nohant too was overrun, it now seemed to Chopin, by homespun local activists, as Sand once again began the struggle to raise money, solicit subscribers, and find a publisher and printer for the new venture. Endless meetings crowded the family rooms, sending Chopin in retreat to his quarters upstairs. It was not only the company but the ideology that estranged him.

He, too, had been horrified by the callous exploitation and attempted disposal of a retarded orphan girl. (Among those "patriots" Sand named as supporters of the new journal, Chopin was down for fifty francs.) But he did not see Fanchette's martyrdom in class terms, as proof of the abuses of both church and state, demanding drastic reform. Such terrible acts were evidence, as he had been taught, of human sin—as old and unchanging as history. But one could not say these things to George; she would only hold him to be more childish, naive, and useless than poor Fanchette herself.

On September 1, the Viardots returned from Pauline's triumphant tour to reclaim their child. When they left, her surrogate parents were desolate. "The house feels so empty and sad without you and our darling Louisette that we can hardly bear it," Sand wrote to her Fifille.

At the end of October 1843, Chopin and Maurice—"my two little boys," as Sand called them—set out for Paris together. Depositing them at the coach, George had to leave for home before their departure, and she worried over a noisy altercation among the passengers. She was concerned that, whatever its cause, the consequences might be a less comfortable seat for Chopin. On their arrival in Paris, the travelers reassured her in a joint letter. The only disaster Chopin reported was that "there was a Jewess in the coach"; Maurice merely noted that the temperature inside was raised uncomfortably by six fellow passengers "all reeking of garlic."

Before leaving, Chopin had pleaded with George that Solange be allowed to remain in Nohant with her mother instead of being shipped back to her hated boarding school. This time, he was clever: he did not try to make his case by expressing sympathy for Solange or appealing to Sand's maternal indulgence. Instead, he argued that with George's recent stomach troubles, he would worry about her less if Solange remained with her mother. Sand relented. But she dreaded the prospect of being alone with the daughter who did nothing but irritate her. There was so much to do before leaving Nohant for the winter—in house, garden, and stables, with accounts and repairs—she would be driven to fury by Solange's typically unhelpful and hostile behavior.

Thus, it was with amazement that Sand reported a Solange transformed: In her joy and gratitude at having her adored "Mamoune" to herself, the resentful adolescent had become a model daughter, sweet tempered, cheerful, and, most touchingly, protective of her mother.

From Paris, Maurice griped about the bad weather, bad health, and bad moods endured by both of Sand's boys without her. Please come soon, he begged. Chopin's letters to Nohant, terse and laconic, hinted at illness. Now, it was Solange's chance to turn the tables on the demanding males who always received all of the maternal attentions.

"You and Chopin are both little egoists. Just because you're bored, why do you have to complain to Mommy—Chopin indirectly and you openly," she wrote to Maurice. "The day before yesterday, she was all set to rush back to Paris. Since she's leaving anyway in eight days, at least let her enjoy autumn here—her favorite time—without nagging and worrying her." Indeed, an anxious Sand had written to Maurice: "Please let me know whether Chopin is ill; his letters are so short and sad. If he does feel sick, can't you stay in his room?"* Once again she urged, "Be another me," underlining her next words: *"He would do the same for you."*

From late November, when Sand and Solange returned to Paris, through the winter and the spring, Chopin was sick, first with the influenza that felled many Parisians that year; no sooner had he recovered than he succumbed to a "nervous depression from which he had suffered for some time." Sand wrote an urgent note to Dr. Molin; some medication must be found—and immediately—to relieve him. She was sending a good friend of theirs, the promising young radical journalist Louis Blanc, to pick it up. A drug given him earlier by the same doctor had "calmed [him] too much," Chopin told Molin, adding that he was always tired "without having done a thing." Whatever relief the new medication provided, the courier himself was not part of the remedy: Louis Blanc would shortly become Sand's lover.

Normally, as spring advanced, Chopin's health and spirits lifted. But on May 3, 1844, he learned of his father's death three weeks earlier in Warsaw. He heard the news on returning with Sand from the theater, where he had been politely applauding a performance of Sophocles' *Antigone,* starring Pierre Bocage as Creon.

He locked himself in his darkened rooms and refused to speak

---

*The first editor of his mother's letters, Maurice Dudevant-Sand (as he subsequently called himself) suppressed this sentence.

to anyone for days. Sand's pleadings went unanswered. Dr. Molin was summoned, but Chopin would not see him. Desperate, George asked Auguste Franchomme to come, hoping that the musician closest to Chopin could penetrate his solitary grief. Others paid the traditional condolence call uninvited, Liszt among them. He had visited Chopin's parents in Warsaw during a recent tour, giving them box seats for his concert. Following this kindness, Nicolas Chopin had written to his son—his last known letter—urging him to make it up with Liszt, who, he argued, not only wished him well but was too useful an ally to alienate. But Chopin had confined himself to an exchange of notes, and he made no exception by seeing Liszt now.

The devastation he felt at his father's death was more than the loss of a parent, however painful. He was mourning for home, the idealized home of childhood, now forever shuttered by death. He had never been close to Nicolas; his father's unflagging support and the many sacrifices it entailed were felt as a burden. Paternal urgings to thrift and the healthy life, and the son's avoidance of both, did nothing to draw them closer in separation. Letters from Warsaw, moreover, made it clear that their father had been failing for several years; he only left the house in the most benign weather to tend his beloved fruit trees. Finances were precarious at home. The czarist occupation had seen to his early retirement with small probability of a pension, and it seems likely that Nicolas and Justyna survived only through the help of their two daughters and their husbands. At the height of his earning power, Chopin does not seem to have offered to help.*

In 1833, Czar Nicholas had offered an amnesty to those who had not played a leading role in the insurrection. At that point, or at any time in the eleven intervening years, Chopin could have taken advantage of the "thaw," enabling him to visit Poland whenever he wished. He never applied. He could not confront exile as a

---

*In the early spring of 1842, his mother wrote to Chopin asking to borrow three thousand florins to repay a personal debt, begging him to keep the matter a secret from his father. His response has not survived.

choice then; now, he had no choice but to add guilt to grief. He begged the family for every detail of his father's death, which his brother-in-law Antoni Barcinski tried to be truthful in supplying, while offering consoling bromides. Of course, the good man had died a peaceful Christian death, with all the comforts of the sacraments and surrounded by his loving family. But he had suffered a morbid terror of being buried alive, exacting a pledge from the undertaker that they would check his body for vital signs before burial. In the face of Chopin's inconsolable grief, Sand invited his favorite sister, Ludwika, and her husband, an agronomist turned judge, for an extended visit. This was the wisest decision Sand could have made. When the couple arrived in Paris on July 15, 1844, they were showered with hospitality by the Polish colony: Chopin arranged evenings at the opera and tickets for a royal concert, along with a performance by the mythic tragedienne Rachel.

Exhausted, the sightseers repaired to Nohant on August 9. For Ludwika and George it was love at first sight. She had expected a devout, disapproving provincial and instead had encountered a woman "totally superior to her age and her country, and of an angelic character." For her part, Ludwika expressed only gratitude for the care and love with which Sand had surrounded her brother for almost a decade. Guarding his health and talent, she had saved his life. His sister's presence, and the instant and profound sympathy between the two women he loved, restored Nohant to its state of miraculous happiness, an Eden before the Fall.

"We're all mad with joy here," Chopin wrote to Marie de Rozières. Ludwika's departure for Paris at the end of August, accompanied by Chopin and Maurice, left Sand "brokenhearted." She would now tease Chopin by asking why he couldn't be more like his sister, his better in every way. Following her return to Poland, Sand entrusted her half-brother, Hippolyte, to send Ludwika the manuscript of *The Devil's Pool*, her masterpiece; it was dedicated "to my friend, Frédérick Chopin."

When Chopin returned on September 4, he left Maurice in Paris. At Nohant, he found mother and daughter affectionate and peaceful. With Solange eager to work, Chopin taught her a Beethoven sonata. Drawing inspiration from the master of the form, Chopin labored on his own B Minor Sonata, one of "a satchel of new compositions," Sand reported. The sonata, opus 58, is Chopin's autumnal distillation of summer's riches. Expansive and confident, it seems to overflow the boundaries of the form, marrying Chopin the classicist's mastery of part writing to his romantic exaltation of Bellini's endless melodic line. Solos, duets, and full orchestra—all the voices that Chopin loved as his touchstones—receive their homage, reinvented for a piano unmistakably his own.

Sand, meanwhile, put up forty pounds of jam made from the late-ripening local plums. No one was allowed to help her in this labor. To conserve the fall's rich harvest was a way of husbanding the joys of late summer and autumn, certain the fruit would see them through the lean times to come.

"It would be impossible to savor so much happiness in one month," Sand wrote to Ludwika, "without preserving some, without healing old wounds, without laying in new stores of hope and trust in God."

THIRTEEN

A Victim of Time

Composed in the summer of 1844, the Berceuse in D-flat Major surprises us, like happiness itself. Chopin had originally called the piece "Variations" (*Variantes*) before settling on the more evocative name for lullaby or cradle song, from *bercer*, to rock. It was the only composition to which Chopin ever gave this title, and the lulling enchantment of the music evokes the grace of Louisette's presence in their summer of restored peace. Melodic shifts float over the hypnotic rocking ostinato of the left hand; the modulations are as subtly varied, yet as dramatic in texture and shape as those formed by the barest turn of a kaleidoscope whose bits of colored glass, shivering into patterns, defy us to explain their magic. "Who will open the nightingale's throat," one Chopin scholar asked of the Berceuse, "to discover where the song comes from?"

The rooms at Nohant were unheatable at the end of November. Chopin returned to Paris, preceding Sand by almost a month. They wrote to each other daily, and the few notes that survive deal with the small change of domestic life that, bit by bit, becomes the accumulated capital of intimacy. Delegated by George to choose the fabric for her new dress, Chopin decided on a black silk twill (the most expensive of nine samples he had inspected). He had also found the dressmaker, leading him to feel particularly pleased by the elegance of the finished work and confident that George would approve. At the Square d'Orléans, heavy snow blanketed her garden plot, making a white-on-white still life whose shadings he playfully enumerated: snowballs, sugar, swans, cream cheese, Solange's hands, Maurice's teeth. He had sorted George's mail (nothing urgent) and moved her plants indoors. Putting in a good word for his Polish servant, not famous for industry, he reported that Jan had worked at polishing the mirrors in Sand's apartment. And he reassured her about his eating habits, noting when he had dined chez Marliani, Franchomme, or Rozières. George, for her part, should not overtire herself with packing, and she must not think of traveling to Paris by coach on the icy roads.

Despite the good care taken of him, Chopin admitted to feeling weak and exhausted—feeble—and his debility gave him the sense of having, suddenly, aged. The cold afflicted him more keenly than ever; visiting the Franchommes, he dwelled on the disparities between their guest, huddled by the fire, wrapped in his heaviest overcoat and still shivering under three layers of flannel under-wear, his skin waxen, and his hosts' little son, romping near him on the floor, bare-legged, his rosy face glowing with warmth. And Chopin signed himself "Yours always, older than ever, dreadfully, terribly, incredibly old," or else, "Mummifiedly yours."

His piano had just arrived, but so far, none of his old pupils had reappeared; still, he claimed not to be worried—yet.

If he were of a mind to count his blessings, he wrote, news from the Polish colony early in the New Year of 1845 would incline him to cross himself. Yielding to his own undertow of fanaticism, Adam Mickiewicz had become the disciple of a messianic religious leader, Andrezj Towianski. By an act of public notary, Mickiewicz had had himself officially declared a "slave" of the new messiah— "a *thing*," Chopin underlined in horror. This public profession of abject faith in a madman, one who also advocated violent revolu-tion, had caused the poet, burdened with a sick wife and seven chil-dren, to lose his appointment at the Collège de France.

Demagogues and rabble rousers, political or religious, repelled

Chopin. But he particularly dreaded hearing the raised voice shriek in a Polish accent. His dandyism, the obsession with style as a sign of grace, was also a flight from the lure of darkness, from rage and melancholy. The doomed pursuit of perfection in art might be redeemed by the perfection of a boot.

Now, Chopin and Delacroix (the painter housebound with a winter's worth of ailments) exchanged messages on the vital subject of the best bootmaker. Delacroix counseled that stylishness in the matter of boots was determined by "tip," the most fashionable purveyor of the round tip, or English-style boot, being a Mr. Arrowsmith. In exchange for the reference, the painter delegated Chopin to write to Mr. Brown, sales agent, asking the latter to come to his house for a fitting.

Meanwhile, Chopin divided between two other friends chores formerly undertaken by Fontana alone: He assigned to the "serviceable" Marie de Rozières all domestic errands in Paris, while Franchomme took on Chopin's professional chores. In detailed letters from Nohant, the composer coached the cellist in the tactics of negotiation with publishers. Schlesinger wanted to delay publication of Chopin's three new mazurkas (opus 59), which at 600 francs each would provide badly needed income; Chopin himself had already placed German and English sales for this same price. If the publisher refused to reconsider, Chopin instructed, Franchomme should threaten to take the works elsewhere.

Money seemed to disappear. Chopin had recently borrowed 500 francs from Franchomme himself and, sounding somewhat embarrassed—as well he might, since his friend had a young family to support—Chopin now urged the cellist to apply to his banker, Auguste Léo, for prompt reimbursement. By way of interest, Chopin provided Franchomme with a rich and hardworking pupil: Miss Jane Wilhelmina Stirling, a Scots heiress, had, for a year now, arranged her life to spend several months in Paris studying with Chopin, who now urged that she supplement training in piano with cello lessons.

. . .

As it happened, Chopin was wise to insist on the best terms for the three new mazurkas. They would be the only compositions he would complete in the new year, 1845.

Less energy was needed for teaching than for composing, but that was a relative matter. Discipline could not disguise Chopin's weakened state. Visitors and pupils alike were shocked by his appearance. The more observant could see what effort it cost the master just to receive them. An English musician, Lindsay Sloper, recalled his teacher as impeccably attired when he arrived at eight o'clock in the morning, but often so weak that he had to conduct the lesson lying down, sniffing at the potion in his bottle. And when Franchomme brought another visitor from Britain, the émigré German pianist and conductor Charles Hallé, they found Chopin "hardly able to move, bent like a half-opened pen knife and evidently in great pain." He insisted, nonetheless, upon playing for them. He had promised, and he hated pleading illness. His guests were relieved to see that "as he warmed to his work, his body gradually resumed its normal position, the spirit having mastered the flesh."

When George returned to Paris in mid-December, she found the "patient as usual," coughing, with intermittent attacks of neuralgia and asthma. But now she could empathize; the city had never seemed to her so noxious. She felt suffocated. After six months in the country, she was unused to the noises of a large apartment complex, especially one that was home to many musicians and their pupils. Her morning sleep would be interrupted by the sound of a horn or a human voice singing off key; neighbors dropped in to welcome her back. She was so exhausted, she told her new confidant Louis Blanc, she feared she might be dying of brain fever. At the very least, she suspected rheumatism lurking in every drafty corridor, and quinsy throat in each salon.

Sand's finances, however, looked promising: installments of her latest novel, *Isadora*, were about to appear in *La Revue Indépendante*, the journal she had helped found, and she had signed a two-book contract with Louis Blanc, whose new newspaper, *La Reforme*, would serialize the completed work, *The Miller of*

Angibault, followed by another novel, as yet unwritten. Her income assured, she was planning to take Chopin away from Paris just before another bitter winter set in; a year in a warm climate followed by a long summer in Nohant would give him eighteen months' respite from the cold, she explained to Ludwika. The problem would be persuading that urban creature to give up autumn in Paris: the balls, receptions, and concerts. Always anxious about money, moreover, Chopin was never convinced that his pupils would return. His newest student was one whose devotion proved unwavering. Princess Radziwill before her marriage to Prince Aleksander Czartoryski, Marcelina Czartoryska, at twenty-three, was acknowledged to be a pianist of the first order. But there was also a deep affinity—human as well as musical—between teacher and pupil. Those who had heard them both play agreed that Marcelina's pianism was eerily close to the master's.

A young woman of warmth and charm as well as talent, the princess drew Chopin closer to her world, the Polish court in exile at the Hôtel Lambert. And a world it was. Along with several branches and generations of Czartoryskis and Radziwills, the town house on the Ile Saint-Louis, as large as a small palace, housed a school for young ladies and even printed its own newspaper. Host to lavish celebrations of holidays like Polish Easter, the Lambert ballroom was also the setting for Marcelina's benefit bazaars, balls, and musicales, which coaxed Chopin into the freezing night and across the Seine to perform as a star attraction. He was more grateful to be welcomed alone or with other regulars like Grzymala, any time he cared to visit.

Sand, too, was fond of Princess Marcelina—a singular affection, as she was rarely drawn to aristocratic women. In a party that included Delacroix, Solange, and Titine, Sand's young relative, she accompanied Chopin to a grand ball at the Lambert. It may be that she was relieved that Chopin had found another *foyer* where he felt at home. Madame Marliani had departed the Square d'Orléans for less expensive quarters, leaving Chopin and Sand in their separate apartments deprived of a family hearth and, more important, a communal kitchen. The good-hearted Charlotte urged

moving their dinners to her new apartment in the rue de la Ville-
l'Evêque, but Sand declined on the grounds of Chopin's reluc-
tance to leave his rooms on these cold nights (the Marlianis not
being Czartoryskis).

With too many claims on his time and failing strength, Chopin
chose his outings carefully, and these were mostly musical. With
Delacroix, he attended performances of Mozart's Requiem and
Haydn's *Creation*—a parenthesis whose reversed order had to
pique his sense of irony. (He let Solange accompany her mother to
hear Victor Hugo deliver his acceptance speech to the French
Academy.) When a tearful Louis Blanc appeared bearing the last
request of a dying friend and colleague, the republican journalist
Godefroi Cavaignac, that Chopin play for him, the composer
rushed off to the writer's bedside, where he stayed for hours at the
piano. He scarcely knew Cavaignac and had little sympathy for the
politics of either man; it was the terror of death that spoke to him
intimately. He was grateful that his music consoled Cavaignac's
last hours.

In May, Sand and Chopin were among thousands of Parisians
enthralled by a visiting troupe of Native Americans. Members of
the Ioway tribe of Plains Indians, they were touring Europe under
the management of the painter George Catlin; their performances
of tribal dances formed a living accompaniment to Catlin's famed
Indian Gallery, consisting of the artist's portraits of his subjects in
native dress together with their own marvels of feather and bead-
work. (Sand went twice to see the exhibition and performances.)
Chopin was moved less by the artifacts or ceremonial dances than
by the death of one of their number. The young wife of a brave
called Little Wolf, "the poor creature had died of homesickness,"
he told Ludwika. O-kee-wee-mee had been baptized on her
deathbed, and a monument in her memory was to be placed in
Montmartre Cemetery*—where Jan Matuszynski was buried, he
reminded his sister. He went on to describe—in obsessive detail—

---

*The design, commissioned from the noted sculptor Auguste Préault, failed to receive
the expected funding through public subscription and the monument was never built.

the oddly beautiful design (as reported in the press), a likeness of the dead woman and decorative frieze carved on a stone cenotaph.

In fact, O-kee-wee-mee had died of a "rapid consumption of the lungs," already diagnosed earlier during the company's visit to London. Chopin's version of her mortal illness exposes his identification with the foreign visitor: Like him, she had been an exile and wanderer, powerless to return home, steadily sickening until she died far from the rocky banks of the Missouri River. Her death was proof of homesickness as a wasting disease—like consumption itself. He would have another, final connection with the Ioway woman. Mobbed by crowds of the curious, her funeral at the Madeleine shivers with prophecy.

He covered pages of a letter home, written from Nohant in July of 1845, with musings on that death; normally, Chopin found writing to his family painful. One of Nicolas Chopin's last letters to his son ends with a plea not to let another three months go by without word from him. Now, his father's death freed him; he wrote to his mother and sisters more often and less guardedly. No longer fearing disapproval or criticism, writing home offered consolation.

"I feel a strange atmosphere here this year," he told them. "Many mornings, I look into the room next to mine but there's no one there. Sometimes it's occupied by a friend who's staying for a few days—the reason why I don't drink my hot chocolate in there any more and why I've moved the piano; it's now against the wall where the sofa used to be, along with the little table where Ludwika used to sit, embroidering bedroom slippers for me while the lady of the house was working."

The room next door felt empty, as though all the air had been sucked out; objects left behind by his family took on the numinous aura of relics: "In front of me," he told his sister, "in its case, is the repeater watch that you gave me (at this very minute, it reads four o'clock); there are some roses, carnations, also a quill and a bit of sealing wax left by Kalasanty. One part of me is always with you while the rest remains in the room on the other side of mine where the lady of the house is working; at the moment, I don't feel at home here at all but, as is often the case, I'm in some strange world elsewhere, a place that exists only in my imagination, but this doesn't embarrass me in the least. Don't we have a saying in Polish, 'In his daydreams, he's gone to the coronation'?" Pages follow with news of mutual friends, gossip about Victor Hugo's sexual adventures, gleanings from the newspapers—all run together in a free association that echoes with the unmistakable voice of someone who lives too much in isolation; the important thing is to keep talking and hope that somebody is listening.

Paris was preparing for another official celebration, he told Ludwika; instead of the annual fireworks over the Tuileries honoring the king's birthday—much enjoyed the year before by the Polish visitors—the forthcoming event, commemorating the fifteenth anniversary of the fraying July Monarchy, was to take place on the Seine. Chopin viewed this latest extravaganza—organized, so he claimed, by "speculators in festivities for the masses"—with a sourness that curdled into disgust. The stage for this year's version of "bread-and-circuses" was the river itself, where small craft, including imported Venetian gondolas decorated for the occasion, would converge on the water, while on the banks, thousands of Parisians would gather to gasp as night flamed into day, thanks to the new gaslights, moved for the occasion from the boulevards to the quays.

The plan aroused all Chopin's aristocratic horror of the mob and its raucous pleasures, and his gloating tone as he evokes the scenario of disaster sure to be unleashed—drownings, fire, panic, tramplings—verges on an apocalyptic wish for destruction. Like the earlier fantasies of his Stuttgart journals, crazed with images of Cossacks brutalizing his family, Chopin once again injects a collective event with his own rage.

In Nohant, Maurice had finished biding his time. He was twenty-two now, a year past his majority, a birthday celebrated quietly, but with outpourings of tenderness from Sand. Both mother and son were eager for Maurice to assume the role of man of the house.

Certainly, there were few competing demands upon his time. The dutiful apprenticeship in Delacroix's studio had ended amicably, without firing the dilettante into ambition or industry; now, his adoring mama could keep Maurice at her side while he tried to learn the day-to-day responsibilities of a gentleman landowner. Managing Nohant, moreover, would still allow him to pursue his amateur interests: sketching, producing homemade theatricals (to which Chopin contributed his "characters"—imitations of an Englishman or a Jew), and collecting local specimens of plants and rocks. In return for easing her burdens in the business of rents and leaking roofs, Maurice persuaded Sand to yield some of her authority as well. His first act was to fire Jan, Chopin's dim but conscientious manservant, "because he worked hard and steadily," Chopin wrote in the bitter tone that, more often now, sliced through his words.

It was the opening salvo in the first offensive of a long war. Insofar as he had a strategy, Maurice appeared to be mounting a siege whose goal was to isolate the enemy while gradually starving him of crucial nourishment; in this round, Jan's dismissal deprived Chopin of speaking and hearing his native language. But he was almost as upset by Maurice's success in persuading Sand to retire Françoise, along with the old gardener who had reigned over everything grown on the property since the final years of the first Aurore Dupin. Their replacements, Maurice made clear, would answer to him alone.

The young master preened in the attentions of Pauline Viardot, now his lover. Sand certainly knew about Maurice's pursuit of her beloved Fifille and seems to have smiled upon his conquest. If any woman could make a man out of her immature, indecisive son, it would be the worldly young diva, wife, and mother, with her great talent and brilliant career. Before she tired of him, the enchanting Pauline would provide Maurice with the perfect sentimental education. George always preferred to have matters under her control; in Nohant, at least, she could monitor the affair.

With characteristic discretion, Chopin gives no hint of whether or not he was aware of the liaison. If he managed to remain oblivious to the erotic tremors from the lovers themselves, Solange, with the sexual obsession of a sixteen-year-old with little else to occupy her, would certainly have enlightened him. Pushed out of the magic circle—together—they played four hands at the piano, endless games of checkers, and went for rides in the buggy. When he tried to work, Solange—if no other distractions summoned—interrupted him with little treats and welcome attentions. "She has such a kind heart," he told Ludwika.

At the end of summer, Pauline left to rejoin her family and embark on a new season of concert engagements. But Sand had seen to her replacement. From being an occasional guest, Titine arrived on September 10, escorted by Maurice from Paris for an indefinite stay. Then, at the end of January 1846, Titine returned to Paris and moved into Square d'Orléans with Sand and the children. No longer a visitor, she had become a member of the family.

Augustine Marie Brault—Titine—remains a blank canvas. Only one likeness of her seems to have survived: a caricature in pencil, depicting her and Solange flanking a tall and bearded young man, Fernand de Preaux, a scion of local nobility and Solange's new suitor. In contrast to her stepcousin's cameo features, Titine's profile is dominated by a huge hooked nose—much like Chopin's. Recent accounts exalt her as "prettier and cleverer" than Solange—a Cinderella scenario to account for the daughter's antipathy to her poor relation; but Solange, in fact, was described by all who saw her as a lush beauty, of superior, if undirected, intelligence. Her hatred and jealousy, then, were aroused not by Titine's attributes but by her mother's displaced love.

What attracted Sand was the vitality of this child of the people; in contrast to Solange's languor, Maurice's passivity, and Chopin's sickly ennui, her young relative's purposeful energy—the attribute of a penniless girl who had to make her way in the world—promised a transfusion of Sand's own proudly declared "plebian blood" into a family threatened by moral anemia.

George acted quickly on her hopes for Titine. She had dropped out of the Conservatory five years earlier, but Sand now arranged for the girl to have private lessons with Pauline's brother, a famous voice coach.* Persuaded that her protégée was another Viardot, her benefactress planned to replace the unavailable siren with the charming younger singer. As for Titine, she was only too willing to become whatever her new family wanted her to be. Sand longed, first, for another daughter: From there, Titine might be groomed into an ideal daughter-in-law.

Like everything else about this unhappy scheme, the actual adoption remains a murky affair. The young woman's parents were not only poor, they were a disreputable pair. Adèle Philbert, Sand's stepcousin and Titine's mother, had borne several children by different fathers. When she married Joseph Brault, a sporadically employed stonemason, he chose to legitimize Titine, possibly because she was in fact his daughter. Meanwhile, her mother, so gossip claimed, returned to her sluttish ways, often taking the child with her on assignations. When Sand undertook the girl's rescue, the father shrewdly decided that he had found a buyer for his daughter—and right in the family. For an undisclosed sum, in the form of ongoing payments to the parents, Sand "adopted" Titine.

For Solange, her replacement at this time came as a catastrophic shock; for the past year, relations between mother and daughter had been happier than ever before. She was devastated; her only recourse—and one, ironically, that had Sand's wholehearted blessing—was to find a husband and leave home as quickly as possible.

Chopin loathed Titine. He suffered for Solange, for the pain the adopted daughter inflicted upon the real one. But on a deeper level, he shared her humiliation at being supplanted—exiled—within her own family. Beyond Titine's appointed role, everything about her offended him, particularly the voice and accent and manners (or lack thereof) that betrayed her as a prole, a child of the Parisian working class. Chopin had learned to tolerate the sweaty, loud, ill-mannered journalists, organizers, and worker-poets with whom George surrounded herself, but he could never hide his dis-

---

*Besides his renown as a teacher, Manuel García was a theorist of music and voice whose research into physiology led to his invention of the laryngoscope.

taste for Titine's coarseness, for the gall with which she acted the lady, presuming to behave as their social equal. In his letters, he refused even to refer to her by her name (itself suggesting an off-color joke); she was designated, anonymously, "the cousin."

For Maurice, Titine was a gift provided by his mother as an alluring distraction from Pauline. But the twenty-year-old had larger ambitions. Titine cast her loyalties with the man of the house and against those who challenged his shaky claim to authority. In turn, Maurice, as he made clear in his flattering and flirting, was prepared to act as her defender. If he chose to take liberties, permitting himself intimacies with her in front of the others, that was his *droit de seigneur*. Titine was mindful of her father's promise: If she played her cards right, she might one day be young Baroness Dudevant.

In Nohant, the lines were drawn.

Soon enough, hostilities broke through the surface of the everyday life whose peace had been maintained with such care and cost. Once more, it was another "Polish question" that wrenched aside the curtain of civility. Countess Laure Czosnowska, a family friend from Warsaw, arrived, accompanied by Albert Grzymala. Sand had never been fond of the lady, but neither would she have ever denied Chopin's request that the countess be invited, coming at a time when his moods of good humor were increasingly rare. In the event, Sand had a ready excuse to avoid a tiresome guest: She disappeared upstairs to work. The countess's only sins seem to have been a fondness for overdressing and for dousing herself with a musk-scented perfume that Sand claimed to be as as evil-smelling as the breath of Laure's poodle, Lili. Left to the mercy of her enemies—namely, Maurice and Titine—the poor lady became the favorite object of their mockery. Egged on by Maurice, Titine now showed her true colors, Chopin reported, making smutty jokes that smacked of the streets where she belonged. This time, he did not retreat haughtily to his room; he exploded in rage, instructing the young woman that her indecent remarks would not be allowed while he was in this house. His lecture to Titine provoked a counterattack from Maurice: There was only one man in charge here; only *he* was permitted to remonstrate with women and servants. Titine became bolder and more spiteful; when their visitors left, she took to sneering at Solange and Chopin.

As head of a household of fractious children, Sand tried to appear neutral. Privately, she was relieved to see her adored son and future heir assert himself, grasping the mettle of masculine authority. Moreover, after exalting Titine to friends as "perfect—beautiful, charming, virtuous, hardworking"—she would have been obliged, in siding with Chopin, to admit that she had been wrong; that the daughter she had chosen over her own child was, in fact, a nasty, vulgar little tart.

Now, the father who, in effect, had sold Titine to Sand denounced her for "prostituting" his daughter, buying her as a whore for Maurice. The source of Brault's affronted paternal feelings was a letter from Sand in which she tactfully explained why Maurice could never marry Titine. He was far too young, and his affections were engaged—however unsuitably—elsewhere. Reading Sand's obvious second thoughts on Titine's suitability as a daughter-in-law, Joseph Brault decided that they had been robbed and their child violated. Not trusting in gossip alone to spread the scandal, Joseph Brault, impoverished though he was, would soon manage to publish his seamy version of events in a pamphlet which enjoyed wide distribution in the Berry. Sand sued—successfully—to have the pamphlet withdrawn, but the damage had been done.

Only months before, Chopin had playfully referred to George as "they," explaining to Ludwika that her kindnesses to him were so numberless, she herself had to be pluralized. Laboring over this fall's preserves, Sand's past hope that their summer's store of happiness could nourish them through the winter was starting to sound like a cruel joke.

Another promise had vaporized: the dream of Italy. Sand's plan to take Chopin away for a year in the sun had yielded to Maurice's veto. He preferred the country, Chopin told Ludwika, "so we didn't go." He would never see the magical Venice that was so much part of Aurore's youth or the golden Roman countryside that infused the music of his contemporaries.

The Berceuse had emerged from the halcyon summer of 1844, its lyric tenderness lofted with such ease as to suggest that its intricacies and inventions were as natural as breathing. Begun the following year, the Barcarolle, op. 60, is almost twice the length of the earlier work, but the two pieces are almost always paired; they share the same rocking ostinato; their natural rhythm of breath or water girding a helix of melody and ornamentation has led the Barcarolle to be spoken of as a fifth ballade. In its continuous melodic line, the Barcarolle also evokes a nocturne in several acts. As in other of his late works, these referrals are acts of memory reaching into Chopin's musical past, but the Barcarolle, a traditional gondolier's song, pushes off with its boatman's oar into the future.

Later composers loved and borrowed more from the Barcarolle than from any other composition by Chopin: Brahms, for the ending of his F-sharp Minor Sonata, Debussy, in *L'Isle joyeuse*. Ravel wrote lengthily about its meaning for him. Composed in the same key of F-sharp major, the Adagio of Mahler's unfinished Tenth Symphony invokes remembrances of Chopin's daring harmonies along, perhaps, with those of the Austrian composer's own *ile joyeuse*, his first sight of Venice on a sunlit morning. Like a memory of experience missed, summoning what he himself would never see, Chopin's Barcarolle sailed triumphantly into uncharted waters.

FOURTEEN

Lucrezia Floriani

I n Berry, the summer of 1846, the summer that Maurice took over the house, had begun with heavy rains. Swollen rivers and streams overflowed; low-lying fields remained flooded, threatening farmers with ruin. All this came at a time of steep increases in the price of wheat, and rumors were rife of imminent riots. Government bread vouchers for the poorest did little to quell spreading anger. One local landowner, a neighbor of Sand's half brother, Hippolyte Chatiron, had been slashed to death in his house by an enraged mob.

The resentments that overflowed Nohant in midsummer had been long festering. The Paris winter had exhausted everyone. At the Square d'Orléans, George's throat infection had dragged on for weeks; Solange had been diagnosed with anemia. But Chopin had been sickest of all; along with the flu and grippe that felled most of Paris, he had succumbed to coughing attacks that no longer ended by mid-morning, and when they did subside, he was left too weak too walk. Freezing weather made it hard for him to breathe out of doors: he was not able to get downtown to buy a Christmas gift for his nephew and godson, he told Ludwika, and with his spending habits, he could scarcely promise him a legacy by way of compensation.

For the first time, that winter and spring, Sand was less than sympathetic. In her letters, accounts of Chopin—many fewer in number now—no longer depict him as patient, stoical, angelic; he was *souffreteux*—a word suggesting not chronic sickness so much as sickliness, with a whiff of hypochondria. He was the child who claims the privileged attentions of illness. Yet, he appeared even-tempered and less prone to mood swings. At thirty-five, he had turned a corner, she declared, with evident relief. But the corner was a hiding place. He felt less safe with George now, unwilling to risk irritating her. He could hardly disguise his weakened physical state, but he could keep his feelings to himself.

In early spring, Sand had started work on a new novel, and by April, it was far enough along for her to sign a contract for serialization in *Le Courrier Français*, the installments to begin in late June and run through the end of July. As she always did, George read each day's work aloud to Chopin. Then, on May 5, Sand left for Nohant—alone. Over the next three weeks, she rewrote the novel from beginning to end, a labor of revision without precedent in her work. She finished the new version on May 24, "making a fat volume," and on the next day, she met Chopin at the Châteauroux coach.

Following the strains of midsummer—the visit of Madame Czosnowska, the skirmishes between Chopin, Titine, and Maurice—Delacroix's arrival on August 16 was greeted with unanimous relief. The painter had not visited for three years, but Nohant remained "in my heart and thoughts as one of those rare places, where everything delights, captivates and consoles me," he told George; and, as though he had never been away, he yielded to the spell of its restoring rhythms: days of freedom, and in the evenings, entertainment provided by his hosts. He was primed to hear his friend's new compositions. But if Chopin played the works with which he had struggled these past months, Delacroix made no mention of them. He records only his amazement at the composer's performance of Beethoven sonatas: "divinely" inspired, and worth every lecture on beauty.

With only Chopin and Delacroix for her audience, Sand read

aloud from her new work. Although he always had polite praise for the novels that she regularly sent to him, Delacroix harbored growing reservations about Sand's recent themes: dangerous exposures of class injustice and visions of social leveling. But now, for the first time, he was shocked by what he heard.

Lucrezia Floriani is a double portrait of two mismatched lovers. Floriani, an actress and playwright who left the stage at the peak of a fabled career, has retired with her young children to her childhood home on a remote lake in the north of Italy. There her earnings have purchased a large property, including the fisherman's hut where she was born and where her miserly old father still lives and her present villa, former residence of the noblewoman who helped transform the fisherman's daughter into a great artist.

At the same time that she retired from the stage, Lucrezia retreated from love. Never married, her affairs had always ended badly, their only happy outcome being four children by as many fathers. Her consecration to motherhood wants no relief; Floriani sleeps in a hammock slung in the center of a large bedroom, surrounded by her slumbering brood.

Into this matriarchal paradise fate delivers two travelers: an old admirer, Count Salvator Albani, accompanied by his closest friend, Prince Karol de Roswald. Their brief stopover turns into weeks when the prince falls suddenly and critically ill; he is nursed back to health by his hostess, and Karol and Lucrezia succumb to the fatal disease of love.

This much is established by Sand in the early pages of the novel. The narrative that follows traces the fever chart of their affair. More revealing of its author than the many volumes of her autobiographical works, Lucrezia is Sand, sanitized and sanctified: George as she saw herself and wanted others to see her. For Lucrezia's only sin is loving too much—too generously, too purely, too sacrificingly. Falling in love out of sympathy, she has given herself to men who, in every way, prove unworthy of her.

Prince Karol, a German nobleman with a Polish name, stands as Lucrezia's polar opposite: aristocratic where she is plebian in origin, sheltered where she is worldly, reserved and inhibited where she is open and expressive, morally rigid and conformist where she is independent and indifferent to convention. Until his encounter with Lucrezia, Karol's affections have been confined to an idealized love for his devout late mother and dead fiancée. At twenty-four, he is without sexual experience; offering his purity on the altar of a perfect spiritual love, he dismisses the erotic with disgust and fear.

His fall from innocence is shattering. From initial repulsion towards this actress of scandalous reputation, Karol moves from admiration, gratitude, friendship, and, finally, when they become lovers, to obsessive passion.

An indolent aristocrat, the prince does nothing—the life for which he was trained. His relations with the world mediated by others, his intelligence and sensibilities have turned inward. Locked in the solitary confinement of his own making, Karol's love for Lucrezia, exclusive and devouring, demands her as fellow prisoner.

"The absolute and continual possession of the being he loved was the only existence that Karol could endure," his author wrote. Soon, his suffocating passion accuses all other claims upon Lucrezia as a threat, the granting of her attentions elsewhere a betrayal. The second half of the novel maps the murderous effects of Karol's jealousy: Lucrezia's every living attachment—her father, former lovers, his own best friend, her children, even her dog—becomes an instrument of his torment. Each reminder of her life before they met reopens wounds of suspicion.

An unexpected visit from one of Lucrezia's old loves is the event that unhinges the prince, unleashing the novel's final tragedy. An actor and the father of her little daughter, Onorio Vandoni leads a debauched and extravagant life that has destroyed his career; but his present pathetic circumstances summon all of Floriani's sympathies. Her fatal error is believing Karol to be secure enough in their love to accept her expressions of affection and friendship for the failed artist.

Instead, this tribute to his trust arouses Karol's festering suspicions. As jealous rage blasts all other feelings, a fundamental nastiness—"something harsh and bitter"—takes over. "Of all angers, of all vengeances, the darkest, the most atrocious and the most agonizing is the one which remains cold and polite," the author notes of her tormented hero. Turning on his lover, Karol now speaks to her "in the language of spite and affectation." Rage, accusations—even physical abuse—all these Lucrezia would have tolerated, even welcomed. But she cannot tolerate Karol's withdrawal, his abandonment. "I prefer the coarseness of the jealous peasant who beats his wife to the delicacy of the prince who rends his mistress's heart without turning a hair. I prefer the child who scratches and bites to the one who sulks in silence. By all means, let us lose our tempers, be violent, ill-bred, let us insult one another, break mirrors and clocks! It would be absurd but it would not prove we hate one another. Whereas, if we turn our backs on each other very politely as we leave, uttering a bitter and contemptuous word, we are doomed, and no matter what we do to be reconciled we will be driven farther and farther apart."

Nothing else Sand would ever write seized the emotional polarities of two lovers so well as this chasm dug by blindness and incomprehension.

Their punishment was mutual: a decade spent together in a "desperate struggle as to which would consume the other." Her attempt to flee her captor and his crazed pursuit end with Floriani dead of a stroke. Her real death, however, had been a long and slow one. In our last image of Lucrezia, the woman we met in the bloom of life has shrunk to a withered crone of forty. Her end is her deliverance.

In place of love, Sand sacrificed her heroine to loyalty and compassion. She would not accept a similar fate.

As he listened to Sand's reading of *Lucreẓia Floriani*, Delacroix heard his own unfinished likeness of the couple brought to demonic completion, the recognizable features of its subjects flayed by exposure of their intimate relations. Sand's novel barely held the fig leaf of fiction over the private hell of its protagonists. Foreshadowing Wilde's *Picture of Dorian Gray*, *Lucreẓia*, too, predicts what its subjects would become. The "weariness of boredom," Delacroix said, stamped every page. He was "in agony" for Chopin as they both listened to Sand's low, velvety voice in its hypnotic monotone describe Karol/Chopin's "stubborn adoration" of Lucrezia, and his progressive derangement, all painted, Delacroix said, in the "transparency of truth." And he went on to explain how her hero can only understand those who are exactly like himself, "having no sense of others' reality"; in his "intolerance of mind and unbridled jealousy, despotism comes naturally to him. With exquisite manners, he persecutes the woman he loves politely and graciously, while, at every turn and on every issue, he wages war on her ideas."

For this hero, Delacroix observed, "a woman only exists, relatively speaking. Thus, when Lucrezia stopped loving Karol, there was no oblique way she could express her feelings; she can only reach him harshly and brutally." As to the reactions of their prototypes, Delacroix found himself "equally mystified by victim and executioner": "Madame Sand was perfectly at ease and Chopin could hardly stop making admiring comments." At midnight, when his host suggested that Delacroix accompany him upstairs, the painter leapt at the opportunity to be alone with his friend, when he could "plumb his real feelings about the book and learn whether he had earlier been putting on a performance." Their talk left Delacroix still more astounded.

Chopin's enthusiasm had not been an act, after all: "He hadn't understood a single word."

Lucrezia Floriani was Sand's first foray into the roman à clef and, helped by the author's own well-publicized love affairs, was guaranteed to fan speculation, gossip, and debate about the boundaries between life and art. More than a decade later, she returned with *Elle et lui* (She and He), a nostalgic chronicle of her Venetian escapade with the younger poet Alfred de Musset. (That same year, 1859, Musset's brother cashed in with a sequel, *Lui et elle*.) These romantic hybrids of memoir and fiction have produced robust offspring in our own day, along with similar outrage, denials, titillation, and argument about genres, invented documentary and truthful fictions, the morality and motives behind the pillaging of intimate relationships (including use of real letters), of exposing another to the glare of public scrutiny against which the unpublished victim has no defense.

Critics continue to produce charts showing the analogies between Sand's literary doubles in *Lucreçia* and their real-life counterparts: the six-year difference in ages, the "German" prince's Polish name; the physical resemblance between the author—small, plump, dark—and her heroine. Claiming that such literal borrowings were the merest coincidence, and using similarly superficial examples of differences between her protagonists and any living couple, Sand would later deny that the novel was anything other than fiction.

In their gossipy, jealous circle, judgments bore the stamp of the writer; past grievances colored present opinion—the loudest clucking came from Sainte-Beuve, the powerful critic who had been George's mentor early in her career and who now envied her success. Most of the others, too, professed sympathy for "poor Chopin" while condemning the "unworthy" Sand. Ever political, Heinrich Heine, who wrote a cultural column, "Lutece," for German readers, made sure to sweeten his blame for George the woman with praise for Sand the artist: "She has treated my friend Chopin outrageously in a divinely written novel."

Hortense Allart, a divorced woman of letters with more lovers to her credit than Sand herself, worried about what such printed indiscretions could cost other literary women in male trust: "She has handed us a Chopin complete with his ugliest little habits," she wrote (cracking his knuckles was one of them), "described with a coldness towards his literary double that nothing can justify. . . . Women cannot protest too much against such betrayals of bedroom secrets which could drive away all our lovers."

Incensed by favorable reviews of the novel which had swept every copy from Paris bookstores, the Liszt-d'Agoult wheels were spinning overtime, decrying the "vulgarity of confessions." Most galling was the critical reception of d'Agoult's roman à clef, called *Nélida,* about which one reviewer was so unkind as to suggest that, by way of penance, she should read more Sand in view of trying to capture the "natural" style of this great writer.

Whether fueled by malice, envy, or sincere distaste for art that copied life so nakedly, outrage was aimed at what Sand had revealed—not invented. Indiscretion, not calumny, was the issue. It was *Lucrezia* as a case study that offended, laying bare in anatomical detail a sickness unto death, the progression of physical disease into a poisoning of the spirit. Could it be that the artist deemed by friends and admirers as "angelic" (by implication, free of the darker passions), and socially a man of the most exquisite tact and refinement, was inhabited by a doppelgänger, that romantic invention, a psychopath who had become his monomania, destroying and destroyed by jealousy and rage?

Three years earlier, Chopin had taken on a new pupil. The daughter of a prosperous Warsaw restaurateur, Zofia Rosengardt had been highly recommended by Chopin's friend the poet Bohdan Zaleski (soon to be Zofia's husband), who praised the nineteen-year-old student's talent and seriousness. She was also highly intelligent, and the journal she kept of her Paris years leaves a portrait of her teacher that confirms Delacroix's shock at hearing *Lucrezia Floriani* lay bare the "transparency of truth."

His moods veered wildly, as the young woman would come to learn all too well: warm, teasing, charming one day; cold, sarcastic, hostile another. These swings were nothing new. What seems to have changed was Chopin's will—or capacity—to control his behavior. Astute and naive at the same time, Zofia attested to the fits of rage—screaming, foot stamping, chair smashing—produced by a mixup about the hour of a lesson (the fault of Jan, the dim-witted servant later dismissed by Maurice), and her teacher's fury when, having learned by heart the assigned nocturne, she forgot to bring the sheet music. He had no time for people to waste, he shouted.

Where pupils were concerned, title and fortune ensured that Chopin could master his demons. He gave vent to tantrums only with students—women or men—training to be professional musicians. The rich and aristocratic recall their teacher as possessed of infinite patience; unfailingly, he praised, encouraged, and only gently corrected or criticized. He was a snob, certainly, but these two faces also point to an awareness of his needs: It was maddening to train the less talented to follow where he himself could no longer go, but the princesses were his life blood—not only their fees but their great houses, where he felt cared for and cosseted, sheltered from the specters of poverty and sickness. Waste, the loss of time, irrecoverable and running out, was the hair trigger of his outbursts. Zofia could not know how sick her teacher was, or that wrath was a *Liebestod* for his waning powers. But she grasped the wear of disease and disappointment upon the character of a man who had always been "strange and incomprehensible." "He is polite to excess, and yet there is so much irony, so much spite hidden inside it! . . . He can be as petulant as a small child, bullying his pupils and being very cold with his friends. These are usually days of suffering, physical exhaustion or quarrels with Madame Sand."

Along with the causes of anger and frustration that Zofia observed, Chopin's volatility was exacerbated by behavioral change held by some to be characteristic of tuberculosis. Called "consumptive rage," the particular disease, not progressive illness in general, has been related to episodes of paranoid suspicion, furious attacks upon intimates, accusations of abandonment and treachery leveled at the most loyal of friends and servants.

William Cullen, the eighteenth-century English physician who first distinguished the pulmonary form of consumption, attributed the disease to an "acrimony" in the blood. All the external symptoms of pathology (the only diagnostic evidence available to medicine before the invention of the stethoscope) confirmed, he believed, the temperamental and physical duality of tuberculosis. The disease started with a predisposition of the victim, followed by steady degeneration that attacked body and soul: the hectic flush, distracted state, and extreme agitation were all outward signs of *consumption* that "invisibly (at first) inflamed, irritated, corroded, melted and wasted the lungs and chest."

Trained as a physician, John Keats clinically observed his own emotional and physical devastation: "My Chest is in so nervous a State, that any thing extra such as speaking to an Unaccustomed person or writing a Note half suffocates me. . . ." In Rome, where he had been brought in the hopes of recovery and where he died, Keats described the sufferings brought on by separation from his fiancée, Fanny Brawne, in terms of physical torment: "Every thing that I have in my Trunks that reminds me of her goes through me like a spear. The silk lining she put in my traveling cap scalds my head."

Chopin's suffering was inflicted by emotional, not physical, distance. He could choose to see the portraits in *Lucrezia Floriani* as fiction, but not the author's dismissal of him. In a burst of anger, George told Marie de Rozières, "I found the courage to tell him some unpleasant truths about his behavior along with the threat that I wasn't going to take it any more. From that moment on, he came to his senses and you know how good, excellent and admirable he can be when he's not acting crazy."

He had been served notice. Nohant was no longer his home; he was there on sufferance, not welcomed but tolerated—as long as he could disguise his sickness of flesh and spirit.

"In the nineteenth century," Michel Foucault claims, "a man, in becoming tubercular, in the fever that hastens things and betrays them, fulfills his incommunicable secret. That is why chest diseases are of exactly the same nature as diseases of love: They are the Passion, a life to which death gives a face that cannot be exchanged."

Created in "the fever that hastens things" and the betrayal of love, Chopin's last style indeed fulfilled his incommunicable secret, and for the short time that his powers lasted, his art diverted him from the face of death.

FIFTEEN

Winter Journeys

O n the last day of October 1846, Chopin set off for Paris. The autumn had been so unseasonably warm and rainy that the Loire rose to flood levels as though it were spring. When they reached the bridge at Olivet, Chopin and another departing guest, Sand's old friend Emanuel Arago, had to turn back. Abandoning the carriage, the two men clambered down a rope ladder hung from the break in the bridge and, swinging twenty feet above the rushing waters, returned to the same riverbank and made their way back to Nohant. Eleven days later, Chopin set out again, alone. The earlier false start—the flooded roads, the broken bridge, the perilous return—followed by another round of good-byes, sounds a warning tocsin: This was a final leavetaking; he would never see Nohant again.

In fact, he was not much missed. Solange's suitor, the sweet gan-gly young knight Fernand de Preaux, had been elevated to fiancé; he was expected two days after Chopin's departure. Meanwhile, the bride-to-be reveled in her new status. The others, forced by the sudden cold and unheatable upstairs rooms to spend most days and evenings below, threw themselves into nightly theatricals, loosely written by Sand, but largely improvised by the actors themselves. Relieved of Chopin's presence, George sent him frequent and detailed synopses of plots and casts. With his absence, animosities subsided and the family drew closer, warmed by wedding plans and makeshift footlights. The door to Chopin's icy rooms was shut.

In a wintry Paris, he returned to his lessons, thawing at the fires of Polish hospitality. When he felt strong enough, he rehearsed with Franchomme the piece he had written for and dedicated to his friend, finally finished after two years of work.

Of the two monuments of Chopin's last style, the Polonaise-Fantaisie in A-flat Major, op. 61, and the Sonata for Cello and Piano in G Minor, op. 65, the second seems to have caused him the deeper anguish. Evidence of the frustrations impeding his work—cries and tears and tantrums—had occasioned another of Sand's incredulous reports on the agony of creation. And he had written to Ludwika of his alternations of satisfaction and despair at its progress. (His sketches for this work alone fill a volume.) He had not composed for another instrument since shortly after his arrival in Paris, when he had written the frothy Grand Duo Concertant, also for Franchomme's cello, based on operatic airs from Meyerbeer's popular *Robert le diable*.

His last sonata for piano, no. 3 in B minor, op. 58, of 1844, had been completed in a time of confidence and tranquility, bolstered by relative good health. Within two years, Chopin's own world of order and calm was fracturing; the entire structure tottered crazily, on the verge of crumbling around him.

Haunting in its melodic variety, this final sonata, as Chopin's worksheets reveal, echoes with the fragmentation and discontinuities of the composer's life. Despite an outpouring of exquisite melodies for both cello and piano, the voices of the two instruments suggest those of a couple who speak of the same things but each in a language incomprehensible to the other. Duets break down into accompanied soliloquies—the cello at moments reduced to helpless growling. In the first movement, the richness of texture conferred by the paired instruments weaving between two themes chokes into scrambled signals. Called "an undervalued masterpiece," Chopin's final sonata is performed less frequently than his solo piano compositions but also less often than most chamber works by Haydn, Mozart, Beethoven, Brahms, and César Franck. Even cellists, known for complaining about the dearth of great music written for their instrument, largely avoid it; the long and intricate piece frustrates expectations of both Chopin and chamber music, of audiences and instrumentalists.

A song without words, the sonata's opening piano solo in its artless simplicity borrows from a work by a contemporary whose name Chopin never mentions: Schubert's *Winterreise*, the last of his great song cycles, was written a year before the composer's death in 1828. The twenty-four poems (curiously, the same number as Chopin's Preludes, op. 28) that Schubert set to music track the wanderings of a rejected lover through a hostile winter landscape. With the first lines of the opening song, "Gute Nacht," we hear the impact of both the poet's words and Schubert's melodic line on Chopin's final sonata:

> A stranger I came
> And a stranger I depart . . .

Loss of love is a contagion from which others flee; dogs drive him from the town and he stumbles, confused, through the frozen waste. He falls deeper into solitude and madness, a descent through ice-bound circles of hell. Even death—a graveyard imagined as an inn—turns him away (*Das Wirtshaus*).

In his sonata, Chopin quoted those songs in *Winterreise* which spoke directly to his own condition of banishment and despair. Schubert's leading motive, like the phrase of the fictional composer Vinteuil that haunts Proust's Swann, flickers through the sonata's first movement, the Allegro moderato, where the cello's opening notes continue the ending of the piano solo. Schubert's phrase threads through his own entire work, but emerges most clearly in those songs that address loss, separation, and exile; from "Erstarrung" (Numbness) ("I look in vain in the snow, / for a trace of her footprints") through texts dark with images of the flesh as food for predators "Die Krähe" (The Crow) ("Do you mean, carrion bird, soon / to seize my body as prey?") until in the final terrible image of "Der Leiermann" (The Hurdy-Gurdy Man) the dying poet sees his double in the beggar-musician:

Barefoot on the ice,
He shifts back and forth,
And his little tray
Is always empty.

Chopin would have had ample occasion to hear *Winterreise* performed in Paris. His publisher Maurice Schlesinger also published Schubert in France, and the song cycles were widely appreciated among Paris's discerning music lovers through recitals by the singers that Chopin most admired: Luigi Lablache, Adolphe Nourrit, and Pauline Viardot. Among amateurs, one of the Viennese composer's most ardent admirers was George Sand.

Begun in 1845, the Polonaise-Fantaisie, like the last sonata, tested the composer's waning powers over his last productive year. Its gestation period, too, points to resistant problems, solutions tried and rejected, the contested uphill terrain that separates new ideas and their resolution. Exceptionally for Chopin, he left the piece untitled while work was well underway, writing to his family at the end of 1845, in the same weeks which found him too weakened to buy Christmas gifts, "Now I would like to finish the Sonata for violoncello, the barcarolle and something else that I do not know how to name, but I doubt whether I will have time, for already the frenzy begins."

Two earlier works include a version of the word "fantasy": Chopin wrote the first, the Fantasia on Polish Airs, for piano and orchestra when he was eighteen, and it wears the conventional colors of the title, as a melange or rhapsody on popular or familiar themes. Then, thirteen years later, he composed the only surviving work to which he gave that unmodified title: the Fantaisie in A-flat Major of 1841. One of the glories of Chopin's mature period, the Fantaisie leaps from the measured pedestrian cadences of its opening march to extravagant acrobatics, passagework of high drama, lyrical and playful interludes, before returning to sober chromatic rationality. For all the indecision suggested by its yoked working title of a name, the Polonaise-Fantaisie emerges as a distillation of Chopin's experience as both composer and performer. The capacious form itself is a declaration of freedom, alerting us to the character of improvisation in the piece that lets us imagine ourselves among Chopin's privileged listeners.

From the illusory tentativeness of the opening notes, we hear the composer feeling his way into the work, privy to the very process of creation, including its uncertainties. The Polonaise-Fantaisie sounds almost like a series of introductions to pieces Chopin would not live to write, a sequence of beginnings. Confounded by the harmonic daring of shifts from major to minor keys and strange inversions of phrase, Chopin's contemporary the virtuoso pianist and composer Ignaz Moscheles dismissed the Polonaise-Fantaisie as all "preluding." It's still easier to admire discrete events in the music, the whole managing to elude us. Unfamiliar territory is made stranger by fleeting appearances of the familiar—a mazurka within a polonaise, strands of nocturne, the impress of a sonata form; all of these add to our sense of disorientation in a wild and unmapped land.

Like Chopin's other polonaises—big pieces that require a big pounding technique—the Polonaise-Fantaisie is a test of stamina. Unlike them, however, the work doesn't invite recognition of its virtuosic hurdles. Audiences do not rise to their feet at its thunderous conclusion, an invitation for the pianist to slump, Liszt-like, over the keys. Instead, the hush of concentration lingers. Difficult and demanding of performer and listener alike, the piece confounds our expectations of the Chopin we think we know. Vaulting into the future, the Polonaise-Fantaisie declares its modernity in the freedom to displease.

Writing of Beethoven's last sonatas, Theodor Adorno insisted that "in the history of art, late works are the catastrophes." This perspective, in Chopin's case and others, owes more to what we know of the artists' lives than of their art: the tragedies of age and failing powers, of genius or talent cut off in its prime; or the broken promises of youth. As we project our own feelings of loss onto these final efforts, they take on the nimbus of relics fraught with both the suffering and the transcendence of martyrdom. Pliny's reminder that "sorrow for the hand that perished at its work beguiles us into the bestowal of praise" was never more true than in the romantic era, with its cult of death. Poets and composers, particularly, whose art was made to be recreated—recited, played, and sung—were readily drafted into the ranks of secular saints; "Schubert's Last Songs" (a swan gliding on the cover) was a publishing bonanza when Chopin first came to Paris, while many witnesses, alive and dead, were summoned in the attempt to identify with certainty the deaf Beethoven's last composition.

"Late style" as a cluster of characteristics held to recur in final works by artists across centuries and cultures has been subject to growing scrutiny, but these examinations have focused on stylistic changes at the end of the aged artist's career: Rembrandt, Titian, Goya, and Beethoven himself, pointing to looser execution, an impatience with "finished" effect, with beauty or harmony for its own sake, in favor of more expressive and open forms.

Yet, another current of "late style" flows in the opposite direction: a return to basic principles of structure, a stripping away, including a rejection of what is "contemporary" in the artist's own time (think of Chopin's disdain for Berlioz) in favor of revisiting earliest lessons. Fusing the formal and the expressive, Chopin's last style seems to embrace both possibilities. In the early 1840s, he had returned to the classical works on counterpoint and polyphony, bringing to lessons of his student days the experience of his own mastery; from what he had already achieved, he started to rethink the basic building blocks of his art. At the same time, the freedom of the last works is purged of the violence, the painful assault on heart and nerves, that explodes from the ballades and scherzos; the inwardness of the Polonaise-Fantaisie seems scarcely to address us. Solitary and spiritualized, aloof and unknowable, the work declares a lifetime's meditation on form and structure, from the baroque to the folkloric, that he had long since made his own. He made greater room for the play of experiment. Stripping his melody of ornamentation, welding stable and unstable elements, hazarding daring continuities, he used so many elements new to him that the forward sweep of the music projected this last long masterwork beyond the composer's own sightlines.

Frail and ill, Chopin saw only the struggle, not the triumph of his achievement. "Where has my art gone?" he would ask. His art reached for music yet unwritten: the music of those contemporaries—some much younger—who would survive him. We hear his seductive intimacy in Liszt, who called the Polonaise-Fantaisie "the portrayal of extreme moments"; in Brahms's orchestral conquest of the piano; and, later still, in the color washes of Debussy and Ravel, in the claims of Rachmaninoff to a shared Slavic legacy—and in the visionary mission of Wagner himself.

Marooned by the cold at the Square d'Orléans, Chopin consoled himself with Sand's faithful notes. Like a starving prisoner, he pounced on crumbs of dailiness from Nohant—even on news of Titine's progress at checkers. He hugged George's homely little commissions, assuring her that the semisoft *stracchino* cheese she loved, along with her favorite cold cream, should arrive together with his gift of the traditional New Year's candy. To quash any rumors of a rift, he underlined their continued closeness, reporting to friends on the progress of Sand's new novel set in Sicily, *Le Piccinino*—"The Little One," once her pet name for him.

He worked on a set of mazurkas and waltzes, but the energy to compose seemed to have ebbed with the effort needed to finish the Polonaise-Fantaisie and the sonata. Money, the expenses of the holiday season, but loneliness, too, drove him to squeeze in as many lessons as there were hours in his day. On one afternoon alone, he had seven pupils. In the evening, in freezing temperatures or snow, he dragged himself on his nightly rounds: a dinner, followed by "several soirées." Only on one occasion did he beg off, when he was literally too weak to change into evening clothes. He spared George news of bouts of illness, saving for Grzymala word that he was "sick as a dog" or waiting for the doctor who had still not come.

Then, on February 6, Sand and her "two girls," Titine and

Solange, accompanied by the latter's fiancé, Fernand de Preaux, returned to Paris. Eleven days later, on Ash Wednesday, Chopin was host and performer at a musical evening at home. Before an audience that included, besides Sand, Delacroix, Grzymala, Baron and Baroness de Rothschild, and Prince and Princess Czartoryski, Chopin and Franchomme gave the first performance of the Sonata for Cello and Piano. He was especially pleased that another guest, Delfina Potocka, was able to hear the new work before she left Paris for Nice.

The next day, Sand and Solange visited the studio of a sculptor that everyone was talking about. Jean-Baptiste Auguste Clésinger had settled in the capital two years earlier, but he was already well established as the talented bad boy of the Paris art world. At thirty-three, his dark good looks, muscular build, and swaggering manner served as reminders that the former cavalryman was no effete artist. He was also gifted with a keen political sense—a crucial component of success in the competition for public commissions and private patrons. For the last year, he had wooed Sand in a series of letters professing his fervent admiration for her novels and begging the honor of immortalizing their author in a portrait bust. With little vanity about her looks, Sand arrived at the studio with Solange, planning to ask the sculptor, instead, to provide the traditional likeness of the younger woman at the time of her marriage, whose contract was to be signed in the next weeks. Gallantly, Clésinger insisted upon offering both. A separate series of sittings was arranged. Now the artist mounted his siege. Certain of his conquest of the daughter, he directed his flattery to the mother, maternal approval and a handsome dowry being key to his plans.

With an eye sharpened by jealousy, Chopin noted the daily arrivals at the Square d'Orléans of flowers, delicacies, even a puppy, all addressed to Sand. Within weeks, the sculptor had seduced Solange, not yet eighteen, who now announced that her wedding to Fernand was to be put off—indefinitely.

Alarmed by the Clésinger juggernaut, Chopin made inquiries. What he heard was worse than he could have imagined. The sculptor's past—in both his native city of Besançon and in Florence, where he had spent several years—was littered with debt to the tune of hundreds of thousands of francs. From other artists, Delacroix learned that Clésinger drank heavily; a principal cause of his borrowing was a chronic inability to deliver on lucrative commissions. When drinking, he was notorious for brutalizing his mistress, whom he had recently abandoned, pregnant, as soon as he saw the possibility of marriage to the daughter of the successful novelist.

All this was reported to Sand, but she would hear none of it. If possible, she was even more smitten by the sculptor than Solange. Surrounded by weak, dependent men, she had become persuaded that the energetic, domineering Clésinger would be the salvation of the family. She left Paris for Nohant with the girls on April 6, and a week later, the sculptor appeared with an ultimatum: He gave Sand twenty-four hours to agree to the marriage, during which time she must also set in motion the steps to secure the permission of Baron Dudevant. Sand was even more enchanted by this last maneuver. Who could possibly stand in the way of this "Caesar," she sighed, who "swept all before him by sheer force of will"?

George not only agreed to the match, she became a gleeful co-conspirator. When the sculptor left Nohant for Paris, she advised him on a strategy of secrecy. No rumors must reach Solange's father until Clésinger, accompanied by Maurice, appeared at Guillery to make his case in person. More important: "Not a word to Chopin. It's none of his business." Continuing her imperial metaphor, she explained: "Once the Rubicon has been crossed, any ifs and buts can only do harm."

Of course, Chopin already knew—as did everyone in their gossipy circle. Writing to his family, he relayed all the seamy reports about Clésinger, refusing even to grant the sculptor's acknowledged talent. The only ambition of this "second Michelangelo," he sneered (the title bestowed by his adoring fiancée), was to titillate a jaded public; Clésinger's recent submission to the Salon des Artistes Français had indeed caused considerable scandal. The model for his nude *Woman Stung by a Serpent* had been a well-known courtesan whose *contrapposto* pose—a thrusting display of breasts and pudenda suggestive of orgasm—was made the more impudent by the placement of the coiled snake that directed the viewer's gaze to the offending parts.* With savage prurience, Chopin wondered whether in next year's Salon, the sculptor would exhibit his bride, her "bare little ass" immortalized in white marble.

Horrified by Clésinger's swift seduction of mother, daughter, and son ("God help them all," he wrote to his sister), Chopin was still more humiliated by his exclusion. Sand and the children were his family. For nine years—since Solange was nine years old—he had shared their lives. Now he was being treated like one of the aged domestics, recently dismissed after years of service. His first knowledge of the forthcoming marriage was its formal announcement in a Paris newspaper on May 4.

Nonetheless, he managed a tender letter to Solange telling her of his pleasure in (finally) receiving a lovely note from her; she had never sounded so happy and he counted on always seeing her that way.

He was too hurt to agree to Sand's request that he wait for her in Paris, where she planned to convene the family in the middle of May to make the marriage arrangements. In fact, he had been terribly sick for most of April and barely convalescent now, he decided to visit friends in suburban Ville d'Avray, making sure to be out of town when George and the others returned to the Square d'Orléans. Even had he been invited, he wrote to Ludwika, he would not have been well enough to attend the wedding, which took place on May 19 in the tiny church just outside the gates of Nohant. And besides, what sort of face could he have managed for the occasion?

Sand's shabby treatment of the composer, along with news of his deteriorating health, led George to do what she always did when she was feeling guilty: She fired off a round of letters justi-

---

*This figure is one of the few privately commissioned works by Clésinger to have survived; most of the public commissions in Paris that he managed to complete were destroyed by bombardments during the Commune of 1870–71. Clésinger died in 1883.

fying her actions. There was no point in telling Chopin anything, as he understood nothing about human nature or the realities of life, she told Delacroix and Grzymala. "He can't abide anyone who isn't exactly like himself. Since his soul is all music and poetry," this meant just about everyone. "He is full of rigid preconceptions, moreover, which refuse to yield to the facts of life."

But Chopin understood everything about Solange's marriage, from the facts of Clésinger's past to his strategic wooing of George and Maurice, and finally, how Sand's obsession with secrecy, her romantic infatuation with the "artist," coupled with the bridegroom's insistence upon haste, had deprived her of the counsel of friends, and her daughter of a mother's better judgment.

"Mama is adorable, but she doesn't have a grain of common sense," he told Ludwika. He didn't give the marriage a year after their first child was born.

By late June, the honeymoon was over. Clésinger had revealed himself to Sand as a liar and extortionist who, failing to mention his huge debts and lack of work, expected George to underwrite the newlyweds' extravagant Paris life—servants, lavish parties, a carriage, and daily deliveries of hothouse flowers. When his mother-in-law urged economy, he became furious, blaming everything upon his spoiled young bride and concluding with no subtle threats about the future of the marriage if Sand failed to subsidize their present style.

She promptly invited "the children" to Nohant, hoping that a dose of simple country life—days of walks and visits and work followed by homemade entertainments—would restore their sense of what was needed to be happy.

Instead, they arrived in early July brimming with rancor and spoiling for a fight. By way of a dowry, Sand had made over to Solange a valuable Paris property whose rents were to provide them with an income. On learning that Sand planned to make the conventional cash settlement upon Titine and her probable future husband, the painter Théodore Rousseau, the newlyweds were outraged. After a week of quarreling with everyone, Solange and

Clésinger appeared in the front hall while the others were at dinner, demanding a family conference. Probably in his cups, the sculptor bellowed his grievances to Sand and Maurice, insisting that his mother-in-law arrange to mortgage Nohant, giving them an allowance—to begin immediately. When Sand coldly refused, insults were exchanged. Solange accused Maurice of seducing Titine with Sand's encouragement. Her stepcousin's dowry was blood money to wash away their guilt.* A fight erupted. Maurice struck or tried to strike Clésinger; the sculptor picked up a hammer and went for his brother-in-law; Sand rushed between them, slapping Clésinger twice in the face. He then punched her in the chest. Maurice, meanwhile, rushed to his room, returning with a loaded pistol. At this point, servants and dinner guests (who included the parish priest) intervened. Sand ordered Solange, now in the first months of pregnancy, and her husband from the house, forbidding either of them to set foot on her property ever again.

Chopin knew nothing of the events that had taken place at Nohant. The first he heard was a frantic note from Solange, alluding to the "most appalling scenes" that had led to banishment from her mother's house. She was ill and stranded at nearby La Châtre without money to return to Paris. She made no mention of Clésinger. As Chopin had left his carriage at Nohant, would he please write to Sand immediately giving her permission to take it? Her mother had refused her earlier request.

Solange's plea for help reached Chopin at the same time as a long letter from Sand, now lost. If Chopin was distressed by news from the bride, George's letter rendered him so distraught he rushed off to see Delacroix, to whom he read it aloud. In brief, Sand decreed that Chopin could return to Nohant only if he agreed to close his door to Solange and Clésinger. Second, he must

---

*Rousseau broke off the engagement on learning from an anonymous source that Titine had been Maurice's lover. His informant is assumed to have been Solange, but recalling M. Brault's pamphlet, the painter could have learned that his intended was "defiled" (as he wrote to Sand) from other sources.

never again mention the name Solange in her presence; as far as she was concerned, her daughter had ceased to exist.

Delacroix was appalled. The letter, he said, was "just as atrocious" as Chopin described. Sand's "cruelest passions, long suppressed, had finally surfaced."

Chopin's polite reply could not soften his message. There was no way to refuse George's conditions without also accusing the one who imposed them. He could have nothing to say about Monsieur Clésinger, he wrote, since "I never even heard of the man until you gave him your daughter." As for Solange, "she can never be a matter of indifference to me." But far from always taking her daughter's side, as George had claimed, he pointed out the many occasions when he had interceded with Sand "on behalf of both children."

"Surely, you are fated to *always* love them," he reminded George, "because a mother's feelings are the only ones that never change. Troubles can disguise but never destroy them."

If those remarks didn't suffice to render Sand apoplectic, he closed with a direct hit: "Your pain must be overpowering indeed to harden your heart against your child, to the point of refusing even to hear her name, and this on the threshold of her life as a woman, a time more than any other when her condition requires a mother's care." Faced with the gravity of matters "touching on the most Holy of your affections," this was not the moment to talk about himself, and he concluded simply, "I shall wait," underlining the next words, "*ever the same,* Your all devoted Ch."

Sand's reply was all martyred virtue. She had been betrayed, first by her monstrous child and now by Chopin. After nine years of her "exclusive love," he had "gone over to the enemy," and since he had confessed as much, there was nothing else but to forgive him and wish him well. "Goodbye, my friend," she wrote. "Let me know how you are once in a while. As far as we're concerned, there's nothing more to be said."

Along with the dime-novel speechifying that Delacroix had also observed, Sand's long-festering jealousy had indeed imploded. To Marliani, George raved that Chopin had been in love with Solange all along; his betrayal of her now only proved it. His worst blow could not even be mentioned. He had exposed Sand's image of herself as the perfect mother for a delusion. He—and others—had warned her about Clésinger, begging her to treat the affair as an escapade, an infatuation that would run its course, urging her to do everything in her power to save Solange from a disastrous marriage. Instead, George had dismissed his remarks as fueled by envy, obtuseness, and snobbery, writing to everyone she knew exalting the sculptor as a man, an artist, and an ideal husband and son-in-law.

This was Chopin's unforgivable sin: his knowledge that she had failed her child, a failure from which all of her own miseries flowed. When both Viardots wrote to Sand protesting her unjust indictment of Chopin as a conspirator who was gathering a "faction" against her, and pointing to his unwavering loyalty and devotion, she replied: "If I had made mistakes, even committed crimes, Chopin should not have believed them, should not have *seen them*. There is a certain point of respect and gratitude past which we no longer have the right to examine the behavior of those beings who have become sacred to us."

Chopin had examined her and judged her. She had ceased to be sacred, and he claimed the right to love her as merely human and flawed. But this was also the excuse she had been seeking. For too long, she said, he had made her existence a "prison." Now, the jailer would be banished from her life.

SIXTEEN

The Expulsion from Paradise

Nothing had prepared Chopin for the series of blows whose impact he had only begun to feel. He had lost the being closest to him—lover, muse, mother, nurse, friend, and manager. Her roles had changed over the years, but each had become crucial to his survival. His banishment from Nohant had deprived him of a family and home.

He went through each day in a limbo of shock and disbelief, quickened by flashes of hope. George had made overtures to Solange, nearing her confinement. Surely, he would hear from her, too.

But the silence continued and he began to lose hope.

"I'm like an old cobweb whose walls are crumbling," he told a friend.

With such energy as he could muster, he fled Paris for short visits. There were no cobwebs or crumbling walls at Ferrières, the vast estate of Baron James and Betty de Rothschild; its hundred rooms with their profusion of gilt and brocade invited guests to sink into "a luxury that surpasses imagination," where every material need and wish was gratified. More modestly, he made a return visit to Ville d'Avray, where his friends the Albrechts, parents of his godchild, had diverted him from the wedding to which he had not been invited. He continued to see Solange, chastened and matured by money worries and impending motherhood. He had even come to sympathize with Clésinger; with all his faults, the disordered sculptor was struggling to meet the demands of both domesticity and art. Separately, Clésinger and Solange thanked Chopin for his friendship, and not least, his five-hundred-franc loan, desperately needed to meet a mortgage payment. Without his help, Solange assured him, they would have been ruined.

Sand now gave up her apartment across the courtyard at the Square d'Orléans. Like seeing the final hammer come down on an auction lot, Chopin watched (or avoided watching) while the contents of rooms as familiar to him as his own were carted off. As long as her possessions remained, the apartment had held the promise of a return.

He had come to that most terrible of acceptances: the finality of separation. Sand's life, crowded with people, causes, events, new friends and lovers, moved with the force of a rushing river. By the sheer momentum of the present, he had been pushed to George's past.

"Madame Sand cannot but find a good memory of me in her soul when she looks back," he wrote to Ludwika.

With Solange, he felt no need to invoke happy memories:

"This horrible year must end."

Late in January 1848, a few friends, including Auguste Léo and Camille Pleyel, persuaded the composer to give a concert. His last public performance, six years earlier, had been arranged down to every detail by Sand. The glittering event in Pleyel's rooms had enjoyed a huge success, critically and financially. In the interim, Chopin's failing health warned of reduced income from lessons and sales of new work: The energy and invention that infused the Polonaise-Fantaisie and the Sonata for Cello and Piano had deserted him, the knowledge of this loss more devastating even than its actuality. Even his playing, he insisted, had never been so bad. But he agreed to the proposal nonetheless. He hardly needed reminders of unpaid bills. And in his state of mourning, even worry over the performance was a welcome diversion.

With only the most general announcement of a concert by Monsieur Chopin, to take place "sometime soon," the rush for tickets began. The court being the first to reserve forty places, the rest of the three hundred seats were gone (almost all of them to the same select list) before the date—February 16—was announced or tickets, in the form of an engraved invitation, were printed. The managerial tasks that Sand had dispatched so effortlessly had been taken over by the bustling Jane Stirling: from overseeing the temperature of Pleyel's rooms (free of drafts but not stuffy) to making sure that the pianist would see a frieze of reassuring faces on the dais, Count Grzymala, the poet Bogdan Zaleski, Delacroix, the Marquis de Custine, and the Prince and Princess Czartoryski.

Easing his way into the program, Chopin began with a Mozart trio, accompanied by the noted violinist Jean-Delphin Alard* and by Franchomme at the cello. Alternating with two soprano solos, he continued alone with one nocturne and several etudes, including the flowing perfection of both the Barcarolle and the Berceuse. And this was only the first half of the performance.

He had arrived in the green room late, suffering from an attack of nerves. A bout of influenza that week, he said, had not given him enough time to practice the Cello Sonata. (In fact, there had been a dress rehearsal of the instrumental works in the program days before at Delfina Potocka's apartment.) Then, he could not decide what to wear. There was a frenzied last-minute discussion with Franchomme about the sonata and the decision taken that they would begin with the second movement, the Scherzo.

Like the haunting voices of the unplayed opening measures, the question lingers: Why was the work's first movement omitted, on this, its public premiere? The most obvious reason is that his recent bout of flu had left him too weak to attack the movement's exposed

---

*A composer and professor of violin at the Conservatory, Alard also owned the famous "Messiah" Stradivari. With Chopin at the piano, joined by two great string instrumentalists, this had to have ranked among the most memorable accounts of a Mozart trio ever performed.

arpeggios. Whatever argument Chopin offered to Franchomme, there is one explanation he is unlikely to have given: The missing Allegro moderato pays clear homage to Schubert's *Winterreise*, and it's been suggested that the omission on this occasion was dictated by Chopin's fear that the knowledgeable among the audience would hear, in the wanderer's banishment by his beloved, allusions to his own dismissal by Sand. Certainly, Chopin's horror of gossip, of the merest possibility that by quoting Schubert's opening phrases he might seem to be exhibiting his own stigmata, could have led him to omit this first movement. Then again, the sonata was one of the last works that Chopin composed at Nohant, and its first measures, the plangent chain of piano and cello voices echoing one another before joining in duet, may simply have been too painful to play.

As much to reassure himself on the eve of the concert, he had written to Ludwika of the ordeal to come: "I shall be completely at home and see only familiar faces." But the sonata's first movement was a reminder that he had no home and that the face most familiar to him would not be among those applauding his triumphant return.

Reviewers reached for celestial imagery to describe the perfection of the performances; Chopin's playing, one wrote, "has no equal in our earthly realm." Only his friend Custine grasped the new emotional depths that recent months had granted the composer in exchange for what he had lost: "You have gained in suffering and poetry; the melancholy of your compositions penetrates ever deeper into the heart. Each of us feels alone with you in the midst of the crowd. It's not a piano that you play, but a soul. Take care of yourself for your friends' sake; we need the consolation of listening to you. In the hard times ahead, only an art like yours has the power to unite men otherwise divided by the harsh realities of life. We love and understand each other through Chopin . . . the man and the artist are one. What else is there to say?"

Seizing the moment, Pleyel announced a second concert, to take place on March 10. Typically, Chopin had not initially objected; now he told friends he was planning to cancel. History spared him the trouble, for on February 22, the July Monarchy fell, literally overnight. Launched by the Revolution of 1830, Louis Philippe's reign had begun as a middle-of-the-road, middle-class, cautiously liberal regime, symbolized by its "Citizen King" carrying his own umbrella. In eighteen years, the only evidence of its republican promises was an alliance with the new aristocracy of wealth over the feudal claims of the ancien régime. Money ruled, as the surge of new fortunes from real estate, banking, railroads, and industry ushered in an era of voluptuous and visible consumption never before seen in Paris. Money commanded the favors of ministers and deputies to a degree that left few areas of government untouched by scandal. France was compared to a "joint stock company run for the benefit of those who could afford to buy shares."

Strangely, the most hated symbol of corruption was Louis Philippe's only incorruptible minister. François Guizot was Protestant and raised in Calvinist Geneva, but where social ills were concerned, the brilliant historian turned bureaucrat proved more absolutist than any royal. Moving swiftly through the administration to his present post, minister of foreign affairs, Guizot's attempts to stabilize the shaky monarchy made him the architect of its fall. On his advice, dissent was stifled, organizations and political clubs outlawed; his infamous response to the widening gulf between wealth and poverty, "Get rich" (*Enrichessez-vous*), conveyed the regime's philosophy: Greed would continue to be rewarded, since nothing must interfere with a free market.

Class hatred erupted with increasing regularity. The failures of potato and wheat crops in 1845 and 1846 (the latter, followed by rioting and attacks on local landowners, were witnessed by Chopin and Sand in the Berry) produced an economic slump and a drastic decline in living standards for all but the very rich. In Paris, bankruptcies soared, unemployment was rife; crowds of gaunt, hollow-eyed men lined up before dawn for a few jobs, visual evidence that working-class Parisians were near starvation. By the winter of 1846–47 in the Prefecture of the Seine, 450,000 had applied for government bread vouchers.

As a lightning rod to deflect violence, the regime planned a "campaign of banquets," at which grievances and proposals for reform could be aired. But with growing unease at the incendiary potential of gatherings of the disaffected, the government canceled the last of these events, to have taken place on February 22.

Almost at once, betrayal ignited revolution. The next day, the king dismissed Guizot, but it was too late. Already, the famous Parisian barricades, constructed of overturned carriages, tree trunks, and paving stones, barred the way to streets throughout the city, made more impassible by housewives who strewed broken china and bottles in the vicinity. By ten p.m. on the twenty-third, a demonstration that had begun peacefully outside the Ministry of Foreign Affairs (where Guizot also lived) on the boulevard des Capucines turned violent: A single shot fired into the crowd became a fusillade. Within minutes, fifty-three demonstrators were dead, including one woman. Most of the bodies had been stacked one upon another in the nearby rue Fosse-du-Remparts; sixteen corpses were piled on chariots by the insurgents and paraded around the city, to mobs shouting, "Down with the killers!"

These first volleys of revolution took place a few blocks south of the Square d'Orléans and Chopin's ground-floor rooms. Recovering from an attack of his chronic winter "asthma," he would have needed a carriage to get about more than ever; now he was marooned, as isolated as if under house arrest—or quarantined by deadly disease.

At noon on February 24, the king abdicated in favor of his ten-year-old grandson. Within the hour, the royal family had fled the Tuileries for exile in England. In 1830, it had taken a week for the Bourbon Restoration to fall, placing Louis Philippe on the throne. The July Monarchy, born with Chopin's arrival in Paris, toppled in twenty-four hours.

Political uncertainty and fears of further bloodshed continued to keep him at home and in isolation. Visits dropped off. The faithful Solange had gone to her father's estate in Guillery for the birth of her child. There were no more letters to Ludwika reporting seven lessons a day. The Count de Perthuis, one of the friends who had arranged the concert, and his wife, a pupil of Chopin's, had left with the royals for England. James de Rothschild sent the women in his family to London for safety, remaining himself only because of warnings that his departure would cause financial panic and the failure of his bank.

Receptions, soirées, and salons ceased. Shops and theaters closed. Chopin's second concert was only one of many such events to be canceled. Berlioz remained in Britain, where he had been touring. In Paris, music was dead, Berlioz declared.

Rejecting the royal grandson and a regency, the deputies allowed Alphonse de Lamartine, poet and aspiring statesman, to declare the Second Republic. A provisional government was installed in the Hôtel de Ville. Among its founding members was Sand's intimate Louis Blanc, head of a new Labor Department. Their dreams of a socialist France seemed about to come true.

On March 1, George arrived in Paris in time to watch the funeral procession of those killed on February 23—mostly workers and students—from the windows of the Ministry of Foreign Affairs. Within days, she had become the pen of the new republic, issued an official pass to every government office and a contract to provide reports and analysis of events for the administration's organ, the *Bulletin de la République.*

Three days later, on one of his first forays outside, Chopin dined with Countess Marliani. Leaving her apartment with a fellow guest, Edmond de Combes, a young diplomat, they encountered Sand, arriving, in the doorway. Visibly shaken, Chopin summoned himself for an exchange of greetings. He asked whether George had heard the great news of the birth of her granddaughter, Jeanne-Gabrielle Clésinger, on February 28. She had not been told, so Chopin expressed pleasure at being the first to congratulate her. He extended his hand, which, Sand recalled, felt icy to the touch; and turning away, he proceeded slowly down the narrow staircase. But when he reached the bottom, Chopin remembered what he had forgotten to say: Too weak to climb back, he dispatched Combes to run up and add that mother and baby were both doing well. Sand herself now descended, asking Chopin for further details of Solange and her family. She also asked about Chopin's health. "I told her that I was doing well," Chopin wrote to the new mother, "then I said my goodbyes and asked the concierge to open the door to the street."

It was the last time they would see each other. Walking Chopin home, Combes felt enveloped in a vast and silent sadness. "He seemed utterly defeated," he told Sand.

Slowly, the city returned to normal. Members of the young provisional government were busy quarreling among themselves, but their hearts were in the right place, Sand insisted to friends. Nor had the European powers used the chaos in France during the crisis as a pretext for attack, as had been widely feared. Social legislation was passed extending the franchise to some million more Frenchmen, creating jobs, ending child labor at home and slavery in the colonies.

Moments of collective hope make individual hopelessness harder to bear. Despite the baby's apparent good health, Jeanne-Gabrielle Clésinger failed to thrive and lived for only five days. Chopin wrote consoling letters to the stricken Solange, trying to make her feel less alone. He gave her news of Clésinger, who had stayed in Paris to finish a bust of Liberté commissioned by the provisional government and cheered the letters that she had finally received from Sand. He could not disguise his pessimism about a new Polish uprising, which depended upon support from the Prussian-controlled province of Poznan. Many of the émigré colony were setting off to join the liberation forces, but he tried to dissuade Fontana, struggling to survive in New York, from rash action. He foresaw more bloodshed before a new Poland would arise.

For months now, Jane Stirling had tried persuading Chopin of the possibilities offered by a tour of Britain. His music was much admired across the Channel and he had excellent relations with his publisher there. European composers and virtuosi, Liszt and

Mendelssohn among them, filled concert halls throughout England and Scotland. Why should he not enjoy equal success? Miss Stirling may have been too discreet to urge a change of scene as a prescription for melancholy, but this seems to have been the deciding force in his decision. There was nothing left for him in Paris.

SEVENTEEN

"The Abyss Called London"

He crossed the Channel on April 19, without seasickness, arriving in London on the twentieth. Rooms had been arranged for him by Miss Stirling at 10 Bentinck Street, Cavendish Square, and furnished with every comfort; he found notepaper engraved with his monogram and his favorite French cocoa for hot chocolate. What Miss Stirling could not effect was a change in climate. In late April, when spring would be warming Paris and flowering in Nohant, London was cold and rainy, the air heavy with the coal dust that trapped moisture, producing the infamous pea-soup fog: On Good Friday, he could see nothing outside, and he felt further suffocated by the gloom with its strangely livid color. No letters of introduction could be presented during Holy Week, so Chopin took the occasion to call on the exiled Louis Philippe and his family and, on another evening, to dine with Guizot.

After ten days of feeling ill and "good for nothing," the sun finally shone "in the abyss called London," and his miasma lifted. Mornings, he no longer felt himself choking.

Jane Stirling now scheduled a dizzying round of calls, receptions, soirées, salons; together, they crisscrossed the sprawling city several times a day in her carriage, meeting, so it seemed, the entire peerage and all the cultural stars to be found in the capital. Stirling has been accused of displaying her musical lion to enhance her own status, but it seems likelier that the practical Scotswoman recognized that Chopin's earnings—from both pupils and performances—depended upon meeting the right people. Within weeks, he had invitations to play at matinées: at Lady Gainsborough's, and the Marquess of Douglas's, for which he charged twenty guineas. (Lady Rothschild, sister-in-law of his beloved Baroness Betty, had advised him that, London not being Paris, he must keep his fees there low.) His first and most glittering summons came from the Duchess of Sutherland, Queen Victoria's Mistress of the Robes, to give a concert on May 15, on the occasion of her newest daughter's christening. Stafford House (now Lancaster House), St. James's, was one of the few establishments grand enough to receive the queen as guest of honor. The evening, which began with a dinner for eighty, ended with a concert in the gilt and crystal State Drawing Room. Not usually given to pictorial images, Chopin, gazing at Her Majesty "sparkling in her diamonds and decorations," her courtiers moving up and down the grand double staircase, compared the scene to a procession in a Veronese painting. Following convention, Chopin shared the program, this time with the renowned singers Mario, Lablache, and Tamburini, along with another pianist, with whom he played Mozart's Variations in G arranged for two pianos. Then, alone, he performed several of his own mazurkas and waltzes. While he was still playing, Prince Albert left his seat to stand next to the piano. But Chopin was still more elated when, following the musical offerings, the queen chatted with him—twice. He was confident of an invitation to play before Their Royal Highnesses at Buckingham Palace or at Windsor. He could not know that in the queen's diary, she had reported ecstatically on the three singers by name, noting only that "several pianists" had also performed.

Competition among visiting virtuosi was keen; the brushfires of revolution were spreading through Europe. A continental exodus of musicians and singers had preceded Chopin to London, including Jenny Lind, the "Swedish Nightingale," and his friend Pauline Viardot. "All the Parisian pianists are here," Chopin reported, along with news that the Viennese Sigismund Thalberg, "Iron Wrists," was booked for twelve concerts.

In Paris, Chopin had been enthroned high above the fray of musical politics. As a teacher, he occupied a legendary place, with fees to match. At salons or soirées, from the royals to the Rothschilds, he might play (or not) as an honored guest, accepting gifts but no money. The rarity of his performances organized by Sand and Pleyel, public in name only, made it unthinkable that he would ever need personally negotiate halls and tickets.

With his acute social antennae, he was alert to the "thousand rules" that governed relations among the British upper classes. But innocent of the most basic stratagems of the professional, he had missed the rules governing the small world of English music. He had declined the signal honor of an invitation to play with the orchestra of the London Philharmonic Society; like that of English roast beef or turtle soup, its reputation, he said, was undeserved. He had been shocked to learn, moreover, that in London, time was money; there was only one rehearsal—open to the public—before each performance. He had not known that visiting musicians were expected to call upon the society's director (all the more crucial, in Chopin's case, to soften the insult of rejection) or that the same gentleman was also the queen's director of music. He never received an invitation to play for Her Royal Highness.

By early June, he was spitting blood again and sleepless with money worries. Longing for sun, he had moved to larger, lighter rooms at 48 Dover Street, off Piccadilly. The drawing room, he reported happily, was big enough to house three pianos—his own Pleyel, a Broadwood provided by the son of the firm's founder, and the deep-voiced Erard. Exorbitant to begin with, the rent of his new apartment was suddenly doubled. His Italian valet was so grand that he disdained to accompany a master who traveled in a hackney cab; Chopin obliged by hiring a carriage and coachman. In the event, the conveyance gave useful evidence that he was the social equal of his hosts.

Until recently, the English had roped off musicians so that they would not mingle with the guests. Only because his boots were clean and he didn't produce a business card had he been able to breach the social barrier, Chopin noted. Heard everywhere—at

garden shows, charity bazaars, and receptions—music was background noise, the "cocktail piano" of a later era or, at its most elevated, entertainment. Art was understood solely as commodity,
"luxury goods," Chopin observed: architecture, painting, and
sculpture. Only opera, in a culture crazed for theater, had managed
to cross the boundary.

Just as well, since performances had to pay his way. One former
professional who understood and sympathized was Mrs. Sartoris.
The former Adelaide Kemble, of the legendary theatrical family,
she had made a brilliant Covent Garden debut, only to be rescued
from the stage by a rich husband. She lent Chopin her Belgravia
house at 99 Eaton Place for a benefit matinée on June 23—the
composer being the beneficiary. In the double drawing room,
before an audience of 150 of the titled, rich, or celebrated (including Jane Carlyle and Thackeray), Chopin was at his best, as
reflected in the first of the two most strenuous programs he would
play in Britain. Alternating with the fashionable tenor Mario, he
performed four sets, the Ballade in F Major, a gathering of nocturnes, two mazurkas, two waltzes, an impromptu, and the
Berceuse. Two reviewers pointed to the power of his sound; he
played "with the greatest energy," while the same critic noted
approvingly "the loudness of his *fortes*"; the performance, in all,
"unrivalled by any executant in the present day." Not least, after
paying Mario, Chopin had earned 150 guineas.

Two weeks later, he repeated this triumph at Lord Falmouth's
house at 2 St. James's Square, adding to the ballade one of the
demanding scherzos of opus 31. This display of stamina was not
lost on the *Atheneum*'s critic, who heard "more force and *brio*" than
had reverberated through Mrs. Sartoris's salon. For Chopin, it was
a performance to summon the most bittersweet memories. He had
asked Pauline Viardot to share the program with him. Joined by a
young cousin, she sang, among other works, her own settings of
Chopin mazurkas, which she and the composer had first played
and sung together at Nohant.

The London season now over, the court led the exodus to country estates. To his distress, Chopin found that one of his pupils had

decamped owing him for nine lessons. "I suffer from idiotic attacks of nostalgia, of nerves and worry about the future," he wrote to Grzymala.

For nine years, Chopin had preceded his pupils and patrons, leaving Paris for Nohant as early as May, and remaining through November. In the dusty heat of a London July, he was abandoned once more.

He had spent the hundred guineas from this last benefit on paying old bills. He would need two thousand more to see him through another London season. At the moment, he had almost no cash on hand, and his calendar of engagements—lessons, concerts, social life—was blank. He had little choice but to accept Jane Stirling's proposal for a tour combined with a holiday in the north, resting between concerts at the far-flung Stirling fiefdoms. Thus, in early August, he found himself on the train heading to Edinburgh. From there he joined his "two Scottish ladies"—Stirling and her sister—at Calder House in Midlothian, seat of their elderly, widowed brother-in-law, Lord Torphichen.

In the next four months, moving from mansion to castle, trying to rest between concerts, Chopin lost strength and heart. The houses were grand; the paintings and parks admirable; his hosts warm and attentive. Both the climate and the conversation, however, were worse than in London; most guests (including neighbors) were related, and genealogy was the favorite topic: The succession of "begats," Chopin observed, was rivaled only by the Old Testament, all the way down to Jesus. Once more, he thought he would "cough up [his] very soul" in the mornings. And he was spitting blood again. "I'm suffocating in beautiful Scotland," he told Pleyel.

But in Paris, fighting had erupted again, more violent this time than the earlier round of uprisings and reprisals. A fragile Second Republic reacted defensively to insurgents, becoming more repressive than the July Monarchy had dared to be, and making the "Days of June" far bloodier than those of February. Idealistic supporters of the early days of revolution, like George Sand, had been branded dangerous "communists" for reporting that teenaged students were being "murdered," gunned down in cold blood. In a vacuum of leadership, civil war threatened.

Knowing he could not return while Paris was in chaos, Chopin fell into the despair and hopelessness of a prisoner. He was afraid of dying in England if he stayed the winter. In the dark galleries of Calder House, lined with gloomy portraits of Stirling ancestors, he dreamed the consumptive's dream of Rome. He wondered aloud to Franchomme whether he could get a government pension "for not composing anything."

Exiled from France, he turned his resentment on the radicals, those, in his view, causing the bloodshed; the British monarchy fed his nostalgia for a golden age of authority. He recalled to his family the stirring moment when the queen made her entrance at Her Majesty's Theatre for Jenny Lind's performance in *La sonnambula*. The sovereign had received more applause than the star. When the audience, including the Duke of Wellington, rose to sing "God Save the Queen," "it was an imposing sight, that real respect and reverence for the throne, for law and order," he said. When a fellow musician and Polish exile in London had suggested that the archreactionary pope, Pius IX, should stop meddling in politics, Chopin flew into a rage, shouting that His Holiness was the *only* authority fit to rule nations.

He arrived in Manchester on August 28, a day before his scheduled concert. The great manufacturing city was his first experience of a provincial center of serious music. His host, Salis Schwabe, like their mutual friend Auguste Léo, was a converted German Jew and founder of the local "Gentlemen's Concert" series, where, in their neoclassical auditorium, the rich and cultured gathered to hear those reigning virtuosi willing to travel northward. Schwabe was so successful that the chimney of his printing plant alone had cost five thousand pounds, Chopin reported in some awe, and Crumpsall House, his elegant Regency mansion well outside the chimney's belching reach, received a steady stream of celebrated musical guests.

Chopin filled the twelve hundred seats of the hall, but his music was swallowed by the vast space. Acoustical disparities between his familiar drawing rooms and the cavernous theater accounts for differing reports of his powers. But the pianist's condition had also deteriorated visibly. At least one reviewer noted that he mounted the stage with "an almost painful air of feebleness in his appearance and gait." Even after two cuts in the program (omitting the longest work, a draining ballade, and a second nocturne) and the rest between sets provided by three celebrated singers, he was exhausted. Critics praised his "finesse and purity of tone" but felt obliged to point to the lack of force in his playing. The works themselves were ignored, except for one writer, who complained that they were "incomprehensible." Similar perplexity was voiced after his next engagements, in Glasgow and Edinburgh. Unlike Brahms, Chopin never found a George Bernard Shaw to champion his work in Britain. The composer himself was beyond caring. He wanted only to take his sixty guineas and leave. Had he been a "machine," he said, he could have gone through the motions, "banging out music" and making a great career in Britain, but it was too late for that now.

By train and carriage, he zigzagged between the two cities where he was playing next and the great Stirling houses where he had committed himself to visits, Johnstone Castle and Keir Castle, in Perthshire, as well as Lady Murray's home, Strachur, on Loch Fyne. The social strain far outweighed the creature comforts. "I cannot work and I cannot rest. Surrounded by people, I feel alone, alone, alone," he wrote to Grzymala. He was ecstatic to learn that the Czartoryskis would be in Edinburgh, and he rushed from Glasgow for the first of two reunions with the adorable Princess Marcelina.

"I breathed again their Polish spirit and it gave me enough strength to play in Glasgow," he wrote. He had similar hopes of comfort and refuge as the guest of a Polish émigré, Dr. Lyszczynski. But the small house, where he promptly took to his bed, was ill equipped to care for a demanding invalid. Squeezed into a tiny former nursery, he descended only to huddle by the stove. After weeks of feudal splendor, assigned his own servants, he could not adjust to a middle-class household. Speaking Polish failed to compensate for the poor service; he snapped at the doctor's wife for failing to have his boots polished to a gleam and his linen dazzling white.

His irascibility worsened as his condition deteriorated: "I'm angry and sad and people irritate me with their excessive care," he complained—or by their lack of same. Glasgow was shocked by his appearance: A "small grey person, he looked thin, ashen, bent over and marked for doom," one recalled.

His performance in Edinburgh was Chopin's only solo recital; but this time, it was because he lacked the energy to find other musicians to appear with him. That evening he seemed possessed: Electric with fevered energy, he played for two and a half hours, including five encores. Omitting only the polonaise, the evening formed an anthology of his inventions; like a drowning man, he seemed to summon his entire creative life before him.

Escorted by the unflagging Stirling sisters, he dragged himself from Lady Belhaven's at Wishaw House to the Duchess of Hamilton's at Hamilton Palace; the forced march ended where it began, at Calder House.

In the last weeks, his health had gone "from bad to worse," he told Grzymala. Feeling ever weaker, he lay immobilized until two in the afternoon; then, when he dressed, "everything hurt" and he just sat "panting until dinner," after which he had to remain at table with the gentlemen, "watching them talk and listening to them drink." Aware that their guest could barely speak or understand English,* they tried out their schoolboy French. "Bored to death," Chopin moved into the drawing room where, knowing he was expected to play for a while, he tried his best to revive. After the music, his manservant carried him upstairs, undressed him, and put him to bed, where he lay "gasping and dreaming" until the round began again.

Finally, on October 31, he was helped onto the London train.

---

*Jane Stirling had warned Carlyle—a great admirer of Chopin's music—about the composer's difficulty with spoken English. Carlyle had then asked whether he could read the language, in which case he would write to him. The answer was probably negative, as no letters from the writer to Chopin survive.

Through the Czartoryskis' agent, new rooms had been found for him at number 4 St. James's Place. For the next two weeks, he was too sick to move. He could only breathe if he kept the windows wide open to the freezing air outside, so he sat propped up by the fire wrapped in his overcoat. Determined to honor his commitment to play at a concert and ball for Polish relief, he appeared at the Guildhall on November 16. Most of the subscribers had come for the dancing; the music, consisting of singers, a little orchestra, and Chopin playing on a small upright, was shunted into a side room (probably the Common Council Chamber) along with the refreshments. Chopin's "divine" playing, Princess Marcelina reported, was wasted on this audience.

Cold fog descended on the city and the Stirling sisters returned. Chopin could hardly claim to be unaware of Jane's tender feelings, or that she nurtured hopes of replacing Sand in his life. He was horrified, nonetheless, to learn that rumors of marriage had reached Paris; he hastened to remind Grzymala that he was closer to a coffin than to a marriage bed. Even were his health better, he felt no physical attraction to the statuesque Scotswoman, like Sand, six years his senior. But he had clearly considered the possibility; they were too much alike, he had told Grzymala earlier, and besides, how could he ever support a wife?

Princess Marcelina had taken over his care, and she now had Chopin examined by an eminent homeopath (his preference) as well as by a specialist in tuberculosis, Sir James Clark, the royal physician, who had treated Keats in Rome; at the least, he knew a dying man when he saw one. There was nothing to be done for his present patient except to make him less miserable. Clark urged him to return to Paris as soon as he could travel.

His suffering, of body and spirit, would only end with his life. "Why does God not kill me right away, instead of piece by piece?" he demanded. His thoughts turned to another instrument of his suffering: "I have never cursed anyone, but my life now is so unbearable, that I imagine feeling better if I could curse Lucrezia."

He had known all along. But his pride could never have allowed him to face Delacroix's pity. Playing the dandy, insouciant, even a bit obtuse, applauding Sand's truth as fiction, had been another memorable performance.

He left London on November 23. Alerting Grzymala to prepare his rooms, he asked his friend to put a bunch of violets in the salon at the Square d'Orléans, a "breath of poetry" to greet him on his return.

EIGHTEEN

Recordare

S ome time after his return to Paris, Chopin sat for a camera portrait.* In this posed likeness, he is shown seated, turning towards us and away from an upright secretary. Along with books on the shelves, its glass front appears to show the reflection of a window across the room. A bound folio volume lies on top of the desk.

Huddled in a gray overcoat worn above a waistcoated dress suit, the composer seems to be shivering, arms held close to a torso thickened by layers of clothing. But it's Chopin's face that shocks us: swollen with the edema that accompanies the last stages of tuberculosis; the iconic images—frail sylph or the fiery romantic artist of Delacroix's portrait—have disappeared. Under frowning brows, his eyes are ringed with bruised shadows; the thin aquiline nose is now bulbous. A stranger stares from the doughy flesh, accusing in his pain.

For a man dying alone, friends are a reminder of solitude. Visitors come and go, leaving only memories in constant attendance. On his return to the Square d'Orléans, Chopin was greeted by a committee of the faithful: Marie de Rozières, Grzymala, Franchomme.

*For problems surrounding the photograph itself, see Appendix.

Photograph of Chopin, c. 1846

But the place itself was peopled with ghosts. Of his community of friends and fellow artists, only the reclusive and melancholy pianist Alkan remained. The Czartoryskis were abroad until March, while Grzymala himself had crept into town as a quasi-fugitive; financial scandal and membership in a now-outlawed political club had forced him to leave Paris. Only a scattering of pupils remained; a few, including Delfina Potocka and Betty de Rothschild, were also friends. The most faithful in his attentions was Delacroix. Ill himself, working frenziedly on the ceiling for the Louvre's Galerie d'Apollon, he nonetheless came by most afternoons to take Chopin for a drive.

Medical scrutiny of the sick man intensified, bringing no improvement. The trusted homeopath Dr. Molin had died while Chopin was in England; and without his special medication, his patient had no relief from the choking cough, to which he now added swollen limbs. In the course of the new year of 1849, no fewer than seven doctors would ponder Chopin's case. By the end of January, four had already examined him. Some came twice a day, and with fees of ten francs a visit, medical bills soared as his earnings plummeted. All the physicians agreed that he needed a healthier climate, quiet, and rest.

"Soon, I'll have rest enough without their advice," he wrote to Solange.

In the meantime, peace held in Paris, quelling fears of an uprising against National Guard units called from outside the capital. On January 30, the day before he began his letter to Solange, Chopin reported "troops and cannons *everywhere*"; he felt thankful for this "show of force that discouraged elements bent on creating disorder."

Despite Sand's operatic dismissal of Chopin from her life and her guilty insistence that he was slandering her, she continued to ask friends for news of him. Although Pauline Viardot hadn't seen the composer since they met in London, she reported to George that he was "declining slowly" with occasional "good days" during which he sparkled with the old gaiety. But his pupils were few, and he no longer went out at night, she said. In April, he made an exception to hear Pauline herself sing in the premiere of Meyerbeer's new opera, *Le Prophète*. For weeks, Paris had been abuzz with word of the spectacular effects to be unveiled on stage, including ice skaters (actually, roller skaters with hidden wheels), a sun ablaze with electrical filaments, and a huge fire. Only the music was a disappointment. Recalling his delight in Meyerbeer's earlier spectacle *Robert le diable*, which had inspired his piano variations, Chopin found the present opera a sad reminder of his own musical decline.

Tradition has cast the Mazurka in F Minor, op. 68, no. 4, as Chopin's last work. Published posthumously, the unfinished sketch speaks of the life that was failing. A maze of indecipherable markings, the one-page manuscript of the F-minor mazurka has drawn scholars into a labor of cryptography for over a century; starting with Franchomme and Fontana, who edited his unpublished works posthumously, the piece has exerted the siren call to completion. Teasing out the private notations, abbreviations, memos to himself, everyone who tries to solve the puzzle gets, literally, to play Chopin.

Fragments within a fragment, this brief piece shifts keys, slipping in quavers and "chromatic digressions" all in a seemingly futile effort to gain momentum and take off. The sense of collapse evoked by these few measures (99 or 101, depending on the reading), the unfinished jumble of the manuscript, and the conviction of friends and fellow musicians have enshrined the sketch as the composer's "last thoughts," which pain and weakness did not allow him to finish. The most recent scholarship, however, rejects this dating, proposing, instead, the work as a discarded section of an earlier mazurka, the F minor, op. 63, no. 2, begun in 1846. In this analysis, Chopin rejected the unfinished sketch as a failed attempt to infuse a traditional genre with radical innovation, an experiment that had succeeded with the expansive structure of the Polonaise-Fantaisie.

At mid-century, new ideas were in the air, ideas whose daring Chopin's last style had helped initiate. (One has only to think of English critics' shock at the harsh dissonances they heard from his piano.) Approaching death condemned him to abandon his attempts to forge a "tradition of the new"; the failed mazurka proved its modernity nonetheless, laying bare the anatomy of process. A fragment of past failure or a shard of the future, the mazurka's last bar, with its eerie prefiguration of Wagner's *Tristan* harmonies, encodes directions to roads he himself could not take, but which, like a signpost's sudden illumination, emerged clearly for others to follow.

Unable to work, Chopin found his greatest suffering was boredom. But in early May he was cheered by the birth of Solange's second child. Named for her sister, Jeanne-Gabrielle but called "Nini," she was all the more beloved by her mother as a reincarnation of her firstborn who had lived only days. For Clésinger, however, the new daughter dealt a blow to his desire for a son. His disappointment, along with his continuing failure to find (or, in his wife's view, to seek) work led to mounting dissension between the couple. Mustering what little strength he had, Chopin tried to help. In response to Solange's pleas, he inquired of Princess Obreskoff, a rich and influential Russian friend, about possibilities for commissions in Saint Petersburg; his own experience, however, made him discouraging about prospects in London.

Chopin's ground-floor rooms in the Square d'Orléans, with their spectral reminders of loss, were damp and sunless. By April, the ranks of visitors were thinning; within weeks, everyone had left Paris. Some feared another outbreak of revolution; others were terrified of cholera, Chopin wrote to Grzymala. Delacroix, on the way to his rented country house, felt anxious in abandoning "my dying friend."

At least something could be done about his insalubrious surroundings and lack of proper care. Well away from the swirling dust of Paris streets, Princess Obreskoff found an airy apartment, flooded with sunlight, on the second floor of a two-story house at 74, avenue de Chaillot in the village of that name.* Chopin could never have afforded the rent: a staggering 400 francs a month. His earnings were so tiny now, he had joked to Solange that "come autumn, I'll be foraging for food." But Obreskoff, as tactful as she was generous, quoted half this figure to Chopin, paying the balance herself.

---

*Since razed to make way for the Trocadéro.

By the time he was moved to Chaillot at the end of May, he was too sick to manage with only his valet, Daniel, who, in any case, left evenings. Princess Czartoryska sent Chopin her daughter's old nanny to act as night nurse, and arranged with another young Polish woman to help during the day.

He was too weak to leave his apartment, except for the occasional drive to the Bois de Boulogne nearby. For these outings, Daniel would carry him up and down stairs, placing his master gently into the carriage. For the rest, he was grateful for what he called the "Roman view" from his five windows. Rising from the expanse of gardens separating Chaillot from the city, he could see the Tuileries, the Chamber of Deputies, Notre-Dame, the Panthéon, and Saint-Sulpice. But the panoramic sweep of domes and steeples, so familiar yet so far away, might as well have been Warsaw.

His "good" days he ascribed to his latest physician, a homeopathic doctor who took him off medication. This, together with the fresh air, improved his appetite, and he felt better. Now, with the cholera receding, he talked of moving back to the Square d'Orléans the following month, of visiting Delfina in Nice, even of a trip to Poland. Meanwhile, from their respective retreats, the faithful came to Chaillot.

He had dodged his "Scottish ladies" in his last weeks in London: the elder sister, Mrs. Erskine, wanted to convert him to Calvinism; Miss Stirling, to marry him—and she refused to be dismissed, neither by plague, by revolution, or by Chopin himself. The only concession she and her sister made to danger was to join Chopin's other friends who had moved from Paris to suburban Saint-Germain-en-Laye.

Jenny Lind found time, between a round of Paris engagements, to make the trip to Chaillot. It was the last musical evening where Chopin presided as host. Lind and Delfina Potocka alternated songs and arias to the applause of a small group including Delfina's sister, the Princess de Beauvau, Marcelina Czartoryska, and Betty de Rothschild.

By the end of June there were fewer good days. He was now hemorrhaging heavily and suffered from chronic diarrhea; even in bed, he received visitors dressed in trousers and pumps, but his legs and feet were visibly swollen. Now the most famous of his physicians appeared. Chopin could not have been unaware that the reputation of Dr. Jean Cruveiller, professor of medicine and clinician, was based upon his study of consumption. The doctor prescribed new medication, an extract of lichen, which did nothing to help.

He began writing letters to Ludwika at the beginning of July, imploring her to come and care for him. The sight of her would do him more good than all of Cruveiller's useless remedies. Weeks earlier, others had decided that his sister's presence could ease the dying man's despair; nothing, they knew now, could arrest the disease or even alleviate his symptoms. Princess Obreskoff and Marcelina Czartoryska had pulled strings in Russia to speed passports through the czarist bureaucracy. Borrowing money from her mother, Ludwika, accompanied by her husband and fifteen-year-old daughter, set out on the long journey that her younger brother had made with so much hope and ambition less than twenty years before.

Franchomme now took on the management of Chopin's finances. Not that there was much to manage. Savings from his British tour were almost gone. Desperately, the cellist took stock of his friend's few valuables, looking for something to sell but trying, at the same time, to shield the sick man from the truth: He had only a few hundred francs left. At this point, Franchomme must have talked to Jane Stirling. She was horrified by what she heard, but for reasons Franchomme could never have anticipated. In March, Stirling reported, she had left a packet containing 25,000 francs in cash for the composer with the concierge at the Square d'Orléans. As the gift had been anonymous, Stirling had no reason to expect any acknowledgment of its receipt. Now, of course, Chopin had to be told of the money's disappearance. A byword for honesty, the concierge, Madame Etienne, was never herself a suspect. With no leads, Stirling decided to engage the service of the most famous clairvoyant in Paris. Known only as "Alexis," this celebrated personage required a lock of Madame Etienne's hair.

Lest she be offended, a pretext was found to bring her to Chaillot and to divest her of the crucial cutting. From this evidence, Alexis was able to divine that the missing packet had been stuck behind a table lamp on the concierge's desk and then forgotten. And there it was!

In Chopin's eyes, Jane Stirling could do nothing right. He claimed that she had invented the whole story of leaving the money earlier, first to assuage her guilt at having failed to help him sooner, and second, because she was no longer satisfied with the role of anonymous benefactress but wanted full credit for her grand gesture. To punish her, he would accept only 15,000 of the 25,000 francs she had given him, and that only as a loan.

Finally, on August 9, Ludwika and her family arrived. The sick man rallied briefly. For weeks he had been plagued with insomnia; now his sister stayed up with him, talking through the night. Hearing in detail the sorrows of the last years, Ludwika was grateful for the darkness, in which she could weep unseen, she told their sister in Warsaw. At the end of the month, the irascible Kalasanty returned to Poland, unable to persuade his wife to accompany him. Two more doctors now appeared to consult with Dr. Cruveiller. Together, they decided that living in Chaillot, Chopin was too far from medical help, advice that suggests that they were unwilling to make any future trips for a hopeless case. They prescribed a move to well-heated rooms with a southern exposure in the center of town.

In the middle of September, then, Chopin now confined to his bed, was moved to a splendid apartment at the most fashionable address in Paris. His new rooms were on the ground floor giving on the courtyard of 12, place Vendôme; although the view of the square with its famous column of melted cannons from Napoleon's campaigns was reserved for the principal tenant, the Russian embassy, his was the sunnier space.* The same building housed the offices of his friend Thomas Albrecht, Saxon consul

---

*Now occupied by the accounting department of Chaumet jewelers; light and sun were not yet blocked by the Ministry of Justice.

and father of Chopin's little godson. This time, several other friends contributed to make up the rent. With Stirling's loan, the stored contents of his rooms at the Square d'Orléans were moved and his upright Pleyel placed in one of the two drawing rooms closest to the bedroom. Unable to make the tour of the apartment more than once or twice in the next month, he rallied to advise on the purchase of new furnishings and the reupholstering of worn ones.

Word spread in Paris that Chopin was dying. Crowds of visitors had to be screened; some were tactfully confined to the anteroom, others were admitted to the bedside for a few final words. His childhood acquaintance Father Aleksander Jelowicki was a constant presence. Once a writer and publisher, he had recently taken holy orders, and his sights were set on reclaiming this prized soul for the Church. According to his own rapturous account of his victory, the dying man at first agreed to confess to him "as a friend," holding that his lack of faith would make a mockery of the sacraments. But Jelowicki persisted, and close to the end, he announced, Chopin relented joyfully, embracing the Cross and thanking his confessor for not allowing him to "die like a pig." Others have disputed the priest's version of Chopin's salvation, insisting that last rites were forced upon a weak and terrified man.

Contradiction and conflict blur every version of Chopin's four-day agony. The ranks kept swelling of those who offered eyewitness accounts of the composer's last hours. A cartoon featured a weeping countess, identified in the caption as the only noblewoman who had not been present at Chopin's deathbed.

Along with the assiduous Father Jelowicki, those known to have kept the vigil include Ludwika and her daughter; Marcelina Czartoryska; Franchomme; Adolf Gutmann; Charles Gavard, husband of one of Chopin's students; and, later, Dr. Cruveiller. Then, on October 16, when Delfina Potocka arrived from Nice, Chopin asked her to play and sing to him. The Pleyel was rolled next to the open bedroom door, but there is little certainty about what Delfina sang—a Marcello hymn, a Bellini aria, or Mozart? Another recalled that she had begun playing the opening measures

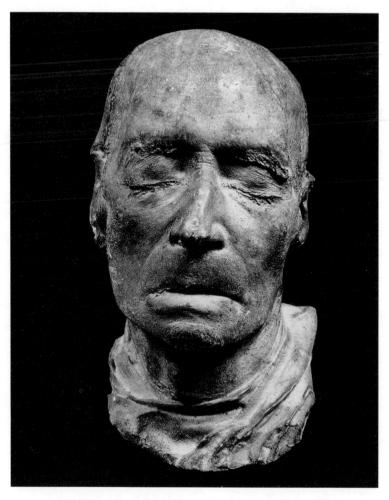

Jean Baptiste-Auguste Clésinger's death mask of Chopin, 1849

of Chopin's Sonata for Cello and Piano when the composer, choking, motioned for her to stop. "A stranger I came / And a stranger I depart"—if the phrase recalled the first words of Schubert's *Winterreise*, memories would be unendurable, beyond all physical pain.

Towards evening, he could no longer breathe; like a hanged man's, his face turned black in suffocation. But when those gathered around the bed asked if he was in pain, he whispered, "Non plus"—No longer.

Solange was summoned, and when she arrived no one seemed to question her privileged place near the bed. Banished from Eden, they had consoled each other's losses for so long. Shortly after two a.m., Solange, holding the dying man to offer him water, saw that his eyes had filmed over—his gaze "tarnished," she said. He was gone.

The room where the dead man lay was still dark when two photographers arrived. No one knows who alerted them or let them in. A new and nimble breed, they came with the barest of equipment and, deciding they needed more light, started to move the bed with Chopin's body next to the window to catch the first streaks of dawn. The stunned little group was galvanized; the intruders were ushered to the door.

Too late. Their glass plates were blank, but they had already claimed the deathbed as public domain. Heralds of a new era, these larval paparazzi announced the end of Chopin's world of aristocratic privacy and discreet patronage. His musical heirs would be the artist as professional, requiring larger concert halls, bigger audiences, more publicity.

The revolution that surged through the streets of Paris ended for all time the role of the artist as courtier. Following Chopin's death, art bifurcated into high and low, popular and obscure; commercially viable spectacles like opera with mass appeal or the hermetic language of a modernism for the few.

After Chopin, nationalism no longer breathed the poignancy of exile from which a patriot artist, evoking dances of peasants and nobles, mazurkas and polonaises, affirmed ties to a violated country. The new nationalism, expressed in the music of Richard Wagner, exalted the composer as prophet of a mythical past sweeping towards an apocalyptic future "beyond good and evil."

Chopin's mocking spirit would have savored the ironies revealed by his art. The salons at which he was both guest and performer, conservative redoubts of power and privilege, heard compositions as radical as any ever written. At his rare concerts, the chosen audiences cheered music whose democratic genius touches every heart.

Like his father, Chopin feared being buried alive, and he asked Dr. Cruveiller to make certain it would not happen. To this end, the doctor performed an autopsy—a report that was lost, along with other archives in the Hôtel de Ville, during the Commune of 1870–71.

Ludwika quoted Cruveiller as reporting that Chopin's heart appeared more damaged than the lungs, giving rise to the questions that still linger as to the cause of death. But it is also true that tuberculosis, with its taint of contagion, would have been a more troubling diagnosis for his family.

Honoring Chopin's request, his heart was sent to Warsaw. Placed in the Church of the Holy Cross, the heart in its urn survived the bombing of the church during World War II. Many of Chopin's possessions, including manuscript material, accompanied his sister back to Poland, where they were destroyed by the Cossacks in 1863 or by the German bombardment in the Second World War. With the exception of an unfinished *Method* of teaching theory, bequeathed to his neighbor Alkan, Chopin had given instructions for the unpublished manuscripts in his possession to be burned. These orders were ignored.

Almost all of Sand's letters to Chopin found their way back to her, to be destroyed, along with hers to Chopin. In her copious autobiographical writings, it pleased her to portray their relations from the outset as a chaste friendship, in which she played forbearing caretaker to an increasingly destructive genius.

Whatever misfortunes she suffered, Chopin once observed, things always worked out well for George in the end. In the twenty-six years she lived after Chopin's death, adversity only strengthened her: political disillusionment, from the Second Republic to the bloodbath of the Commune; the deaths of another lover and longtime companion, also of tuberculosis, and of her beloved grandchild Nini at six, victim of her parents' hostilities.

Her mother's hatred pursued Solange to the end of her wretched life. Banished again after Nini's death, with no money or skills, she was kept, then deserted, by a series of rich lovers. Her daughter, Sand said, was "no better than a common prostitute." Like an abandoned animal, Solange returned periodically to Nohant. With an inheritance from her father, she bought her uncle's property in nearby Montgivray. When she took to appearing unannounced at meals, Sand issued orders that she could be fed, but that no one in the household was to speak to her or even acknowledge her presence.

Titine, the chosen daughter, also proved a disappointment. When she was jilted by the painter Théodore Rousseau, Sand married her off to another promising young artist. After receiving a large cash dowry from her adoptive mother, Titine dismissed George from her life.

At thirty, Maurice wed a plain and pliant young woman and produced two daughters, one of whom, Aurore, was Sand's namesake and favorite. His talents ultimately found their outlet in Nohant's famous marionette theater. From the wood of local willow trees, he carved and painted the large puppets and, with help from friends, family, and guests, built the stage, scenery, and lighting, with Sand contributing scripts and costumes. In this mechanical universe of his own making, Maurice was, finally, master.

A young man from the provinces, armed with talent or brilliance, ardent with ambition, arrives in the capital. His mix of cynicism and innocence is irresistible—especially to older women. His dandyism is a mirror of distance: He gives himself to no one. From its salons, he conquers Paris: The rich, the titled, the gifted bow to his genius. His distinction of dress and manner is enhanced by the sorrows that have left their mark: the pain of exile, of solitude, of illness, of the struggle to perfect his art. To these will be added other losses: the death of illusions and of love itself.

This is the theme of the great novelists who were Chopin's contemporaries. He is a brother of their invented heroes: Balzac's Eugène de Rastignac, Stendhal's Frédéric Moreau, destroyed by desire fulfilled. Only Chopin's final chapters are his own: a failed life redeemed by art.

Appendix

Chopin's Photograph

The photograph of Chopin reproduced on page 191 is described as being "in the English technique," making it almost certainly a collotype, a slightly more advanced process than the daguerreotype.

Neither the size, nor the format of the image, nor any other conclusive evidence justifies its long-standing attribution to Louis-Auguste Bisson, oldest son of a family of photographers, including a father and younger brothers. Significantly, the Chopin portrait was not included in a 1999 exhibition, *Les Bissons Photographes,* at the Bibliothèque Nationale.

Indeed, with the exception of a wholesale commission of government bureaucrats, there were few portraits in the Bisson exhibit. Those that are illustrated in the catalogue are either small *cartes-de-visite* or daguerreotypes. Only one of the latter, called *Portrait of a Young Man, c. 1845,* and showing an elegantly dressed youth seated at a secretary which could be said to resemble the desk with bookshelves at which Chopin is posed, has a tenuous link to our portrait. In the case of the Chopin image, however, this particular piece of furniture is said to have belonged to Maurice Schlesinger and is cited as evidence that the photograph was taken in the publisher's apartment. This accounts for the dating of the photograph as 1846, by the present owners, The F. Chopin Society of Warsaw, since, in that year, Schlesinger sold his business and shortly thereafter retired to Baden-Baden, Germany. By that date, however, Chopin and his irascible publisher had already parted ways, socially and (except for existing contracts) professionally. More compelling evidence for a later dating, 1848–49, or following the composer's return from England, is the physical state of the sitter. Chopin's appearance exhibits all the symptoms of the edema characteristic of the final stages of his illness, along with an expression that suggests pain or extreme discomfort. Even if the Bissons kept such a desk as a studio prop, denoting the odd client as an artist or intellectual, it's unlikely that Chopin's condition would have accommodated a studio sitting. No evidence exists that they made "house calls." The behavior of the mysterious intruders at Chopin's death—their attempts to push his bed close to the window—illustrates another obstacle, along with cumbersome equipment, to a portable studio: namely, the problem of improvising adequate lighting. Thus, like the haunting portrait itself, the mystery of the photographer and the setting remain.

Notes and Sources

The source for Chopin's letters is the three-volume *Correspondance de Frédéric Chopin*, edited by Bronislaw Edouard Sydow, with the collaboration of Suzanne and Denise Chainaye, *La Revue Musicale* (Paris, 1981).

Quotations from Sand's letters are based upon the monumental edition of her *Correspondance*, edited by Georges Lubin, 25 volumes (Paris, 1964–85)— Lubin's life work. Not the least of its pleasures are the editor's notes, personal and penetrating in their analyses of people and events.

Unless otherwise indicated, translations from the French are by the author.

For the facts of Chopin's life, I have drawn on the three-volume biography by Gastone Belotti, *Chopin, l'uomo* (Milan, 1974), and on Adam Zamoyski's *Chopin* (New York, 1980), especially for the early years and for Count Zamoyski's translations of letters and other documents from the Polish.

For concert programs and reviews, I have relied upon William Atwood, *Fryderyk Chopin, Pianist from Warsaw* (New York, 1987).

PART I: *Departures*

ONE: *Lacrymosa dies illa:* "What weeping on that day"

3 For eyewitness accounts of Chopin's funeral and burial, see Hector Berlioz to his sister, October 29, 1849, *Correspondance*, edited by Pierre Citron, 3 vols. (Paris, 1978). Also see Hugh Macdonald, ed., *Selected Letters of Berlioz*, translated by Roger Nichols (New York, 1997), 265–66. See also the following for obituaries and accounts of the funeral.
Admission was by invitation: Theophile Gautier, *La Presse*, October 22, 1849.
"many of whom, perhaps": J. W. Davison, *The Musical World*, November 10, 1849.

6 Certain of the fashionable: *Journal des Débats*, October 27, 1849.
"utterly pretentious": Henri Blanchard, *Gazette Musicale de Paris*, November 4, 1849.

7 Although Viardot was a mezzo-soprano, her famous three-octave stretch placed most soprano roles well within her reach. She was also the star of the occasion; the soprano, Madame Castellan, being a minor singer, was

almost certainly relegated to the supporting contralto part whose "solo" is integrated with those of the quartet in the Requiem. My thanks to Mr. Ira Rosenstein for providing this information.

9 "The Great Sinner" was the title bestowed on Potocka by the poet Adam Mickiewicz.

TWO: First Meetings

11 "I can still recognize": Marliani to George Sand, October 18, 1849. Lubin, IX, 297.

17 "We heard wonderful music": George Sand, *Histoire de ma vie*, 4 vols. (Paris: Calmann-Lévy), vol. IV, 405.

THREE: A Genius in the Family

19 "worry and nerves": For the Chopin-Liszt duet, along with an even-handed discussion of the troubled relations between the two artists, I am indebted to Alan Walker's magisterial biography *Franz Liszt*, 3 vols. (New York, 1983, 1989, 1996), especially vol. I passim, together with the author's helpful replies to my questions.

20 The "few people" noted casually by Chopin constituted a cultural "tout Paris." Delacroix was among the other guests at this momentous soirée. Marquis Astolphe de Custine, aesthete, amateur, and one of the composer's greatest admirers, was under the impression that the entire evening had been arranged for him to meet the infamous George Sand. In a letter to Prince Klemens von Metternich, Custine enumerates the writer's many offenses against taste and comportment, principally her refusal to charm him. To the archconservative aristocrat, Sand's ascendancy signaled the decline of the West. More personally, the homosexual Custine already sensed the hold she would soon have over their host.

First published by Jean-René Derré, "Astolphe de Custine, correspon-dant de Metternich," in *Approches des lumières: Mélanges offerts à Jean Fabre* (Paris, 1974), 133–53, the letter is also the subject of a more recent article by Jeffrey Kallberg, "Chez Chopin: New Light on the Soirée of 13 December 1836," in *Muzyka w kontekscie kultury,* edited by Malgorzata Janicka-Slysz et al. (Krakow, 2001). Professor Kallberg kindly drew my attention to this letter, hitherto unknown to Chopin biographers.

23 No research has as yet produced a genealogy for Chopin's mother, Justyna, raising questions about whether she could have been an illegitimate child of Count Skarbek or of his father. She seems to have received less education than the usual employed poor relation who was also a gentlewoman, since instead of attaining the position of governess, she is vaguely described as a housekeeper until her marriage.

25 "my little Chopin": For the raptures of his first aristocratic patronesses, and the role of Professor Zwyny in Chopin's early musical education, see Zamoyski, 10.

FOUR: The Education of an Exile

30 "a true artist": Zamoyski, 46, and Atwood, 200–201.
For an excellent short history of Poland, see Zamoyski, *The Polish Way* (London, 1987; paperback, New York, 1994).

36 Garcia-Vestris is not to be confused with the renowned contralto, director, and theater manager Lucia Vestris.
Emanuel Ax, quoted in liner notes to Chopin: Piano Concerto No. 2 in F Minor, op. 21, performed by Ax with the Orchestra of the Age of Enlightenment, conducted by Sir Charles Mackerras, Sony Catalog #SK63371.

38 Quotations from Chopin's Stuttgart journal in Zamoyski, 88–89.

PART II: *Arrivals*

FIVE: The Capital of Desire

45 Fétis, *Revue Musicale* (Paris), March 3, 1832, in Atwood, 218.

46 Orlowski to his family, December 9, 1832, in F. Hoesick, *Chopin*, vol. II, 91, quoted by Zamoyski, 99.
For an invaluable chapter in the history of music, see Arthur Loesser, *Men, Women, and Pianos: A Social History* (New York, 1954), and James Parakilas, *Piano Roles: Three Hundred Years of Life with the Piano* (New Haven, 2000).

48 Orlowski, in Zamoyski, 113.

50 For recent discussions of Chopin's discovery of the bel canto aria and its relations to the nocturne, see Kornel Michalowski and Jim Samson, "Chopin," in *The New Grove Dictionary of Music* (London, 2001), 706–736; and Jeffrey Kallberg, "Voice and the Nocturne" in *Pianist, Scholar, Connoisseur*, edited by Bruce Brubaker and Jane Gottlieb (Stuyvesant, NY, 2000). Other sources include Jeffrey Kallberg, *Chopin at the Boundaries: Sex, History, and Musical Genre* (Cambridge, MA, 1996); Charles Rosen, *The Classical Style* (New York, 1971), and Jim Samson, *The Cambridge Companion to Chopin* (Cambridge, 1992).

51 expanded form of the Chopin nocturne: Kallberg, in *Chopin at the Boundaries*, 35.

52 "moral vampire": in Z. Markiewicz, *Spotkania Polsko-Francuskie*, quoted by Sydow, vol. II, 279.

55 "You have no idea . . .": Custine to Sophie Gay, October 11, 1838, quoted in Sydow, vol. II, 279.

55 The Sonata's probable date of composition is 1839. For a discussion of the evolution, dating, and reception of the March, see Kallberg, "Chopin's March, Chopin's Death" in *Nineteenth Century Music,* vol. 25, no. 1, summer 2001. Also, Lawrence Kramer, "Chopin at the Funeral: Episodes in the History of Modern Death," *Journal of the American Musicological Society,* 2001.

SIX: Preludes to Paradise

58 The portrait of Sand is now in the Ordrupgaard Museum, outside Copenhagen. The two halves of the canvas were briefly reunited in an exhibition at the Louvre, Paris, in 1998.

62 "Even when he felt well": *Histoire de ma vie,* 4 vols. (Paris, 1893), iv, 439–40.

63 "disturbing and disturbed": Edward Rothstein, *Emblems of Mind: The Inner Life of Music and Mathematics* (New York, 1995), 181.

"impossible objects": Lawrence Kramer, "Impossible Objects: Apparitions, Reclining Nudes, and Chopin's Prelude in A minor," in *Music as Cultural Practice, 1800–1900* (Berkeley and Los Angeles, 1990), 72–101.

"something close to physical terror": from Gide's *Notes on Chopin,* cited in the Norton Critical Score of the Preludes, op. 28, edited by Thomas Higgins (New York, 1973), 96.

64 For the preamble as recitative, see Samson, *The Four Ballades* (Cambridge, 1992), 10.

SEVEN: Homecoming

68 "Come and create": The summons was issued with Sand as intermediary. Marie d'Agoult to George Sand, in Lubin correspondence, vol. III, 807.

71 "Why couldn't Chopin . . . ?": Sand's lengthy description of this process is from *Histoire de ma vie* in *Oeuvres autobiographiques,* ed. G. Lubin, 2 vols. (Paris, 1971) ii, p. 446.

73 "sinister sonorities": from Charles Rosen's elegant analysis of Chopin and the grotesque in *The Romantic Generation,* 427 passim.

EIGHT: Labors of Love

80 "Time, along with the influence of genius": Marquis de Custine to Chopin, June 28, 1840, Sydow, vol. III, 25.

81 For *ange* (angel) as homosexual, see Graham Robb, *Rimbaud* (London, 2000), 65.

"know something about this intimate relationship": Nicolas Chopin to Frédéric, January 9, 1841, Sydow, vol. III, 37.

84 "the most elegant women": Franz Liszt, *Revue et Gazette Musicale,* Paris, May 2, 1841, in Atwood, 231.

85 "A malicious little clique": Marie d'Agoult to Henri Lehmann, April 21,

1841, in Arthur Hedley, *Selected Correspondence of Fryderyk Chopin* (1979), 93.

86 "Even before the concert began": Liszt, quoted in Atwood, 231.

NINE: Earthquakes and Harvests

95 Chopin was said to devote a full hour: Rosen, op cit., 462.

96 The illusion of spontaneity created by the impromptu form, "as though born under the fingers of the performer," in Alfred Cortot's phrase, evokes Chopin's improvisational genius. Quoted in Samson, *The Music of Chopin* (London, 1985), 98.

97 "the faint voices of fairies": *La France Musicale*, February 27, 1842, in Atwood, 239. For an illuminating analysis of how this perception of Chopin colored the reception of both the music and his performances, see Jeffrey Kallberg, "Small Fairy Voices: Sex, History and Meaning in Chopin," in *Chopin at the Boundaries*, 62–89.

"As soon as she appeared with her two charming daughters": "Escudier," *La France Musicale*, February 27, 1842.

TEN: Children of Paradise

102 "Please come on New Year's Day": Solange Dudevant to George Sand, n.d., no. 3, 65. This quote and the following are from Bernadette Chovelon, *George Sand et Solange: Mère et fille* (Saint-Cyr-sur-Loire, 1994). Sixty-eight letters from Solange as a child to her mother are published here for the first time, with a sensitive and even-handed commentary by the author. My thanks to Jeffery Kallberg for calling my attention to this work.

106 "no bed, two mattresses": Balzac to Madame Hanska, May 28, 1843. Balzac, *Lettres à Madame Hanska* (Paris, 1968), vol. II, 126.

108 "When the wind blows through her long blond hair": Marie d'Agoult, *Mémoires* (Paris, 1927), 82.

ELEVEN: Deaths Foretold

111 Delacroix's use of Sand's corseting material for his canvas is quoted by Maurice Serullaz in *Mémorial de l'exposition E. Delacroix* (Paris, 1963).

"God's presence descending": Delacroix to Sand, May 30, 1842, in André Joubin, ed., *Correspondance Générale d'Eugène Delacroix*, vol. II (Paris, 1936), 102.

"Of all those I've known": Delacroix to M. Pierret, June 22, 1842, in Joubin, 112.

112 My discussion of Chopin as a teacher is based upon the invaluable researches of Jean-Jacques Eigeldinger, *Chopin: Pianist and Teacher, As Seen by His Pupils* (Cambridge, 1986; paperback, 1988), 1–21 passim.

113 Sand's tantalizing allusion to Chopin's "blue note" has occasioned much musicological theorizing; see, for example, Eigeldinger, "Chopin and 'la note bleue': An Interpretation of the Prelude, Op. 45," in *Music and Letters*, vol. 78, issue 2 (May 1997).

114 crescendo hoof beats: Rosen, 288.

115 "I had always counted upon one friend": Fontana to his sister, early May 1842, in Zamoyski, 232.

116 For a fascinating history of this *quartier*, see *La Nouvelle Athenes*, Catalogue of an Exhibition at Le Musée de la Vie Romantique (Paris, 1984), 199, 129–131.

117 For Chopin's relationship with Filtsch, see Eigeldinger, *Chopin: Pianist and Teacher*, 66–67.

119 For a complete analysis of the ballades, see Jim Samson, *Chopin: The Four Ballades* (Cambridge, 1992), in particular 14, 62; and for the Fourth Ballade, Samson, *The Music of Chopin*, 187–192.

TWELVE: Forty Pounds of Jam

125 "prophetic harmonies," "premonitions" of the mature Wagner: Jeremy Siepmann, *Chopin, the Reluctant Romantic* (Boston, 1995), among others who have noted the connection.

126 Fanchette: Sand's account of the scandal first appeared in two installments of the *Revue Indépendante* (October 25 and November 25, 1843), followed by a pamphlet, of which no impression seems to have survived. It was then reprinted at the end of Sand's novel *Isadora* in 1846, and again in the same volume as her *Légendes rustiques*, 1877.

128 "there was a Jewess in the coach": This letter was owned by the late Georges Lubin, editor of Sand's *Correspondance*. It is not included in Sydow's three-volume edition of Chopin's *Correspondance*. Lubin, vol. VI, 259, note.

129 "You and Chopin are both little egoists": In Sydow, vol. III, 142–143.

131 "To my friend, Frédérick Chopin": The dedication appeared only in the original edition of the work, published by Desessart in May 1846.

THIRTEEN: A Victim of Time

133 "Who will open the nightingale's throat": Arthur Hedley, quoted in Siepmann, 180.

136 Sloper's and Hallé's recollections: in Charles Hallé, *Life and Letters*, edited by his sons (London, 1896), 36.

142 "prettier and cleverer": Recent Chopin biographers, including Belotti and Zamoyski, appear to accept as fact Titine's attributes over those of Solange in looks and intelligence. As the only visual documentation of Titine's appearance is found in the caricature of both girls, the basis for their judg-

ment is unclear, unless it is Sand's highly prejudiced view of her adopted relative as "perfect."

146 Barcarolle as a fifth ballade: Rosen, 323, while Arthur Hedley has called it "the finest of the nocturnes . . ." Hedley, quoted in Samson, *The Music of Chopin*, 96.

Later composers loved and borrowed more: Rosen, 88, and Siepmann, 162, 191. See also Roy Howat, "Chopin's Influence on the Fin de Siècle and Beyond," in Samson, ed., *The Cambridge Companion to Chopin* (Cambridge, 1992; paperback, 1994), 246–283. For Mahler's Adagio and that composer's memories of Venice, see L. de la Grange, *Mahler*, 4 vols., i, pp. 563–566 and Paolo Petazzi, liner notes to Chopin: 4 Scherzi, Berceuse, Barcarolle, performed by Maurizio Pollini, Deutsche Grammophon Catalog #431623-2.

FOURTEEN: *Lucrezia Floriani*

148 Nohant remained "in my heart and thoughts": Delacroix to Sand, August 10, 1846, *Correspondance*, 277.

150 "The absolute and continual possession": *Lucrezia Floriani* (Paris, 1846). This and the following quotations are from the translation by Julius Eker and Betsy Wing (Chicago, 1985), as modified by the author.

151–152 "The weariness of boredom" and following remarks by Delacroix on Sand's reading of *Lucrezia* were transcribed by his friend the writer Caroline Jaubert and published in her *Souvenirs* (Paris, 1885), 44ff.

153 "She has treated my friend Chopin outrageously": Heinrich Heine, letter to Henri Laube, October 12, 1850, quoted in Marie-Paule Rambeau, *Chopin dans la vie et l'oeuvre de George Sand* (Paris, 1985), 220.

"She has handed us a Chopin complete": Hortense Allart to Sainte-Beuve, May 16, 1847, ibid.

"vulgarity of confessions": Liszt to Caroline de Sayn-Wittgenstein, May 1847, ibid.

154 warm, teasing, charming: quotations and translation from Zofia Rosengardt's diary, in Zamoyski, 139–41.

155 "consumptive rage": Brenda Maddox in *D.H. Lawrence: The Story of a Marriage* (New York: 1994), 71, 226. Also in Claire Tomalin, *Katherine Mansfield: A Secret Life* (Harmondsworth, 1988), 141.

"acrimony" in the blood: This, the quotes from Keats's letters, and the quote from Foucault are in Hermion de Almeida, *Romantic Medicine and John Keats* (Oxford, 1991), 201–207.

FIFTEEN: Winter Journeys

158 His sketches for this work alone: see Samson, *The Music of Chopin*, 137–138.

158 "an undervalued masterpiece": Rosen, 466. Others have noted the failure of the sonata to engage audiences, musicians, or scholars.

159 a contemporary whose name Chopin never mentions: For a discussion of Chopin's "quotations" from Schubert's *Winterreise* in the cello sonata, and his omission of the opening movement at its first public performance, see Anatole Leikin, "The Sonatas," in Samson, *The Cambridge Companion to Chopin*, 185–187.

160 For the most sophisticated discussion of the Polonaise-Fantaisie, its gestation and compositional process, see Jeffrey Kallberg, "Chopin's Last Style," in Kallberg, *Chopin at the Boundaries*, 89–134.

161 "late works are the catastrophes": Theodor W. Adorno, "Moments Musicaux," in *Beethoven: The Philosophy of Music*, translated by Edmund Jephcott (Stanford, 1998), 126.

162 "sorrow for the hand that perished at its work": Pliny the Elder, quoted in David Rosand, "Editor's Statement," "Old-Age Style: Style and the Aging Artist," from a symposium sponsored by the Getty Center for the History of Art and the Humanities, published in *Art Journal*, vol. 46, no. 2 (summer 1987). Along with the elegant introduction by Professor Rosand, I have drawn upon Professor Julius S. Held's "Commentary" for a comparison of the aging artist's "last style" with attempts to account for the "cycle" of artists cut off in their prime or at the start of their careers.

169 "just as atrocious": Delacroix, *Journal*, July 20, 1847, 161.

SIXTEEN: The Expulsion from Paradise

171 "a luxury that surpasses imagination": Count Rodolphe Apponyi, quoted in Philip Mansel, *Paris Between Empires: 1814–1852* (London, 2001), 188.

174 "has no equal in our earthly realm": *Revue et Gazette Musicale* (Paris), February 20, 1848, quoted in Atwood, 244.
   "You have gained in suffering and poetry": Custine to Chopin, quoted in Zamoyski, 285.

175 "joint stock company": Mansel, 390.
   By the winter of 1846–47: ibid., 393.

SEVENTEEN: "The Abyss Called London"

183 "with the greatest energy": *Illustrated London News*, May 20, 1848, in Atwood, 245.
   "unrivalled by any executant": ibid.
   "more force and *brio*": *Athenaeum*, July 15, 1848, in Atwood, 249.

185 When a fellow musician and Polish exile: I owe this unpublished incident to a conversation with Count Adam Zamoyski.

186 "an almost painful air of feebleness": *Manchester Guardian*, August 30, 1848, in Atwood, 299.

186 "finesse and purity of tone": *Musical World* (London), September 9, 1848, in Atwood, 252.

"incomprehensible": *Herald* (Glasgow), September 29, 1848, in Atwood, 254.

187 "small grey person": Sir James Hedderwick, quoted in A. Bone, *Jane Wilhelmina Stirling* (London, 1960), 73–74.

EIGHTEEN: *Recordare*

192 "declining slowly": Pauline Viardot to Sand, in Zamoyski, 311.

193 The most recent scholarship: See Kallberg, "Chopin's Last Style," in *Chopin at the Boundaries*, 118–134, 218.

197 He claimed that she had invented the whole story: Gastone Belotti, Chopin's most exhaustive biographer, appears to accept the composer's view of Stirling's having staged the entire drama. This underhanded behavior, with its inevitable consequences of leaving Chopin in precarious straits for months, seems entirely out of character for the straightforward Scotswoman.

Selected Bibliography

Abraham, Gerald. *Chopin's Musical Style.* Oxford: Oxford Press, 1939. Reprinted by Greenwood Press, Westport, Conn., 1980.

Agulhon, Maurice. *Les Quarante-huitards.* Paris: Gallimard/Juilliard "Archives," 1976.

Atwood, William. *Fryderyk Chopin, Pianist from Warsaw.* New York: Columbia University Press, 1987.

Belotti, Gastone. *Chopin, l'uomo.* Milan: Edizione Sapere, 1974.

Cairns, David. *Berlioz: The Making of an Artist.* Vol. I. London: Andre Deutsch, 1989.

———. *Berlioz: Servitude and Greatness.* Vol. II. London: Penguin/Allen Lane, 1999.

Cate, Curtis. *George Sand.* Boston: Houghton Mifflin, 1975.

Chovelon, Bernadette. *George Sand et Solange: Mère et fille.* Saint-Cyr-sur-Loire: Christian Pirot, 1994.

Cone, Edward T. *The Composer's Voice.* Berkeley: University of California Press, 1974.

Delacroix, Eugene. *Correspondance Générale.* Edited by André Joubin. 5 vols. Paris: Librairie Plon, 1936–45.

———. *Journal, 1822–1863.* Preface by H. Damisch. Introduction and notes by André Joubin. Paris: Editions Plon, 1996.

Delaigue-Moins, Sylvie. *Chopin Chez George Sand à Nohant.* Chateauroux: Les Amis du Nohant, 1986.

Eigeldinger, Jean-Jacques. *Chopin: Pianist and Teacher, As Seen by His Pupils.* Cambridge: Cambridge University Press, 1986. Originally published in French as *Chopin vu par ses élèves.* Neuchâtel: Editions de la Baconnière, 1970–79.

Gide, André. *Notes sur Chopin.* Paris: L'Arche, 1948.

Jack, Belinda. *George Sand.* New York: Alfred A. Knopf, Inc., 2000.

Kallberg, Jeffrey. *Chopin at the Boundaries: Sex, History and Musical Genre.* Cambridge, MA: Harvard University Press, 1996. Paperback, 1998.

Luppé, Marquis de. *Astolphe de Custine.* Monaco, 1957.

Mansel, Philip. *Paris Between Empires: 1814–1852.* London: John Murray, 2001.

Michalowsky, Kornel, and Jim Samson. "Chopin." *The New Grove Dictionary of Music,* vol. II. London: Macmillan, 2001.

Muhlstein, Anka. *A Taste for Freedom: The Life of Astolphe de Custine*. Translated by Teresa Waugh. New York: Helen Marx Books, 1996.

Rambeau, Marie-Paule. *Chopin dans la vie et l'oeuvre de George Sand*. Paris: Société d'Edition Les Belles Lettres, 1985.

Rosen, Charles. *The Classical Style*. New York: Viking Press, 1971.

————. *The Romantic Generation*. Cambridge, MA: Harvard University Press, 1992. Paperback, 1994.

Samson, Jim, ed. *The Cambridge Companion to Chopin*. Cambridge: Cambridge University Press, 1992. Paperback, 1994.

————. *The Four Ballades*. Cambridge: Cambridge University Press, 1992. Paperback, 1996.

————. *The Music of Chopin*. London: Routledge & Kegan Paul, 1985.

Sand, George. *Correspondance*. Edited by Georges Lubin. 25 vols. Paris: Editions Garnier, 1964–85.

————. *Histoire de ma vie*. 4 vols. Paris: Calmann-Lévy, 1884–1916.

————. *Impressions et Souvenirs*. 3rd edition. Paris: Michel Lévy Frères, 1873.

————. *Lucrezia Floriani*. Paris: Calmann-Lévy, 1880. American translation by Julius Eker. Chicago: Academy Chicago Publishers, 1985.

Siepmann, Jeremy. *Chopin: The Reluctant Romantic*. Boston: Northeastern University Press, 1995.

Walker, Alan, ed. *Chopin: Profiles of the Man and the Musician*. New York: Taplinger Publishing Co., 1967.

————. *Franz Liszt*. 3 vols. New York: Knopf, 1983–1996.

Zamoyski, Adam. *Chopin*. New York: Doubleday and Co., 1980.

————. *The Polish Way*. London: John Murray, 1987.

Acknowledgments

The first work of Chopin scholarship that I encountered was Jeffrey Kallberg's collection of articles, gathered under the title *Chopin at the Boundaries*. I've continued to be inspired by his writing and touched by his collegial generosity. Thanks are due other Chopinistes, biographers, and scholars of nineteenth-century music and culture whose texts and conversation have provided both pleasure and profit, among them William Atwood, my friend Frederick Brown, Louis de la Grange, Alan Walker, and Count Adam Zamoyski.

I'm grateful for help from Gordon Baldwin, Anka Muhlstein Begley, Magda Dabrowska, Maria Dzieduszycka, Marzena Szczeniowski, Michael Dellaira, Celia and Henry Eisenberg, Paul Elledge, Francine Goldenhar, Clare Hills-Nova, Robert Kashey, Liliana Leopardi, Beatrice de Plinval, Steven Rattazzi, Harriet Shapiro, Albert Sonnenfeld, Nicholas Fox Weber, and Brenda Wineapple.

I can pay tribute, for the second time, to the taste and talents of my publisher and my editor, Sonny Mehta and Jordan Pavlin, and for the first time, to the artistry of Peter Mendelsund, to the knowledge of Patrick Dillon, and to the care of Sophie Fels.

After more years and favors than I would dare to count, my thanks yet again to Mark Piel, librarian, and to the staff of the New York Society Library. Lisa Le Fevre took on final chores with efficiency and goodwill.

Here and abroad, I've been doubly fortunate in friends who happen also to be my agents: Gloria Loomis, Mary Kling, and Abner Stein.

Colin Eisler was forbearing in the face of domestic tune-outs. I hope these were compensated by the music we heard together, accompanied always by my gratitude and love.

Index

Page numbers in *italics* refer to illustrations.

Adorno, Theodor, 161
Alard, Jean-Delphin, 173 and *n*.
Albert, of Saxe-Coburg-Gotha, prince consort, 181
Albrecht, Thomas, 197–8
Alexander I, Czar of Russia, 31
"Alexis" (clairvoyant), 196
Alkan, Valentin, 116, 191, 201
Allart, Hortense, 153
Arago, Emanuel, 157
Archbishop of Paris, 7, 80
art, 4, 26, 91, 113, 162, 164, 165–6; romanticism, 50–1
Atheneum, 183
Ax, Emanuel, 36

Bach, Johann Sebastian, 4, 24, 61; *Well-Tempered Clavier*, 61
bagpipes, 125
ballade(s), 64, 162; Fourth, 119; Second, in F major, 84, 183; Third, in A-flat, 90, 95, 96
Balzac, Honoré de, 15, 106, 203
Barcarolle, 63, 146, 173
Barcelona, 65
Barcinski, Antoni, 131
Baudelaire, Charles Pierre, 50, 62; *Poèmes nocturnes*, 50
Beauvau, Princess de, 195
Beethoven, Ludwig van, 4, 22, 31, 132, 148, 158; Chopin's early doubts about, 4, 24; late work of, 161–2
Belhaven, Lady, 187
Bellini, Vincenzo, 50, 132

Benjamin, Walter, 50
Berceuse in D-flat Major, 133, 146, 173, 183
Berlin, 29
Berlioz, Hector, 3, 4, 15, 162, 177
Berry, 12, 16, 18, 68, 69, 99, 145, 147, 175
Bibliothèque Nationale, 126
Bisson, Louis-Auguste, 205
Blanc, Louis, 129, 136, 138, 177
Bocage, Pierre, 123, 129
Bourbon Restoration, 4
Bourges, 99
Bourges, Michel de, 123
Brahms, Johannes, 158, 163, 186; F-sharp Minor Sonata, 146
Brault, Adèle Philbert, 143
Brault, Joseph, 143, 145
Brault, Titine (Augustine Marie), 98, 137, 142–5, 148, 163–4, 167–8 and *n*., 202; "adopted" by Sand, 143–5
Brawne, Fanny, 156
Brzezina's music store (Warsaw), 30
Bulletin de la République, 177
Buloz, François, 75, 79, 94, 126–7
Byron, George Gordon, 79

Caillaud, Françoise, 111, 124
Caillaud, Luce, 107, 111, 124
canon, 119
Carlism, 48
Carlos, Don, 48
Carlyle, Jane, 183
Carlyle, Thomas, 187*n*.

Catalani, Angelica, 22

Catlin, George, 138

Cavaignac, Godefroi, 138

cello, 7, 158–9, 173, 174

Chaillot, 13, 194–7

chamber orchestra, 32, 159

Chantilly, 20

Charles X, King of France, 37

Châteauroux, 90, 111, 121, 148

Chatiron, Hippolyte, 68, 72, 131, 147

cholera, 13, 37, 44, 46, 194

Chopin, Emilia, 25, 27–8

Chopin, Frédéric: apartments and
    furnishings of, 12–13, 19–20, 43,
    76–7, 94–5, 105–6, 115–16, 172,
    194–5, 197–8; approaching death,
    6, 189–200; arrival in Paris, 4, 39,
    43; autopsy on, 201; birth of, 23;
    childhood of, 22–8, 69; as child
    prodigy, 22–8; clothing and gloves,
    25, 28, 48, 51, 56, 76, 89, 135, 196;
    "consumptive rage" of, 155–6;
    critics on, 25, 30, 33, 45, 86–7, 97,
    183, 186, 193; dandyism, 5, 25, 51,
    56, 135, 203; death of, 6–14, 94 and
    n., 200–201; death of his father,
    129–31; death mask of, 9, 199;
    declining musical productivity,
    119, 136, 158, 160, 163, 172, 186;
    Delacroix and, 25, 56–8, 78, 84, 96,
    106, 111–14, 135, 138, 148, 151–2,
    169, 188, 192, 194; Delacroix
    portrait of, ii, 5, 56, 57, 58; deterio-
    rating relationship with Sand, 93,
    119, 122–46, 147–55, 157, 163–72;
    early relationship with Sand, 52–5,
    56–67, 68–88, 104; education of,
    23–8; exile from Poland, 5–6, 27,
    38–9, 43–4, 49–51, 105, 114, 130–1,
    200, 203; finances of, 19, 27, 37,
    44–5 and n., 48, 60–1, 66, 78–9, 89,
    95, 114, 135, 172, 182–4, 194, 196–7;
    fingering style, 5, 33, 112; first
    published work, 24–5, 28; funeral

of, 3–4, 6–10, 55n.; genius of, 21–2,
    30, 45, 49, 72, 86–7, 111–12, 119–20,
    193–4, 200–201, 203; homesickness
    for Poland, 44, 48, 114, 130;
    homosexuality and, 80–1; inven-
    tiveness of, 5, 28, 30, 32, 37, 45–6,
    50–1, 62–4, 74, 86, 97, 112, 119–20,
    125, 132, 161–3, 187, 193–4; lan-
    guage, 27; last meeting with Sand,
    177–8; late work of, 158–62, 193;
    Liszt's rivalrous friendship with, 4,
    15, 20–2, 82–7, 97, 117, 130, 163; in
    London, 53–4, 180–9; in Majorca,
    13–14, 55, 58–65, 71, 72, 97, 104–5;
    as mature composer, 37, 80, 90;
    meets Sand, 17–18, 52; mood
    swings of, 154–6; musical influ-
    ences on, 4, 24, 50, 61, 159–60;
    musical style and piano technique
    of, 5–6, 21, 24, 28, 32–7, 45–6,
    49–51, 61–5, 71, 74, 85–7, 97, 112,
    118–20, 125, 132, 133, 146, 158–63,
    174, 183, 186, 193; myths, 3–4, 25;
    at Nohant, 68–78, 89–97, 107–9,
    111–15, 121–8, 131–3, 140–8, 156,
    157, 171, 174; paternal role of, 81,
    104–5, 107–9, 117–18, 121–2, 128,
    131–2, 141–5, 165–72, 177–8, 194;
    personality of, 22, 26–7, 52, 60,
    80–1, 93, 105, 115, 148, 154–5;
    photograph of, 190, 191, 205;
    physical appearance of, 5, 21, 25,
    56, 81, 121, 190–1; plaster busts of,
    91, 92; Polish émigré society and,
    6, 7, 20, 27, 43–51, 114, 131, 134,
    137, 178, 186; Polish roots, 23–39,
    48–9, 85, 114, 201; political views
    of, 4, 31, 48–9, 127, 140, 185;
    posthumous published work of,
    193, 201; public debut in Poland,
    24–5, 32; publishers of, 29, 34, 35,
    47, 60–1, 66, 75, 78, 95, 115, 119,
    135, 160, 193, 201; respiratory
    problems and deteriorating health,

13–14, 35, 38, 54, 55, 58–66, 70, 73, 93, 105, 110, 116, 118, 121, 129, 133, 136, 147–8, 155–6, 163, 176, 186–92, 194–201; salons, 32–3, 34, 164, 200; Sand as caretaker of, 14, 58–9, 65–7, 69, 71–4, 81, 84, 87, 95, 105, 116, 124, 131, 148, 201; separation from Sand, 13–14, 169–72, 174, 177–8, 188–9, 192; sexuality of, 52–5, 72–3, 80–1, 92, 124, 150; social views of, 4–5, 48, 127, 143–4, 155, 182; Stuttgart journals of, 38, 140; success and celebrity of, 19–22, 43–8, 83–7, 112, 173, 203; as a teacher, 12, 45 and *n.*, 61, 78, 95, 112–13, 116–18, 134–7, 154–5, 163, 182, 184, 192; Titine affair, 143–5; in Vienna, 29–30, 34–7; views on painting, 4, 113; Maria Wodzinska and, 53–4, 82 and *n.*, 91, 92; *see also* concerts and performances; *specific musical works and forms*

Chopin, Justyna, 23–8, 30, 38, 48, 53, 130 and *n.*, 139

Chopin, Nicolas, 22–8, 30, 37, 38, 44–5, 53, 81; death of, 129–31, 139

chromatics, 63, 119, 193

Church of the Holy Cross (Warsaw), 201

Church of the Madeleine, Chopin's funeral in, 3, 6–8

Cinti-Damoreau, Laure, 84, 87

Clark, Sir James, 188

classicism, 64, 162

clavichord, 47

Clésinger, Jean-Baptiste Auguste, 9, 164–70; death of, 166*n.;* death mask of Chopin by, 9, *199;* marriage to Solange Dudevant, 164–70, 177–8, 194; *Woman Stung by a Serpent,* 165–6 and *n.*

Clésinger, Jeanne-Gabrielle, 177, 178, 194

Clésinger, Jeanne-Gabrielle (Nini), 194, 201, 202

Clésinger, Solange Dudevant, 9, 11, 16, 59, 70, 77, 81, 92, 93, 97–8, 99–109, 116, 137, 142, 157, 163–4, 176; childhood of, 99–109; Chopin and, 81, 104–5, 107–9, 128, 131–2, 143–5, 165–72, 177–8, 192, 194, 200; marriage to Clésinger, 164–70, 177–8, 194; relationship with her mother, 100–109, 129, 131–2, 142–4, 164–70, 177–8, 201–2; Titine affair, 142–4, 168 and *n.*

Combes, Edmond de, 177–8

concerto(s): in E Minor (no. 1), 33–4, 36, 37, 46, 47, 117–18; in F Minor, 31, 32–3, 45

concerts and performances, 7, 19–22, 200–201; in Britain, 181–8; familial surroundings and chosen audiences, 33, 83, 116–17, 164, 173; with Filtsch, 116–18; with Liszt, 20–2; in Munich, 37; in Paris, 21, 45–6, 55, 80, 83–8, 96–7, 116–18, 172–4; public debut in Poland, 24–5, 32; for royalty, 19, 96, 181; in Vienna, 29–30, 36; in Warsaw, 24–5, 32–4

Congress Kingdom, 31, 38

Congress of Vienna, 30

"consumptive rage," 155–6

counterpoint, 119, 162

Cracow (suburb of Warsaw), 23

Crumpsall House (Manchester), 185

Cruveiller, Dr. Jean, 196, 197, 198, 201

Cullen, William, Dr., 155

Custine, Marquis Astolphe de, 20, 55, 80, 90, 173, 174

Czartoryska, Princess Anna, 24, 44

Czartoryska, Princess Marcelina, 9, 24, 25, 137, 164, 173, 186, 188, 191, 195, 196, 198

Czartoryski, Prince Adam, 7, 24, 31, 44, 51, 164, 173, 186, 191

Czartoryski, Prince Aleksander, 7, 137
Czartoryski family, 44, 114, 137
Czerny exercises, 112
Czosnowska, Countess Laure, 144, 148

d'Agoult, Countess Marie Catherine
    Sophie de Flavigny, 15–18, 20, 21,
    22, 68, 74, 85–7, 153; *Nélida*, 153–4
dandyism, 5, 25, 51, 56, 135, 203
Daniel (valet), 195
Dantan, Jean-Pierre, 91
Dante, 113 and *n.; Inferno*, 64
Debussy, Claude, 163; *L'Isle joyeuse*,
    146
Delacroix, Eugène, 4, 7, 79, 111–14,
    137, 141, 164, 165, 167, 173; Chopin
    and, 25, 56–8, 78, 84, 96, 109,
    111–14, 135, 138, 148, 151–2, 169,
    188, 192, 194; color sense of, 113;
    The Education of the Virgin, 111;
    Journals, 113; Luxembourg Palace
    commission, 113 and *n.;* at Nohant,
    111–14, 122–3, 148–9; portrait of
    Chopin, *ii*, 5, 56, *57*, 58; portrait of
    Sand, 56, *57*, 58
de la Moskova, Prince, 46
Denmark, 59
Dietrichstein, Count, 30, 35
Dorval, Marie, 79
Dresden, 53, 91
Dudevant, Aurore, 202
Dudevant, Aurore Dupin, *see* Sand,
    George
Dudevant, Baron Casimir, 16, 79, 81,
    99–100, 102, 122, 165, 202
Dudevant, Maurice, 16, 54, 59, 70, 77,
    79, 81, 99, 116, 165, 167, 202; as
    apprentice to Delacroix, 122–3,
    141; childhood of, 99–105; Chopin
    and, 81, 104–5, 117, 122, 124, 128–9,
    141–2; as gentleman landowner,
    140–2, 147, 202; relationship with

his mother, 100, 101, 103, 107, 122,
    128–9 and *n.*, 140–2, 145; Titine
    affair, 142–5, 168 and *n.*
Dudevant, Solange, *see* Clésinger,
    Solange Dudevant
Dumas, Alexandre, *père*, 75
Dupin, Marie-Aurore, 68, 69, 141
Dupont, Alexis, 80

earthquake, 90, 91
Eclaireur de l'Indre, L', 126–7
Edinburgh, 184, 186, 187
Elsner, Jozef, 28
England, 13, 50, 176, 177, 178–9;
    Chopin in, 53–4, 180–9
Enlightenment, 26
Erard pianos, 47, 90, 182
Ernst, Heinrich, 84, 87
Erskine, Mrs. (Jane Stirling's sister),
    195
Esterhazy family, 22
etude(s), 21–2, 31, 36–7, 173;
    Chopin's reinvention of, 21–2,
    36–7, 51; opus 10, 22, 37, 46, 47

Falmouth, Lord, 183
Fanchette affair, 126–7
Fantaisie-Impromptu, 97 and *n.*
Fantaisie in A-flat Major, 160
Fantaisie in F Minor, 90
Fantasia on Polish Airs, 34, 37, 160
Feodorovna, Maria, 22
Ferrières, 171
Fétis, François-Joseph, 45
feudalism, 127
Field, John, 50
Filtsch, Karl, 116–18; death of, 118
Flaubert, Gustave, 72
folk songs, 28, 30, 51, 91, 124, 125
Fontana, Julian, 61, 66, 75–7, 89, 90,
    91, 92, 94, 97, 114–15, 135, 178, 193;
    musical career of, 114–15

Foucault, Michel, 156
France, 4, 23, 34, 43; abdication of
    Louis Philippe, 176; July Monar-
    chy, 4, 9, 43, 47, 140, 175–6;
    revolution, 4, 13, 23, 175–8; Second
    Republic, 177, 178, 184–5, 192
France Musicale, La, 97
Franchomme, Auguste, 7, 96, 130,
    134, 135, 136, 158, 173, 174, 185, 190,
    193, 196, 198
Franck, César, 158–9
French Academy, 138

Galeries Lafayette, 19n.
García, Manuel, 142–3 and n.
Gascony, 79, 99, 102, 122
Gavard, Charles, 198
Geneva, 16, 175
Germany, 15, 29, 37–8, 61, 186
Gide, André, 63
Gladowska, Konstancja, 29, 34, 38,
    49
Glasgow, 186, 187
Gluck, Christoph, 91
Goethe, Johann Wolfgang von, 65
Goya, Francisco de, 162
Grabowski, Count, 38
Grand Duo Concertant, 158
Grande Polonaise Brillante, 36
Gransagne, Stêphane Ajasson de, 99
Grisi, Giuditta, 96
Grisi, Giulia, 117
Grzymala, Count Albert, 20, 52,
    54–5, 66, 69, 74, 76, 77, 144, 163,
    164, 167, 173, 188, 189, 190,
    191–2
Guildhall (London), 188
Guizot, François, 175, 176, 180
Gutmann, Adolf, 8, 115, 198

Hallé, Charles, 136
Hamilton, Duchess of, 187

Handel, George Frederick, 91
Hapsburg Empire, 35
harpsichord, 26, 46
Haslinger (publisher and music store
    owner), 29, 34, 35
Haussmann, Georges-Eugène, 102n.
Haydn, Joseph, 4, 24, 91, 158; Cre-
    ation, 138
Heine, Heinrich, 15, 20, 153
Hiller, Ferdinand, 21, 27
homosexuality, 20, 80–1
Hôtel de France, 16–17
Hôtel de Ville, 177, 201
Hôtel Lambert, 137
Houbigant-Chardin, 89
Hugo, Victor, 4, 15, 138, 140
Hummel, Johann Nepomuk, 34
Hungary, 22

impressionism, 119
impromptu(s), 96–7, 183; Chopin's
    reinvention of, 97; Fantaisie-
    Impromptu, 97 and n.; No. 1 in
    A-flat Major, 97
improvisation, 24, 32, 96–7, 161
influenza, 129
Ingres, Jean Auguste Dominique, 4
Italy, 15, 29, 34, 37, 50, 66, 145–6

Jan (manservant), 141
Jedrzejewicz, Józef Kalasanty, 8, 131,
    196, 197
Jedrzejewicz, Ludwika, 8, 14, 23, 82,
    121, 131, 137, 139–40, 142, 145, 158,
    166, 174, 196–8, 201
Jedrzejewicz, Ludwika (Louisette), 8,
    9, 196, 198
Jelowicki, Father Aleksander, 198
Jews, 5, 61, 66, 128, 186
Johnstone Castle, 186
July Monarchy, 4, 9, 43, 47, 140; fall
    of, 175–8

Kalkbrenner, Christian, 45, 46, 112, 116

Kallberg, Jeffrey, 63

Karlsbad, 53

Kärntnertor Theatre, 29, 35

Keats, John, 65, 155–6, 188

Keir Castle, 186

Kumelski, Norbert, 37

Lablache, Luigi, 80, 117, 160, 181

La Châtre, 168

Lamartine, Alphonse de, 177

"late style," 162, 193

Lawrence, D. H., 65

Léo, Auguste, 60, 135, 172, 186

Lind, Jenny, 181, 185, 195

Liszt, Franz, 4, 15, 19, 20, 43, 45, 47, 48, 69, 112, 161, 178; celebrity of, 21, 22, 82; as childhood prodigy, 22; Marie d'Agoult and, 15, 16, 18, 21, 22, 68, 85–7, 153; musical soliloquies, 82; Paris one-man recitals, 82–3, 84; rivalrous friendship with Chopin, 4, 15, 20–2, 82–7, 97, 117, 130, 163

London, 50, 82, 177, 194; Belgravia, 183; Bentinck Street, 180; Cavendish Square, 180; Chopin in, 53–4, 180–9; Dover Street, 182; Eaton Place, 183; St. James's Place, 181, 188; society, 181–3

London Philharmonic Society, 182

London *Times*, 3

Louis (manservant), 93–4

Louis XIV, King of France, 4

Louis Philippe, King of France, 4, 19, 96, 140, 180; abdication, 176; corrupt regime of, 175–6

Louvre, 59, 192

Luxembourg Palace, Delacroix's commission for, 113 and *n*.

Lycée Henri IV (Paris), 101

Lyszczynski, Dr., 186–7

Maberley, Catherine, 125

Mahler, Gustav, Tenth Symphony, 146

Maison Dorée café, 55

Majorca, 13; Chopin and Sand in, 13–14, 55, 58–65, 71, 72, 75, 97, 104–5

Mallefille, Félicien, 54–5, 104

Manchester, 185–6

Marcello, Benedetto Giacomo, 198

Marie Amelie, Queen of France, 96

Marienbad, 53

Mario, Giovanni Matteo, 181, 183

Marliani, Countess Charlotte, 11–14, 66, 76, 116, 124, 137–8, 169, 177

Marliani, Emmanuel, 13, 65, 116, 124

Marseilles, 14, 65–6

Matuszynski, Jan, 20, 35, 94; death of, 110, 114, 118, 138

Mazovia, 69

mazurka(s), 6, 28, 34, 46, 51, 73, 91, 94, 161, 163, 181, 183; Chopin's reinvention of, 73; in F Minor (op. 63, no. 2), 193; in F Minor (op. 68, no. 4), 193; opus 41, 73, 84; opus 56, 125; opus 59, 135, 136

Mendelssohn, Felix, 37–8, 45, 179

Merchants' Resource Hall, Warsaw, 32

Mérimée, Prosper, 123

Metternich, Count, 26, 35

Meyerbeer, Giacomo, 7, 15, 29, 49; *Le Prophète*, 192–3; *Robert le diable*, 49, 82, 158, 193

Mickiewicz, Adam, 52, 86, 134; *Forefathers*, 51; *Pan Tadeusz*, 51

Molin, Dr., 116, 129, 130, 192

Montgivray, 68, 202

Montmartre Cemetery, 138

morphine, 116

Moscheles, Ignaz, 20, 161

Mozart, Wolfgang Amadeus, 4, 22, 24, 30, 91, 111, 158, 173 and *n*., Chopin's variations on, 29, 30, 45; *Don Giovanni*, 29, 30, 91; Requiem, 6, 7, 80, 138; Variations in G, 181

Munich, 37
Musset, Alfred de, 96, 101, 123, 152

Napoleon Bonaparte, 17, 26, 79–80, 197
Native Americans, 138–9
neoclassicism, 4
Nicholas I, Czar of Russia, 31, 130
nocturne(s), 50–1, 96, 119, 161, 173, 183; in B-flat Minor, 50; Chopin's reinvention of, 50–1; in C Minor, 95–6; in E-flat Major, 125; in F Minor, 125; no. 11 in G Minor, 71; no. 12 in G Major, 71; opus 48, 90, 95–6
Nohant, 11, 13, 14, 16, 21, 68–9, 99, 102, 104, 163, 166, 167–8, 174, 183, 202; Delacroix at, 111–14; managed by Maurice Dudevant, 140–2, 147, 202; Sand and Chopin at, 68–78, 89–97, 107–9, 111–15, 121–33, 140–8, 156, 157
Nourrit, Adolphe, 18, 66, 160

Obreskoff, Princess, 194, 196
O-kee-wee-mee, 138 and n., 139
opera, 7, 29, 36, 49–50, 82, 91, 114, 192
opus 7, 73
opus 10, 22, 37, 46, 47
opus 11, 46
opus 18, 36
opus 22, 36
opus 24, 73
opus 25, 22
opus 28, 60, 61–3, 95, 159
opus 29, 97
opus 30, 73
opus 31, 183
opus 35, 55, 70
opus 37, 71
opus 38, 84

opus 40, 85
opus 41, 73–84
opus 44, 90, 94
opus 45, 90, 91
opus 48, 90, 95–6
opus 49, 90
opus 51, 97
opus 53, 114, 119
opus 55, 125
opus 56, 125
opus 58, 132, 158–9
opus 59, 135, 136
opus 60, 63, 146, 173
opus 61, 158, 160–3, 172, 193
opus 63, 193
opus 65, 158–9, 164, 172–4, 199
opus 68, 193
orchestra, 18, 36, 132
Orléans, 4, 80
Orléans, Duke d', 96
Orlowski, Antoni, 45, 47–8

Paër, Ferdinando, 43
Paganini, Niccolò, 29
Palma de Mallorca, 59, 61, 65, 66, 71
Papet, Gustave, 8, 70
Paris, 3, 14, 19 and n., 34, 37, 50, 101; avenue de la Poissonière, 43; Chopin's apartments and furnishings in, 12–13, 19–20, 43, 76–7, 94–5, 105–6, 115–16, 172, 194–5, 197–8; Chopin's arrival in, 4, 39, 43; Chopin's concerts in, 21, 45–6, 55, 80, 83–8, 96–7, 116–18, 172–4; Chopin's funeral in, 3–4, 6–10; Commune, 166n., 201; fall of July Monarchy, 175–8; Faubourg Saint-Germain, 15; Faubourg du Roule (later Faubourg Saint-Honoré), 44; Galeries Royales, 89; place Vendôme, 197; Polish émigrés in, 6, 7, 20, 27, 43–52, 114, 131, 134, 137, 178; revolution, 175–8;

Paris *(continued)*, rue de la Chaussée d'Antin, 19; rue Fosse-du-Ramparts, 176; rue Lafitte, 15, 117; rue Pigalle, 77, 95, 105, 106, 115, 117, 127; rue Saint-Lazare, 12; rue Tronchet, 76, 84, 94; Second Republic, 177, 178, 184–5, 192; society and parties, 15, 17, 20, 43–4, 74, 84

Paris Conservatory, 7, 46, 142

Pavillon de Marsan, 96

Pavlovich, Grand Duke Konstantin, 24, 35

Perdiguier, Agricole, 127

Père Lachaise Cemetery, 9

Perthuis, Count de, 177

piano, 7, 33, 36, 62–3, 158; ballade, 65; Chopin's technique on, 5–6, 21, 24, 28, 32–4, 45–6, 49–51, 61–5, 71, 74, 85–7, 97, 112, 118–20, 125, 132, 133, 146, 158–63, 174, 183, 186, 193; impromptus, 96–7; manufacturers, 7, 47, 53, 57, 61, 66, 84, 89–90, 112, 182; popularity of, 46 and *n.*, 47; *see also specific works by Chopin*

Piano Concerto in E Minor, 33–4, 36, 37, 46, 47, 117–18

pianoforte, 26, 33, 46–7, 49

Pius IX, Pope, 185

Plater family, 44

Pleyel, Camille, 7, 46, 53, 60, 66, 87, 172, 173, 174

Pleyel, Marie, 87

Pleyel pianos, 7, 47, 53, 57, 61, 66, 69, 84–5, 89–90, 112, 182, 198

Pliny the Elder, 162

poetry, 52; troubadour, 65

Poland, 4, 5, 18, 23–39, 81–2, 85, 201; Chopin's exile from, 5–6, 27, 38–9, 43–4, 49–51, 105, 114, 130–1, 200, 203; Chopin's public debut in, 24–5, 32; Chopin's youth in, 23–39, 69; culture, 26–7, 28, 30, 51; diaspora, 6, 7, 20, 27, 43–52, 114, 131, 134, 137, 178, 186; politics, 30–3, 35, 38, 49, 178; Russian rule, 31, 32, 33, 35, 38–9, 130

polonaise, 36, 161; in A-flat Major, 114, 119; -Fantaisie in A-flat Major, 158, 160–3, 172, 193; first, 24–5, 28; in F-sharp Minor, 90, 94; Grande Polonaise Brillante, 36; "Military," 85; for Piano-Forte, 24, 25

polyphony, 162

Potocka, Delfina, 9, 49, 164, 173, 192, 195, 198–9

Potocki, Count, 24

Potocki family, 44

Poznan, 178

Préault, Auguste, 138

Preaux, Fernand de, 142, 157, 164

prelude(s), 61, 62–4, 87, 95, 159; in A Minor, 63; in B Minor, 7; in C-sharp Minor, 90, 91; in E-flat minor, 63; in E Minor, 7

press, on Chopin, 25, 30, 33, 45, 86–7, 97, 183, 186, 193, 200

Proust, Marcel, 159

Prussia, 26

publishers, music, 29, 34, 35, 47, 60–1, 66, 75, 78, 95, 115, 119, 135, 160, 193, 201

Rachmaninoff, Sergei, 163

Raciborski, Dr., 110

Radziwill family, 24, 25, 44, 137

Rameau, Jean-Philppe, 28

Ravallo, 65

Ravel, Maurice, 146, 163

Reforme, La, 136

religion, 48, 49, 198

Rembrandt van Rijn, 162

Revue des Deux Mondes, 75, 127

Revue et Gazette Musicale, 86

Revue Indépendante, La, 127, 136

romanticism, 3–4, 50–1, 63, 73, 79, 96, 113, 120; exiles, 50–1

Rome, 65, 82, 146, 156, 185
rondo, 119
Rosen, Charles, 73
Rosengardt, Zofia, 154, 155
Rossini, Gioacchino Antonio, 15, 90
Rothschild, Lady, 181, 182
Rothschild, Baroness Betty de, 117, 164, 171, 181, 192, 195
Rothschild, Baron James de, 15, 51, 117, 164, 171, 177
Rousseau, Jean-Jacques, 101
Rousseau, Théodore, 167, 168n., 202
Rozierès, Marie de, 92–4, 124, 131, 135, 156, 190
Russia, 23, 24, 26, 194; Poland ruled by, 31, 32, 33, 35, 38–9, 130

Saint-Cloud, castle of, 19
Saint-Germain-en-Laye, 195
Saint-Gratien, 20, 55
Saint Helena, 79
Sainte-Beuve, Charles-Augustin, 15, 153
Salle Pleyel, 84–7, 96
Salon des Artistes Français, 165–6
Sand, George, 4, 9, 15–18, 20, 52; celebrity of, 16, 17, 74, 97, 99; Chopin's death and, 10, 11–14; Consuelo, 126; Cosima, or Hatred at the Heart of Love, 75, 79; Le Courrier Français, 148; critics on, 153–4; Delacroix's portrait of, 56, 57, 58; deteriorating relationship with Chopin, 93, 119, 122–46, 147–55, 157, 163–72; The Devil's Pool, 131; early relationship with Chopin, 52–5, 56–67, 68–88, 104; Elle et lui, 152; Fanchette affair, 126–7; Horace, 79; Indiana, 16; Isadora, 136; Journal des Débats, 16; The Journeyman Carpenter, 79; last meeting with Chopin, 177–8; Lélia, 16; letters and memoirs, 14, 16, 72,

123, 166–7, 201; Lucrezia Floriani, 149–56, 188; in Majorca, 13–14, 55, 58–65, 72, 75, 104–5; marriage to Dudevant, 16, 99; maternal role of, 14, 58–9, 65–70, 71–4, 76, 79, 81, 84, 87, 91, 95, 99–109, 116, 121–2, 124, 128–9, 131, 140–2, 148, 164–70, 201; meets Chopin, 17–18, 52; The Miller of Angibault, 136–7; musical interests, 18, 21, 71, 83, 85, 96, 97, 113, 160; at Nohant, 68–78, 89–97, 104, 107–9, 111–15, 121–32, 136, 140–8, 163, 167–8; physical appearance of, 17–18, 56, 126, 133–4; Le Piccinino, 163; political views, 126–7, 177, 178, 185; relationship with daughter Solange, 100–109, 129, 131–2, 142–4, 164–70, 177–8, 201–2; salons, 12, 17, 51, 100, 106, 117, 127; separation from Chopin, 13–14, 169–72, 174, 177–8, 188–9, 192; sexuality of, 17–18, 52–5, 56, 72–3, 81, 123; social views of, 17, 93, 116, 126–7, 143, 149, 177, 178, 185; Spiridion, 59; Titine affair, 143–5, 202; writing career of, 16, 59, 71–2, 75, 79, 99, 125–7, 136–7, 148–54, 163, 178, 201
Sandeau, Jules, 16, 99, 100, 101
Sapieha, Prince, 24, 44
Sartoris, Mrs., 183
Saxe, Marechal de, 17
Saxon Palace, 23
Scheffer, Ary, 96
scherzo(s), 64, 162, 173, 183; First, 64, 119; Fourth, 119; Third, in C-sharp Minor, 71, 84–5
Schlesinger, Maurice, 47, 49, 60–1, 66, 95, 135, 160
Schubert, Franz, 4, 97; Winterreise, 159–60, 174, 199
Schumann, Robert, 4, 45, 62
Schwabe, Salis, 185
Scotland, 179; Chopin in, 184–7

Shaw, George Bernard, 186
Siberia, 44
Silesia, 28
Skarbek, Count, 23, 24
Skarbek, Countess, 24
Skarbek, Joseph, 82 and *n.*
Sloper, Lindsay, 136
Sociéte des Concerts, 46
sonata(s), 119, 132, 161; in B-flat
    Major, 7; in B-flat Minor, 55, 70; in
    B Minor, 132, 158–9; for Cello and
    Piano in G Minor, 158–9, 164,
    172–4, 199
Sophocles, *Antigone,* 129
Spain, 58–65
Square d'Orléans, 12–13, 116, 134, 137,
    142, 147, 163, 166, 172, 176, 189, 194
Stendhal, 203
Stirling, Jane, 9, 135, 173, 178–9, 180,
    184–7 and *n.*, 188, 195, 196–7
Strauss, Johann (the Elder), 36
Sue, Eugène, 20
Sutherland, Duchess of, 181
Switzerland, 15, 16, 175

Taglioni, Marie, 116
Tamburini, Antonio, 181
tarantella, 90
Thackeray, William Makepeace, 183
Thalberg, Sigismund, 35, 181
Théâtre Français (in Radziwill
    Palace), 25, 75
Titian, 162
Towianski, Andrezj, 134
Troupenas, Eugène-Théodore, 78
tuberculosis, 28, 110, 118, 139, 188, 190,
    201; "consumptive rage" and, 155–6
Tuileries, 19, 96, 140, 195

Valldemosa, 59, 62, 63, 69
variations on duet from *Don Gio-*
    vanni, 29, 30, 45

Venice, 66, 101, 146
Viardot, Louis, 90, 127, 170
Viardot, Louise, 91, 121–2, 127–8, 133
Viardot, Pauline, 7, 80, 83, 90–1, 96,
    108, 117, 124, 126, 127–8, 141–2,
    144, 160, 170, 181, 183, 192
Victoria, Queen of England, 181, 182,
    185
Vienna, 22, 44, 94, 118; Chopin in,
    29–30, 34–7
violin, 29, 173 and *n.*
Ville d'Avray, 166, 171
Visitandine Church (Warsaw), 28
Vosges, 22

Wagner, Richard, 125, 163, 200;
    Tristan, 193
waltz(es), 36, 94, 119, 163, 181, 183; in
    E-flat, 36
Warsaw, 4, 20, 23–39, 44, 48, 69,
    81–2, 91, 111, 129; "Blue Palace"
    in, 24; Chopin's concerts in, 24–5,
    32–4; Chopin's heart sent to, 201;
    fall of, 38
Warsaw Lyceum, 23–8, 45
Wellington, Duke of, 185
Whistler, James Abbott McNeill, 50–1
Wilde, Oscar, *The Picture of Dorian*
    Gray, 151
Witwicki, Stefan, 51, 78–9, 114
Wodzinska, Maria, 53–4, 82 and *n.*,
    91, 92
Wodzinski, Antoni, 53, 91–4, 124
World War II, 201
Woyciechowski, Tytus, 33–4, 35, 51,
    80

Zaleski, Bohdan, 154, 173
Zamoyska, Countess Zofia, 24
Zimmerman, Pierre-Joseph-
    Giullaume, 116
Zwyny, Adalbert, 24, 25, 28, 34, 111

Illustration Credits

A Note About the Author

BENITA EISLER is the author of *O'Keeffe and Stieglitz: An American Romance* and *Byron: Child of Passion, Fool of Fame.* She lives in New York City.

A Note on the Type

This book was set in Fournier, a typeface named for Pierre Simon Fournier fils (1712–1768), a celebrated French type designer. Coming from a family of typefounders, Fournier was an extraordinarily prolific designer of typefaces and of typographic ornaments. He was also the author of the important *Manuel typographique* (1764–1766), in which he attempted to work out a system standardizing type measurement in points, a system that is still in use internationally. Fournier's type is considered transitional in that it drew its inspiration from the old style, yet was ingeniously innovational, providing for an elegant, legible appearance. In 1925 his type was revived by the Monotype Corporation of London.

Composed by North Market Street Graphics,
Lancaster, Pennsylvania
Printed and bound by R. R. Donnelley & Sons,
Harrisonburg, Virginia
Designed by Anthea Lingeman